New Perspectives
in Moral Theology

Other Books by Charles E. Curran

Christian Morality Today
A New Look At Christian Morality
Contemporary Problems in Moral Theology
Catholic Moral Theology in Dialogue
The Crisis in Priestly Ministry
*Politics, Medicine and Christian Ethics: A Dialogue with
    Paul Ramsey*
Dissent In And For The Church (Charles E. Curran, Robert
    E. Hunt, et. al.)
*The Responsibility of Dissent: The Church and Academic
    Freedom* (John F. Hunt and Terrence R. Connelly with
    Charles E. Curran, et. al.)
Absolutes in Moral Theology? (editor)
Contraception: Authority and Dissent (editor)

New Perspectives
in Moral Theology

CHARLES E. CURRAN

Fides Publishers, Inc.,
Notre Dame, Indiana

Curran, Charles E
New perspectives in moral theology.

Includes bibliographical references.
1. Christian ethics—Catholic authors. 2. Social ethics. I. Title.
BX1758.2.C825   241   74-940
ISBN 0-8190-0602-5

TO MY MOTHER
ON HER SEVENTY-FIFTH BIRTHDAY

Preface

This book well illustrates the present state of Catholic moral theology which is described in Chapter One. The changes of the past few years have been so comparatively abrupt that there are now only tentative beginnings to develop new approaches and methodologies. Yet the problems and questions still arise, probably with even greater rapidity and intensity than before. In this context it again seems helpful to bring together seven studies published independently in the last few years under the general title of *New Perspectives in Moral Theology.*

The title of the book indicates the scope of these studies —to give the perspectives and parameters existing today in Catholic moral theology. The original articles have been edited and slightly modified to fit in with this overall picture.

The two chapters on "General Perspectives" try to give an overall picture of the present state of Catholic moral theology and also develop a stance for moral theology which should logically be the first step toward a systematic moral theology. This stance will also be employed in the following chapters. The section on "Perspectives in Social Ethics" discusses the question of a radical Catholic social ethic and then tries to shed light on the very pressing problem of how the Church should teach and structure its own mission in matters of concern to social ethics. "Perspectives in Personal Ethics" treats three very important questions—abortion, sterilization and divorce.

I gladly take this opportunity to thank publicly those at Catholic University who have been most helpful to me in my research and publishing. Once again, I am privileged to express my gratitude to retiring Dean Walter J. Schmitz for his loyal support and encouragement. Carolyn T. Lee of the Catholic University Library and her associates, David Gilson and Bruce Miller, have continued to assist my research as only devoted librarians can. The typing of this and previous manuscripts has been graciously and professionally done by Mrs. Lilian Finan, Marie Floyd and Vada Hummel.

I express gratitude to the following publishers, periodicals and organizations for providing me with opportunities to discuss and publish my research in the first place and then graciously allowing my republication of the material in this book. "Catholic Moral Theology Today" was originally presented as the presidential address to the American Society of Christian Ethics and was published in a somewhat different form in *Theological Studies,* XXXIV (1973). "The Stance of Moral Theology," was read at the Villanova University Theology Institute and published in Vol. IV of The Villanova University Series: *The Pilgrim People: A Vision With Hope,* ed. Joseph Papin (Philadelphia: Villanova University Press, 1970). "The Radical Catholic Social Ethics of Paul Hanly Furfey" was originally prepared as an address celebrating the fiftieth ordination anniversary of Msgr. Furfey and then appeared in a slightly different version in *The American Ecclesiastical Review,* CLXVI (1972). "Theological Reflections on the Social Mission and Teaching of the Church" was delivered at a symposium jointly sponsored by the National Catholic School of Social Service and the National Conference of Catholic Charities and published in *The Social Mission of the Church: A Theological Reflection,* ed. Edward J. Ryle (Washington: Catholic University of America Press, 1973). "Abortion: Its Legal and Moral Aspects in Catholic Theology," appeared in *The Jurist,* XXXIII (1973). "Sterilization: Exposition, Critique and Refutation of Past Teaching" was originally published in *The Linacre Quarterly,* XL (1973). "Divorce: Theory and Practice in American Catholicism" first appeared in *Recherches de Science Religieuse,* LXI (1973).

Contents

1

Catholic Moral Theology Today

The changes that have transpired in the Roman Catholic Church and in Roman Catholic theology in the last decade are enormous. The purpose of this first chapter is to consider the present self-identity of Roman Catholic moral theology especially as it exists in the context of a dialogue with various forms of Protestant ethics. Dialogue with Protestant thought has played an important role in the development of Roman Catholic moral theology in our time, but it is far from the only factor in the developing self-identity of moral theology. Both Roman Catholic and Protestant ethics alike have been involved with an even wider dialogue—an interface with the rapidly changing moral questions of our day and with all forms of philosophical and humanist approaches to these questions. However, this chapter will concentrate on the identity and self-consciousness of Roman Catholic moral theology today as seen in terms of its dialogue with Protestant ethics.

The very existence of dialogue between Protestant and Catholic ethicians is comparatively recent. In 1963 Franz Böckle began a very perceptive series of lectures with the remark that ecumenical discussion is strikingly faint and insignificant in the area of Christian ethics.[1] In the United States one can witness the same growth in ecumenical discussions about Christian ethics. The very influential "Notes on Moral Theology," which have regularly appeared in *Theological Studies,* indicate little or no reference to Protestant ethics in the years before 1966. One moral survey appearing in 1965 did not contain any footnote references to Protestant literature.[2] The history of the American Society of Christian Ethics illustrates the same fact, for it was only in 1965 that Roman Catholics began to participate actively in this society.

The rapid changes which have occurred within such a short time are astounding. In 1963 Böckle indicated some of the practical differences existing between Roman Catholic and Protestant life—Sunday obligation, days of fast and abstinence, contraception, divorce.[3] These practical differences, so pronounced less than ten years ago, have now either been done away with or seriously questioned by Catholic scholars. The dialogue has reached such a level of exchange that no reputable scholar within either tradition can afford to be unaware of the literature and thinking existing in the other tradition.

In the light of these rapid changes of the past few years, what is the self-identity of Roman Catholic moral theology in terms of the dialogue with Protestant ethics? A recent book on the subject by Roger Mehl indicates both convergences and persistent divergences.[4] I fundamentally agree

---

1 Franz Böckle, *Law and Conscience* (New York: Sheed and Ward, 1966), p. 17.

2 John J. Lynch, S.J., "Notes on Moral Theology," *Theological Studies,* XXVI (1965), 242-279. There are a few references to Protestant authors in Richard A. McCormick, S.J., "Notes on Moral Theology," *Theological Studies,* XXVI (1965), 596-662. McCormick has continued to develop and expand this aspect in his highly regarded surveys of literature in moral theology.

3 Böckle, p. 18.

4 Roger Mehl, *Éthique catholique et éthique protestante* (Neuchâtel: Delachaux & Niestle, 1970). Future references will be to the English trans-

with the insistence on the convergences arising from the common source (amounting to a return on the part of Catholic thought) of the Scriptures and also arising from the fact that both traditions are facing new and unprecedented changes in our social life. Mehl also notes persistent divergences in the following areas: nature and supernature—the anthropological problem; natural law and natural morality; the meaning of secularization; soul and body.[5]

GENERAL COMMENTS

In general I deny both the extent and the intensity of the persistent divergences mentioned by Mehl. Three general considerations have apparently influenced the different conclusions reached on this point by Mehl and myself. Although *Catholic Ethics and Protestant Ethics* was published in French in 1970 and in English in 1971, the material was originally presented as the Warfield Lectures at Princeton Theological Seminary in 1968. Obviously there have been many developments since that time, which have indicated that the differences are somewhat disappearing. However, even in 1968 it seems that there were changes already occurring that are not that prominent in Mehl's consideration. Böckle in Germany and Gustafson in this country were well aware that there were developments then in Catholic ethics which were lessening the persistent differences with Protestant ethics.[6]

Secondly, Mehl assumes that Catholic ethics is still a monolothic moral theology, which he frequently refers to as Thomistic ethics. This insistence fails to appreciate the incipient pluralism which was present in Catholic thinking

lation: *Catholic Ethics and Protestant Ethics,* tr. James H. Farley (Philadelphia: Westminster, 1971).

5 *Ibid.,* pp. 43-99.

6 James M. Gustafson, "New Directions in Moral Theology," *Commonweal,* LXXXVII (February 23, 1968), 617-623.

even in 1968. Too often Mehl illustrates his points by quotations of older papal documents (e.g. Pius IX, Leo XIII) which most Catholics even in 1968 realized were somewhat dated.[7]

Thirdly, I believe that the ecumenical dialogue between Protestant and Catholic ethicians has proceeded at a more rapid rate in this country than in Europe. One has to be careful of a hidden chauvinism in such a judgment, but the facts seem to bear out such a conclusion. Catholic and Protestant ethicians in this country have been meeting together more than in European countries. The literature of Catholic ethicians in this country shows a greater ongoing dialogue with Protestant thought.

Perhaps too the conditions for dialogue were more conducive in this country. In Europe the dialogue often exists on a very speculative level, and the Protestant partner in the dialogue frequently belongs to an Orthodox or Neo-Orthodox persuasion so that theological differences appear to stand out. In the United States there has been a greater working together on practical moral issues such as civil rights, peace, and also the dialogue has not been only with Neo-Orthodoxy. Thus the climate in the United States seems to have facilitated the possibility of a better dialogue and exchange between Protestants and Catholics. A recent article by the influential German Jesuit Joseph Fuchs, who teaches at the Gregorian University in Rome, lends some support to this view. In writing on the absoluteness of moral norms Fuchs very frequently refers to the American literature which indicates his appreciation of its significance.[8]

This essay will consider the persistent divergences mentioned by Mehl and others as existing between Protestant

---

[7] Mehl, pp. 67-81.

[8] Josef Fuchs, S.J., "The Absoluteness of Moral Terms," *Gregorianum*, LII (1971), 415-457.

and Catholic ethics. Obviously one cannot speak about Protestant ethics as a monolithic ethical system, since under the umbrella of Protestant ethical thought there are many different methodologies. In the course of the present discussion a somewhat similar pluralism should also become evident in contemporary Catholic moral theology. The questions generally raised in Protestant ethics about Roman Catholic theological ethics can readily be summarized under three headings—natural law, authoritarianism and theological presuppositions.

NATURAL LAW

The category of natural law will include the philosophical questions of methodology, the meaning of nature, the place of law in ethics and the role of norms or principles in the solution of practical questions. This consideration prescinds from the more theological questions connected with natural law such as the relationship of nature-grace, the role of sin, the connection between the order of creation and the order of redemption. These topics will be discussed under theological presuppositions.

In general the critiques against natural law presuppose a monolithic philosophical system based on a "non-temporal and imperceptible nature" and a "reason that is incorrectly postulated not to have a history."[9] "Catholic moral theology seeks a foundation in an original and ontological given, which seems difficult to grasp. It is also led to call certain exigencies eternal, which in fact are relative and sociologically conditioned."[10]

Catholic theology itself in the last decade has been involved in a serious critique and revision of the natural law

[9] Mehl, p. 65.
[10] *Ibid.*, p. 63.

6 New Perspectives in Moral Theology

theory as found in the manuals of moral theology and incorporated into the hierarchical magisterium's pronouncements, especially the papal encyclicals.[11] In this ongoing discussion there are some who reject any change in the methodology or the practical conclusions of the manuals of moral theology.[12] The vast majority of Catholic ethicians today refuse to accept the natural law approach of the manuals. Some have abandoned the concept of natural law altogether and adopted newer and different methodologies; while others, retaining the concept of natural law, have tried to show how the manuals departed from the true natural law approach of the past as seen now in a better appreciation of the exact position adopted by Aquinas and not the one espoused by later scholastics. The concept of natural law as a deductive methodology based on eternal and immutable essences and resulting in specific absolute norms is no longer acceptable to the majority of Catholic moral theologians writing today.

J. M. Aubert stands out as an example of the approach which seeks a revision of the natural law more in accord with its understanding in Saint Thomas and not the conception developed by a later scholasticism. The major problem with the concept of natural law as found in the manuals of moral theology and in papal pronouncements stems from the failure to recognize and employ the Thomistic distinction between *lex naturalis* and *jus naturale*. *Lex naturalis* for

---

11 For an extensive bibliography on recent literature on natural law with a heavy emphasis on German and French publications, see Jean-Marie Aubert, "Pour une herméneutique du droit naturel," *Recherches de Science Religieuse,* LIX (1971), 490-492.

12 E. g., John F. Kippley, "Continued Dissent: Is It Responsible Loyalty?" *Theological Studies,* XXXII (1971), 48-65; Cahal B. Daly, *Morals, Law and Life* (Chicago and Dublin: Scepter, 1966). For a summary of diverse reactions especially in the United States to Pope Paul's encyclical *Humanae Vitae,* see William H. Shannon, *The Lively Debate: Response to Humanae Vitae* (New York: Sheed and Ward, 1970).

Thomas is human reason seeking to regulate the total human reality (body and soul) ; whereas the *jus naturale* comprises the basic human tendencies and inclinations which need to be studied empirically and then regulated and directed by reason.[13]

According to Aubert the textbooks reduced natural law just to the given aspects of *jus naturale* and thereby downplayed the creative and regulative role of reason as well as the function of empirical discovery. Modern natural law theoreticians have concentrated almost exclusively on the naturalist and the *a priori* aspects of human existence; whereas Thomas stressed the rational aspect and an open and changing understanding of the basic human tendencies and inclinations. Aubert thus shows that Thomas did not advocate the physicalism which has characterized so much of Catholic moral theology until the present time. Scholastic thinking after Thomas considered nature in a universal and closed way; whereas for Thomas man as a spiritual being cannot be understood as a simple nature closed and formed once for all, since a spiritual being transcends his given order and is challenged to grow and develop.[14] Personally I believe Aubert is somewhat one-sided, for he fails to appreciate that Thomas did employ Ulpian's understanding of natural law as that which is common to man and all the animals.

Aubert also criticizes a legalistic, voluntaristic interpretation which sees natural law as a source of obligation and restraint rather than a rational guide for the free development of man's existence. A further critique concerns a dehumanization of natural law resulting from the triumph of purely metaphysical and abstract concepts of natural law

---

[13] Jean-Marie Aubert, *Loi de Dieu—Loi des hommes* (Tournai: Desclée, 1964), pp. 43-47; Aubert, "Le droit naturel: ses avatars historiques et son avenir," *Le Supplément de la Vie Spirituelle*, XX (1967), 300-303; Aubert, *Recherches de Science Religieuse*, LIX (1971), 464-467.

[14] Aubert, *Recherches de Science Religieuse*, LIX (1971), 464-467.

thus ignoring the historical and cultural conditioning of the existence of man in this world.[15]

In the light of these inadequacies and misunaerstandings of the true Thomist concept of natural law, Aubert proposes a more functional understanding of natural law. Natural law should express the being of man, but the being of man is more complex, open and changing than was admitted by an essentialist view of man. The reflexive and transcendental aspects of man emphasize the subject more than the object so that human nature is conceived as always deeper and more vast. The empirical and existential character of natural law must become more evident. All these different aspects will bring about a pluralism in our understanding of man so that there can no longer be a monolithic view of human reality. Different interpretations of human and social reality in the more theoretical realm will result in a growing diversity on the level of conclusions and opinions about a particular moral question.[16]

Such a view of natural law obviously responds to many of the critiques proposed by Mehl and others. Aubert's theory of natural law, which he claims to be based on the true interpretation of Thomas, relies on a historical, inductive and empirical understanding of man. As mentioned above, I do not completely accept Aubert's interpretation of Aquinas.

The emphasis on the empirical element in natural law is also found in the natural law theory proposed by Germain Grisez, who has vigorously defended traditional Catholic teaching on artificial contraception, abortion, and generally been a severe critic of newer approaches in moral theology.[17] Grisez acknowledges the first prescription of practical

---

15 *Ibid.*, pp. 471-474.

16 *Ibid.*, pp. 474-488.

17 Germain G. Grisez, *Contraception and the Natural Law* (Milwaukee: Bruce, 1964) ; Grisez, *Abortion: The Myths, the Realities and the Arguments* (New York and Cleveland: Corpus Books, 1970), especially pp. 267-346.

reason as enunciating that good should be pursued. But towards what definite goods should practical reason direct human action? To determine the goods that man should seek, one must examine all the basic tendencies and inclinations of man. Grisez thus admits that man is endowed with basic tendencies prior to acculturation and free choice of his own, but only empirical inquiry can determine what these inclinations are.[18] Grisez's theory illustrates the fact that the empirical has a much greater place in contemporary revisions of natural law theory even among Catholics who have generally opposed newer developments and changes in moral theology.

Other Catholic theologians have discarded the concept of natural law and proposed other moral methodologies which do not claim to be revisions of the natural law. Although these approaches implicitly or explicitly reject natural law, they share natural law's insistence on the capacity of human reason to arrive at ethical truth. Differences do appear about the ontological and metaphysical underpinings of ethics and also about the general ethical models proposed.

At the present time these newer theories are somewhat sketchy and tentative which obviously reflects the fact that they are the first efforts on the part of Catholic theologians to develop newer ethical approaches in the light of the dissatisfactions with the past approach and the rapidly changing historical and cultural circumstances of our contemporary human existence. Many of these newer approaches have appeared in books which are not truly systematic studies but rather collections of essays (e.g., Johann, Milhaven, Antoine), a fact which again underscores the incipient and fledgling state of such developments.[19] However, the basic

---

18 Grisez, *Contraception and the Natural Law,* pp. 62-67.

19 Robert O. Johann, *Building the Human* (New York: Herder and Herder, 1968) ; John Giles Milhaven, *Toward a New Catholic Morality* (Garden City:

fact is very clear—there is now existing in Roman Catholic ethics a plurality of ethical theories and methodologies which will only expand and become more numerous in the future.

A quick survey reveals the diversity already existing. Robert Johann employs a more relational moral model rather than the teleological model of Thomism and acknowledges a strong dependence on American pragmatism.[20] A different philosophical approach emphasizes a transcendental method which has become popular in Catholic theology through the works of Rahner, Lonergan and Coreth. The transcendental method begins not with the object, but with the human knowing subject and the process by which man experiences, understands, judges and decides.[21] Rahner's development of the discernment of the Spirit in decision making corresponds with his transcendental philosophy.[22]

John Giles Milhaven has proposed and developed a love ethic based on a proper empirical evaluation of the consequences of our actions in the light of love.[23] Milhaven recognizes a close relationship between his theory and that proposed by Joseph Fletcher, who also acknowledges that Milhaven is in basic agreement with Fletcher's own ap-

---

Doubleday, 1970) ; Pierre Antoine, *Morale sans anthropologie* (Paris: Epi, 1971) . This book, as well as some of my previous books, illustrates the same reality.

[20] Johann, *Building the Human.*

[21] Donald H. Johnson, S.J., "Lonergan and the Re-Doing of Ethics," *Continuum,* V (1967) , 211-220. For a most interesting attempt to show continuities in seemingly different ethical theories, see Robert O. Johann, "Lonergan and Dewey on Judgment," in *Language, Truth and Meaning,* ed. Philip McShane, S.J. (Notre Dame, Indiana: University of Notre Dame Press, 1972) , pp. 79-92.

[22] Karl Rahner, *The Dynamic Element in the Church* (New York: Herder and Herder, 1964) ; Avery Dulles, S.J., "Finding God's Will," *Woodstock Letters,* XCIV (1965) , 139-152.

[23] Milhaven, *Toward a New Catholic Morality;* Milhaven, "Objective Moral Evaluation of Consequences," *Theological Studies,* XXXII (1971) , 407-430.

proach.[24] Herbert McCabe has argued against both a love-centered, situation ethic derived from empirical consequences and a natural law theory based on the understanding of man as a member of the human community. McCabe views ethics as language and communication which sees meaning in terms of ways of entering into social life and ways of being with each other.[25] A more phenomenological basis marks the Christian ethics proposed more than five years ago by William van der Marck.[26] Enda McDonagh has recently outlined a moral theology built upon reflection on the experience of the moral call in the human situation which has interpersonal, social and historical dimensions. McDonagh likewise rejects the teleological approach as well as the ontology which undergirded the manualist teaching on natural law, for moral obligation is discovered in experience. McDonagh goes from the experience of the "ought" to the "is" and not the other way around.[27]

The radical departure from the natural law theory of the manuals is well illustrated in the theory proposed by Pierre Antoine, S.J., which he negatively describes as a "morality without anthropology" and positively as "praxeology" or "a pragmatic calculus."[28] Morality today cannot be based on anthropology because we cannot develop a model of man or

24 Milhaven, *Theological Studies,* XXXII (1971), nn. 3, 5, 6, 8; Joseph Fletcher, "Reflection and Reply," in *The Situation Ethics Debate,* ed. Harvey Cox (Philadelphia: Westminster, 1968), pp. 255-260.

25 Herbert McCabe, *What Is Ethics All About?* (Washington and Cleveland: Corpus Books, 1969).

26 William H. van der Marck, *Love and Fertility* (London: Sheed and Ward, 1965); *Toward a Christian Ethics* (Westminster, Md.: Newman Press, 1967).

27 Enda McDonagh, "Toward a Christian Theology of Morality," *Irish Theological Quarterly,* XXXVII (1970), 187-198; McDonagh, "The Structure and Basis of the Moral Experience," *Irish Theological Quarterly,* XXXVIII (1971), 3-20.

28 Pierre Antoine, S.J., "Une morale sans anthropologie," *Lumière et Vie,* XVIII (1969), 48-68; Antoine, "Morale et decision calculée," *Projet,* XLII (1970), 131-141.

vision of the world which is applicable. The dimensions of our understanding of man today include artificiality rather than nature, the experimental state of man rather than the fixed essence, relational rather than substantialist understandings. These new emphases do not call for newer applications of older methodologies and principles, but they call for a more radical change in the methodology itself. No *a priori* models of man can exist today. Morality concerns practical reason which involves a pragmatic calculus. Antoine denies the existence of a hierarchy of values and prefers to view morality under the controlling rubric of cost.[29]

This survey has indicated various newer approaches and methodologies which have been emerging in Catholic moral theology in the last few years. In general I agree with the strictures made against the approaches of the past, but it is important to develop some critical stance in the light of the plurality of approaches now being sketched and discussed in Catholic moral theology. Chapter Two attempts to develop a basic stance for Christian ethics. One important critical point of reference concerns the importance of considering all the elements which must enter into a theory. Especially in developing newer approaches and at the beginning stage of development, one is acutely conscious of the danger of failing to consider the complexity of the moral reality and all the elements which must enter into moral theology. For example, some approaches based on a transcendental method fail to give enough importance to the societal and political aspects of reality.[30] Theories based on interpersonal relationships occasionally do not give enough

---

29 *Lumière et Vie,* XXVIII (1969) , 48-68.

30 Johannes B. Metz, *Theology of the World* (New York: Herder and Herder, 1969) , pp. 107-125; Metz, "Foreword," in Karl Rahner, *Spirit in the World* (New York: Herder and Herder, 1968) , pp. xiii-xviii.

importance to societal elements as is evident in discussions of particular questions such as sexuality.[31]

I have also criticized some approaches because of their consequentialism, but in the light of ongoing dialogue I can try to express better my basic concerns and correct some inadequate argumentation. John G. Milhaven has developed more extensively than any other Catholic theologian in this country a moral methodology based on love as known through the consequences of our actions. At times I have felt that such an approach too easily identifies the moral judgment with the findings of empirical and human sciences.[32] Such an approach seems to me to deny the creative and transcendent aspects of any truly human and Christian moral theory. It is not enough just to know the consequences as indicated by the empirical sciences, but one must also have a creative and practical intelligence to direct things to a better future than is now existing. All human morality needs this transcendent and creative aspect which is stressed in transcendental approaches. From a Christian perspective the limitations and sinfulness of the present call for us to work in the direction of an eschatological future which must transcend the present. Take a practical example. One who is planning the future of our cities must have not only the relevant sociological data but also a creative intelligence which can attempt to form new ways for men to live together in cities.

---

[31] See illustrations of this in *Sexual Ethics and Christian Responsibility,* ed. John Charles Wynn (New York: Association Press, 1970).

[32] See my articles, "Homosexuality and Moral Theology: Methodological and Substantive Considerations," *The Thomist,* XXXV (1971), 447-481; "La théologie morale et les sciences," *Recherches de Science Religieuse,* LIX (1971), 419-448. Milhaven in his latest article tries to avoid such a danger, but I still find some dissatisfaction with his approach as will be explained below.

A consequentialist model—especially when it depends so heavily or almost exclusively on the findings of the behavioral sciences— seems to be too similar to a technological view of man. Today people are rightly reacting against such a model of human existence. There is also the danger in such a view of seeing man primarily in terms of his productivity and contributions to life and to society. I believe these are important considerations, but they are not the ultimate reasons for the values we give to human existence. Too often our society wants to treat man only in terms of his ability to contribute and be productive for our society. One has only to think of recent welfare proposals and the facile distinctions between the deserving and the undeserving poor.

The ultimate ethical model for a consequentialist approach is a teleological model, which H. Richard Niebuhr has referred to as the model of man-the-maker.[33] Perhaps because of the somewhat pejorative description proposed by Niebuhr and in light of the obvious analogies with a technological view of man, I tend to reject a teleological model as the ultimate model in theological ethics. Man, despite all the control which he does have over his life and future today, nonetheless does not have the same control over his life that the artisan has over the raw material out of which he is fashioning his product. The limit situation of death too often becomes glossed over in such a concept of man. This model as mentioned does not seem to express enough the aspects of creativity and transcendence. From the Christian perspective it does not seem to do justice to the Christian realities of suffering, death and resurrection, and the hope which always transcends the limits of the present situation.

Rather than the teleological model of man-the-maker or the deontological model I would opt with Niebuhr for the relational-responsibility model as more fundamental in de-

---

[33] H. Richard Niebuhr, *The Responsible Self* (New York: Harper and Row, 1963) , pp. 49-52.

scribing the Christian life—if only because it allows one to incorporate the best elements of the other models. In practical matters the relationality model would share the same diffidence towards absolute norms because one can not absolutize what exists in terms of relationships. Nor would such a model accept a static hierarchy of values because of the multiple and changing relationships seen within a more historical perspective. Such a model realizes the importance of both empirical data and the creative and transcendent aspects of human existence even though these can never exist in a vacuum or merely in the abstract.

Perhaps some forms of consequentialism do not necessarily involve all the negative aspects I have seen in consequentialism. John G. Milhaven has recently insisted that human experience must include affective and creative aspects which correspond to the aesthetic judgment.[34] There seems to me to be a difference between the scientific and the aesthetic judgment which roughly corresponds to the greater emphasis on creativity and transcendence in the aesthetic judgment. Moreover, I have some difficulties with the way in which Milhaven develops his insistence on experience.

Milhaven rightly implies that we have often been insensitive to moral problems because we have not experienced these things ourselves.[35] I personally realize my lack of sensitivities at times because I have not experienced racial discrimination, war, poverty, or hunger. However as a limited human being I cannot experience all these realities. Sometimes experience of only one side of a question will definitely prejudice my understanding of the total human situation with which I am confronted. Actual experience of reality is helpful and important, but it is not sufficient. There is the need for a creative sensitivity and moral sense which does not have to actually experience something before it can

---

34 Milhaven, *Theological Studies,* XXXII (1971), 424-430.
35 *Ibid.,* pp. 426-428.

morally react. The insistence on actual experience seems again to be an indication of the lack of creativity and transcendence in the theological method employed. Especially in the midst of the great complexity existing today and the impossibility of actual experience, the ethician and the individual person must develop a creative moral sensitivity which enables him to go beyond the boundaries of his own limited actual experience. Today we can perhaps accuse our predecessors of white racism, but what will our successors rightly accuse us of?

Perhaps part of the disagreement arises from two different perspectives. Milhaven originally was concentrating primarily on the question of absolute norms in moral theology and denies such norms on the basis of his appeal to the ultimate importance of consequences in determining our actions in these cases. The perspective I have outlined considers rather a very basic posture for our total moral life and thus does not want to reduce our total ethical posture to the model of consequences or of man-the-maker. On particular questions involving the existence of absolute norms, I too would agree on the need to evaluate and weigh all the elements involved in the light of my relational vision of human existence. A relational understanding of reality incorporates the historical and changing aspects while denying any eternal, static hierarchy of relational values. Obviously in particular situations one determines what is good in terms of what will promote his understanding of relational values. In this light I must point out some inadequacies in my own somewhat unnuanced argument against consequentialism based on the inability to know all the consequences of my actions.[36]

Richard McCormick has recently acknowledged the decisive role of consequences in moral theology, but he realizes the importance of Christian intentionalities and

---

[36] *Contemporary Problems in Moral Theology* (Notre Dame, Ind.: Fides Publishers, 1970) , p. 251.

ethos in the light of which consequences are weighed and evaluated.[37] In this way he avoids some of the problems I have with other types of consequentialism, although at least part of the problem may result from the different perspectives mentioned above.

This type of dialogue, discussion and disagreement among Catholic moralists on methodological issues will continue to grow and increase. One must expect to find continuing diversity in the search for more adequate moral theologies. The thrust of this brief survey is to show the diversity of moral methodologies already existing among Catholic moral theologians.

Perhaps the most frequent complaint of Protestant ethicians against Catholic moral theology has been the charge of legalism. The last few years have seen Catholics themselves make the same charge about their own theological tradition, or at least the tradition as it was interpreted in the manuals of moral theology. The discussion has developed from a context of positive law to the context of natural law.[38] Are there certain actions which are always and everywhere wrong?

In the context of the situation ethics debate in the 1960's Catholic theologians have reexamined the role and place of absolute norms in moral theology. I agree with an increasing number of Catholic theologians who deny the existence of negative moral absolutes; that is, actions described solely in terms of the physical structure of the act (a material piece of behavior) which are said to be always and everywhere

---

[37] Richard A. McCormick, S.J., "Notes on Moral Theology," *Theological Studies,* XXXIII (1972) , 90.

[38] One can notice this development in the thought of Bernard Häring who has contributed more than any other Catholic theologian to the contemporary developments in moral theology even though his scholarly contributions have been less in the last five years. Häring first broke away from the theology of the manuals in the name of a more biblical and personalist moral theology.

wrong.[39] There are a variety of reasons for such a denial including both a reexamination of the teaching of the past which does not appear to be as absolute as presented in the manuals and newer methodological approaches to meet our changing understandings of man and reality. Obviously such a denial stems from a more inductive, relational and empirical approach to moral problems. Milhaven, followed now by Crotty, would understand moral norms as empirical generalizations.[40] Note here how Catholic theologians are departing from the ontological foundations upon which the theology of the manuals was based. Others, however, such as McCabe would deny the fact that absolute moral norms are just empirical generalizations.[41]

Perhaps one of the most important principles in the older Catholic moral theology was the principle of the double effect, which decided conflict situations in which an action would have both good and bad effects. As generally understood in the manuals, the differentiation between direct and indirect was based on the physical structure of the act itself as illustrated in such descriptions of the direct effect as the *finis operis* of the act or the act which by its very nature does this particular thing.[42] The literature on the question has been growing in the past five years with more and more Catholics disagreeing with the older understanding of direct and indirect.[43]

---

[39] For an early discussion of this question see the various essays in *Absolutes in Moral Theology?* ed. Charles E. Curran (Washington: Corpus Books, 1968) .

[40] Nicholas Crotty, C. P., "Conscience and Conflict," *Theological Studies* XXXII (1971) , 223-231.

[41] McCabe, *What is Ethics All About?* pp. 29ff.

[42] John McCarthy, *Problems in Theology II: The Commandments* (Westminster, Md.: Newman Press, 1966) , pp. 119-122, 159, 160.

[43] Early rejections of the manualist interpretation of direct and indirect are found in: Van der Marck, *Love and Fertility*, pp. 35-63; P. Knauer, "La détermination du bien et du mal morale par le principe du double effet," *Nouvelle Revue Théologique*, LXXXVII (1965) , 356-376.

The newer approaches call for a weighing and comparison of all the values involved so that I perform the action which brings about the greatest possible good. Note the obvious consequentialist calculus in such a determination but also the fact that the relative importance attached to the different values involved transcends the present limited situation and can be verified only in the context of the fullness of the Christian experience. Richard McCormick has recently suggested that such an understanding of the principle of the double effect based on the proportional weighing of all the consequences of my action also serves as the ultimate basis for the understanding of the principle of totality and also the principle of discrimination in the just war theory.[44]

On more specific ethical questions there is already an ever growing divergence of opinions among Catholic moral theologians. In many ways the criticism of the older teaching on contraception marked just a beginning. The arguments proposed against the teaching on contraception presupposed different theological methodologies which would also lead to different opinions on other complex, specific moral problems. These differences are illustrated in the contemporary literature. On the question of abortion there is now existing among Catholics a plurality of opinions even though the gamut of these opinions at the present time does not seem to be as broad as the spectrum of opinions existing among the population at large.[45] Chapter Six will consider in detail the question of abortion.

---

[44] McCormick, *Theological Studies*, XXXIII (1972), 68-90.

[45] Diversity existing among Catholics is illustrated by two contributions to *Abortion in a Changing World*, ed. Robert S. Hall, Vol. I (New York: Columbia University Press, 1970): Thomas J. O'Donnell, S.J., "A Traditional Catholic's View," pp. 34-38; Joseph F. Donceel, S.J., "A Liberal Catholic's View," pp. 39-45. For a quite comprehensive view of abortion with great emphasis on the empirical data but also summarizing more recent Catholic opinions, see Daniel Callahan, *Abortion: Law, Choice and Morality* (New York: Macmillan, 1970).

Catholic theologians frequently deny the existing teaching of the hierarchical magisterium on such issues as contraception, sterilization, artificial insemination, masturbation, the generic gravity of sexual sins.[46] Newer approaches have recently been taken to the question of homosexuality.[47] Some Catholic theologians have argued against the moral norm condemning all sexual relationships outside marriage.[48] In this particular area, there is not a great number of theologians proposing such views nor is there the range of opinions which exists among the population at large, but there is divergence from the heretofore accepted norm. Another absolute norm in Catholic moral teaching that has been questioned is the absolute prohibition of euthanasia in all cases as distinguished from the traditional teaching on the need to employ only ordinary means to sustain human life.[49] All these questions in the area of medical and sexual morality are being questioned today because some theologians believe that the absolute prohibitions define the forbidden action in terms of the physical structure of the act seen in

---

46 John F. Dedek, *Contemporary Sexual Morality* (New York: Sheed and Ward, 1971).

47 John J. McNeil, S.J., "The Christian Male Homosexual," *Homiletic and Pastoral Review*, LXX (1970), 667-677; 747-758; 828-836; Pierre Claude Noppey, "An Open Letter on Homosexuality," *Cross Currents*, XX (1970), 221-237; Joseph A. McCaffrey, "Homosexuality in the Seventies," *Catholic World*, CCXIII (1971), 121-125.

48 David Darst and Joseph Forgue, "Sexuality on the Island Earth," *The Ecumenist*, VII (1969), 81-87; Gregory Baum, "A Catholic Response," *The Ecumenist*, VII (1969), 90-92. Personally, I do see some exceptions in the general norm, but the exceptions are quite limited. Arguments in favor of pre-marital relationships too often forget about the societal dimension as well as the sinful dimension of human existence. However, I do admit degrees of gravity in terms of the relationship involved. See, *Contemporary Problems in Moral Theology*, pp. 159-188.

49 Kieran Nolan, O.S.B., "The Problem of Caring for the Dying," in *Absolutes in Moral Theology*, pp. 249-260; Daniel Maguire, "The Freedom to Die," *Commonweal*, XCVI (August 11, 1972), 423-427.

itself apart from the context, the existing relationships or the consequences.

The plurality of opinions also exists in other questions where previously there was *the* Catholic opinion. Contemporary theologians are calling for a rethinking of the absolute prohibition against divorce and openly favoring a more benign moral and pastoral attitude to people who are divorced so that they are not excluded from the sacramental life of the Church.[50] Chapter Seven will discuss in detail the teaching and practice of the Church on divorce and advocate a change. In questions of social and political morality there is also a divergence of opinions among Catholic theologians. On the question of war, actual Catholic opinions include pacificism, nuclear pacificism and just war theory.[51] Recent historical research indicates that there has been a just war tradition with different theories even within that tradition.[52] Thus again historical research shows a greater flexibility within the tradition, although contemporary discussions range even beyond the traditional approaches.

The conclusion of this brief overview is evident. Within the context of Roman Catholic moral theology there is not only a growing plurality of ethical methodologies but also an ever more noticeable divergence on particular moral questions. There is a connection between the two statements, for the newer methodologies obviously lead to different conclusions especially in complex issues which are not as simple

---

[50] For a survey of recent literature on the subject, see William W. Bassett, "Divorce and Remarriage: The Catholic Search for A Pastoral Reconciliation," *American Ecclesiastical Review*, CLXII (1970), 100-105; Richard A. McCormick, S.J., *Theological Studies*, XXXII (1971), 107-122; XXXIII (1972), 91-100.

[51] James Finn, *Protest: Pacifism and Politics* (New York: Random House, 1967).

[52] For a helpful bibliographical essay, see Ralph B. Potter, *War and Moral Discourse* (Richmond: John Knox Press, 1969), pp. 87-123.

as they were once thought to be. Recently an American bishop has recognized the fact of this growing pluralism although his reaction to the fact is much different from the generally approving tone of this essay.[53] Thus the myth of a monolithic Roman Catholic moral theology with *the* Catholic opinion on specific, complex matters is exploded.

AUTHORITARIANISM

A second source of critical concern for Protestant ethicians has been the authoritarian intervention of the Roman Catholic Church in moral matters to direct and even bind the consciences of her members. The Catholic Church has claimed a unique competency to interpret authoritatively even the natural law for its adherents and thus supply a sure and reliable guide for conscience in moral matters.

Here again both a reexamination of the tradition and contemporary theological opinions have joined forces to change quite radically the understanding of the role of the teaching authority of the Church in matters of morality. Today there is also emerging within the Catholic Church a proper discussion about the meaning of infallibility as it pertains to the Church and to the papal office, but our discussion can neatly dodge the present furor over infallibility. In my judgment there has never been an infallible, *ex cathedra* pronouncement or an infallible teaching of the ordinary magisterium on a specific moral matter. Our concern is with the so-called authentic or authoritative, noninfallible hierarchical magisterium.

This expression—the authoritative, noninfallible teaching authority—apparently first appears about the time of the

---

[53] Most Rev. John F. Whealon, "Questions and Answers on the Ethical and Religious Directives for Catholic Hospitals," *Hospital Progress*, LII (October, 1971) , 75.

famous letter of Pope Pius IX to the archbishop of Munich in 1863 on the occasion of the conference of intellectuals held under the leadership of Döllinger with the intention of bringing Catholic thought into dialogue with the philosophy and science of the modern world.[54]

The theologians of the time developed this teaching on the authoritative, noninfallible teaching authority and the consent that was required to such teaching on the part of Catholics. The faithful owed to this teaching an internal religious assent of intellect and will as distinguished from the absolute assent of faith which Catholics must give to infallible Church teaching. The 19th and 20th century theologians generally admitted that this assent was conditioned even though they were rather general in describing the conditions. Thus in general the theologians admit the possibility of error in such teaching and even point to historical precedents for error in the teaching function of the popes—e.g., Liberius, Vigilius, Honorius, as well as Celestine III and the heralded Galileo case. Lercher admits at least the possibility of the Church correcting the Pope.[55] Thus the theologians who wrote the theological manuals of the day admit the possibility of error in the papal teaching with the corresponding possibility of nonacceptance on the part of the faithful.

The twentieth century witnessed a growing entrenchment of an overly juridical and authoritative understanding of the Church and of the hierarchical magisterium ever since the insistence in the nineteenth century against a real dialogue with the modern world. The encyclical *Humani Generis* in

---

54 *Enchiridion Symbolorum Definitionum et Declarationum de Rebus Fidei et Morum,* ed. H. Denzinger-A. Schönmetzer, S.I. (ed. XXXII; Barcelona: Herder, 1963), nn. 2875-2880. Hereafter cited as *D.S.*

55 This paragraph summarizes the study of Joseph A. Komonchak, "Ordinary Papal Magisterium and Religious Assent," in *Contraception: Authority and Dissent,* ed. Charles E. Curran (New York: Herder and Herder, 1969), pp. 101-148.

1950 was an attempt to clamp down on the "New Theology" and to reassert the papal teaching authority as a means of controlling theological speculation. In this letter Pope Pius XII applies to the ordinary papal teaching authority as found in encyclicals the biblical words—he who hears you hears Me. If the Pope goes out of his way to deliberately speak on a controverted subject, the subject can no longer be regarded as a matter for free debate among theologians.[56]

Changes occurring in the intervening years are reflected in the teaching of Vatican II and its differences with the teaching of *Humani Generis*. It is interesting to note that conservative opposition to some of the teaching of *Mater et Magistra* brought momentarily to the surface the right of Catholics to dissent from the authoritative, noninfallible teaching of the Pope.[57] The first draft of the Constitution on the Church of Vatican II did contain the teaching of *Humani Generis* mentioned above.[58] The final version of the Constitution purposely left out the teaching of *Humani Generis*. The final document employs the terminology of the manuals in distinguishing the religious assent owed to noninfallible teaching from the assent of faith and describes this religious assent in terms of a religious submission of intellect and will.[59] That the section is to be interpreted in the light of the teaching of the manuals is evident from the response given by the doctrinal commission to the query about an educated person who for solid reasons cannot give internal assent to a noninfallible teaching. The commission responded

---

[56] *D.S.*, n. 3885.

[57] Gary Wills, *Politics and Catholic Freedom* (Chicago: Henry Regnery, 1964).

[58] *Schemata Constitutionum et Decretorum de quibus disceptabitur in Concilii sessionibus: Series Secunda, De Ecclesia et de B. Maria Virgine* (Vatican City: Vatican Press, 1962), pp. 48-49.

[59] Dogmatic Constitution on the Church, n. 25, in *Documents of Vatican II*, ed. Walter M. Abbott (New York: Guild Press, 1966), pp. 47-49.

simply: "For this case approved theological explanations should be consulted."[60]

The ensuing development of this teaching has some interesting aspects. In 1967 the American bishops issued a collective pastoral letter, "The Church in Our Day." One section is devoted to religious assent, but the matter is presented in a confused and an inaccurate manner. This document speaks of religious assent as owed to both infallible and noninfallible teaching, but in the first case the religious assent is definitive, while in the second case such assent is required but not definitively. "A Catholic abides not only by the extraordinary decisions of the Church but by its ordinary life as well where faith and discipline are concerned."[61] Such an assent includes questions touching on dogma, "but it is also required for certain decisions bound up with the good ordering of the Church."[62] In addition to the novel use of religious assent and the confusion between faith and discipline, there is no explicit mention of the possibility of dissent.

On September 22, 1967, the German bishops issued a pastoral letter, which also took up the question of the assent due to noninfallible papal teaching. "To protect individuals and ultimately the substance of faith, the Church must make doctrinal pronouncements which are binding to a limited degree, despite the danger of error in particular matters. Since these are not definitions of faith, they are to some extent provisional and entail the possibility of error. . . . In this kind of situation the individual Christian and indeed the

60 *Schema Constitutionis Dogmaticae De Ecclesia: Modi a Patribus conciliaribus propositi a commissione doctrinali examinati, III: Caput III: De constitutione hierarchica Ecclesiae et in specie de Episcopatu* (Vatican City: Vatican Press, 1964) , p. 42.

61 *The Church in Our Day* (Washington: United States Catholic Conference, 1968) , p. 71.

62 *Ibid.,* p. 72.

Church as a whole is like a man who has to follow the decision of an expert whom he knows is not infallible."[63] Thus
the German bishops rightly interpret the authoritative, noninfallible teaching as provisional.

Before the issuance of Pope Paul's *Humanae Vitae* in
1968, theologians had been developing the possibility of
dissent from such authoritative, noninfallible papal teaching.
Theologians such as Donlon, Rahner and Schueller explicitly
affirmed the right of public dissent which had not been found
in the earlier manualists.[64] Perhaps the most perceptive
discussion of the moral magisterium was by Daniel Maguire,
who realized that the very nature of the search for moral
truth argues for the possibility of dissent from papal moral
teaching on specific issues. Maguire pointed out that the
hierarchical magisterium could not continue to function in
an overly juridical and legalistic style and constructively
suggested ways for the hierarchical magisterium to proceed
in carrying out its function in the changed theological understandings of the post Vatican II Church.[65]

The negative reaction of theologians and even bishops to
the papal encyclical on artificial contraception issued in the
summer of 1968 brought to the attention of all Catholics,
perhaps for the first time, the right to dissent from authoritative, noninfallible papal teaching when there are solid
reasons for so doing. This same reality can and must be
understood in a somewhat broader context and in a more

63 Karl Rahner, S.J., "Disput um das kirchliche Lehramt," *Stimmen der
Zeit*, CLXXXV (1970) , 73-81.

64 S. Donlon, S.J., "Freedom of Speech," *The New Catholic Encyclopedia*,
VI, 123; Bruno Schüller, S.J., "Bemerkungen zur authentischen Verkünding-
ung des Kirchlichen Lehramtes," *Theologie und Philosophie*, XLII (1967) ,
534-551; Karl Rahner, "Demokratie in der Kirche," *Stimmen der Zeit*,
CLXXXII (1968) , 1-15.

65 Daniel C. Maguire, "Moral Absolutes and the Magisterium," in *Absolutes in Moral Theology?* pp. 56-73.

positive manner. Even when the hierarchical magisterium has spoken on a particular issue, there can still be a pluralism of Catholic thinking on this issue. Thus from the viewpoint of a proper understanding of the moral teaching office of the hierarchical magisterium it will be impossible to speak about *the* Roman Catholic position on a particular moral issue as if there could not be any other possible position.

One must understand the reason for such a pluralism not only in methodology but also concerning practical questions. The basic reason for such a pluralism is the complexity of moral issues and the need for relational and empirical considerations which involve many aspects and afford the possibility of arriving at different ethical judgments. In the past when forbidden actions were described in terms of the physical structure of the act, then it was possible to speak about certain actions which were always and everywhere wrong. A relational understanding of morality or an empirical calculus cannot admit such absoluteness. In the midst of all the circumstances which must be considered in complex questions one must admit a possible diversity of concrete, ethical judgments.

The fundamental reason for this possible diversity—the many elements to be considered in the final decision and the complexity of the situation itself—had been acknowledged in the past by Thomas Aquinas himself. Thomas admitted that although the first principles of the natural law were always the same, the proper conclusions of these principles can admit of exceptions because of the complexity of the situation and the diverse elements entering into the final decision. The more one descends into particulars, the greater is the possibility of exceptions because of the complexity of the situation.[66]

---

[66] Thomas Aquinas, *Summa Theologiae*, Ia IIae, q. 94, a. 4.

THEOLOGICAL PRESUPPOSITIONS

Theological presuppositions of Protestant and Catholic ethics do seem to be a source of divergences in the two traditions, but even here the differences are much less today than in the past, and in some cases are negligible so that there really are no outstanding, pertinent theological differences between some Protestant and some Catholic ethicians. Unfortunately Mehl reflects more of the past divergences rather than the present convergences in his assessment.

The question often referred to as the nature-supernature question is of paramount significance in this area. Catholic theology has generally accepted the goodness of man, a continuity between nature and grace as well as between creation and redemption, and the possibility of going from man to God which has been the basis for a natural theology and a natural law. An earlier section has considered the philosophical aspects of the question of natural law, which included the precise understanding of man and nature with the different operative methodologies developed as a result of such understandings. From the theological perspective the natural law theory has asserted that the Christian can arrive at true ethical wisdom and knowledge through his reason and his understanding of man. Some forms of Protestant theology especially in the Orthodox and neo-Orthodox traditions have denied or denigrated the place of reason and the natural in Christian ethical consideration although often some substitute has been proposed. Chapter Two will consider in greater detail some aspects of these differences.

Mehl rejects the Catholic position which he describes as seeing man under two aspects—man as natural being and man as a being with a supernatural vocation. In such a system there seem to be two separate ethics for man—a purely human one and a supernatural one.[67] Although there will

---

[67] Mehl, p. 46.

continue to be differences in this area between some Catholic and some Protestant theologians, there have emerged some developments in Catholic thinking which can and do bridge the former gap at least with some Protestants.

Catholic theology today willingly admits the impossibility of proposing two ethics—an ethic of natural law for those living in the world and an ethic of evangelical perfection for those who choose to enter the religious life. Contemporary Catholic theology recalls that all Christians are called by God in Christ to change their hearts and follow him.[68]

One can notice even in the documents of the hierarchical magisterium a real move away from the notion of an existing natural order to which the supernatural is then added. The Pastoral Constitution on the Church in the Modern World is most instructive in this area—the phrase natural law appears only three times.[69] The anthropology described in this document marks a definite advance over the older anthropologies. The essential nature of man, the same in all possible states of human existence, is not the fundamental concept to which the supernatural order is added. Man is described in terms of the history of salvation which sees man and reality in terms of the work of creation, the reality of sin, the redemptive work of Jesus and final resurrection destiny. I personally have some difficulties with this particular presentation. The older concept of the two separate spheres of the natural and the supernatural is overcome, but the tension and ambiguity of our present existence in the light of the full Christian horizon do not appear. Some chapters of Part One (specifically: 1, 2 and 4) fail to give enough importance to the eschatological future and the discontinuity existing between now and the future. The eschatology of this docu-

---

[68] John D. Gerken, *Toward a Theology of the Layman* (New York: Herder and Herder, 1963).

[69] Pastoral Constitution on the Church in the Modern World, nn. 74, 79, 89; *Acta Apostolicae Sedis*, LVIII (1966), 1096, 1102, 1111. The Latin text employs the word *lex* in n. 74 and n. 89, while n. 79 uses *ius*.

ment has too much emphasis on realization now that Jesus has come. Correlatively, not enough importance is given to sin and its effects on human life.[70]

Even in the document itself, but especially in the light of my personal critique, one can understand the nature-super-nature question or the Christ and culture question in terms of H. Richard Niebuhr's classification of Christ transforming culture or of grace transforming nature rather than the Christ above culture model which characterized Catholic thought in the past.[71] My personal criticism is that this Constitution and the encyclical of Paul VI *Populorum Progressio* do not stress enough the transforming aspect, because sin and the eschatological future as somewhat discontinuous with the present do not receive enough attention. The fact that nature-supernature can be understood in terms of a conversionist or transformationist model in Catholic thought obviously indicates a broad area of agreement with many Protestants. The stance for moral theology to be developed in Chapter Two is most compatible with a transformationist motif.

The ramifications of a transformationist motif have appeared in an interesting way in a study of human sexuality by J-M. Pohier. Pohier rightly acknowledges the unfortunately negative understanding of sexuality in the Catholic tradition, which apparently comes from too easily equating sin with sexuality. Christians should understand sexuality the same way they understand justice, truth, and love. The eschatological future does not call for one to deny these realities or to die to them but rather to transform them. A

---

[70] These criticisms were made in the course of the conciliar debate by a few of the Council Fathers. See Philippe Delhaye, "Histoire des textes de la Constitution Pastorale," in *L'Eglise dans le monde de ce temps,* ed. Yves Congar, O.P. (Paris: Éditions du Cerf, 1967), I, 267-273.

[71] H. Richard Niebuhr, *Christ and Culture* (New York: Harper Torchbook, 1956), pp. 116-148, 190-229.

reconsideration of sexuality calls for a reconsideration of some basic understandings of the Christian faith, especially the resurrection.[72]

In this light Pohier denies the fact that man is by nature immortal. To believe in the resurrection is to believe that God will do to us as his gracious gift what he has done in Jesus. This is entirely different from asserting the natural immortality of man or the soul. These different understandings of immortality affect our understanding of sexuality. If man is by nature immortal, if death is punishment, if recovery of immortality demands that man willingly accept and inflict upon himself the penalty of death, the repression or abolition of sexuality signifies and realizes par excellence this recovery of immortality. If, on the contrary, the resurrection is the work of God, if it is a property of the love of God and not a property of the nature of man, and if it implies a change of man, then sexuality is neither more nor less than all the other dimensions of the present existence of man and the object of this future change.[73]

Certainly it is part of the Catholic theological tradition to uphold a basic goodness present in man, the power of human reason to arrive at some speculative and practical truths, and some continuity between man and grace. Thus Mehl correctly asserts that the Catholic tradition would not accept a total opposition between *agape* and *eros*.[74] There is some continuity between human love and divine love which both transforms and perfects human love. For the same reasons the Catholic theological tradition would have some problems with the theological presuppositions of Paul Ramsey's ethic, such as obedient love, the stress on fidelity with no attention

---

[72] J. M. Pohier, "Recherches sur les fondements de la morale sexuelle chrétienne," *Revue des Sciences Philosophiques et Théologiques*, LIV (1970), 3-23, 201-226.

[73] *Ibid.*, p. 226.

[74] Mehl, pp. 52-54.

to some notion of fulfillment, and his very basic insistence on order because of the prevailing presence of sin.[75] Today Catholic theologians must correct some of the overemphases of the recent past by realizing also the discontinuity between nature and grace and some discontinuity between the present and the eschatological future.[76] Such an insistence makes it easier to adopt a transformationist or conversionist model.

Intimately connected with the nature-grace question is the importance given to the reality of sin. There is no doubt that Protestant theology has generally placed much more emphasis on sin than the Catholic tradition has. The insistence on order in some Protestant social ethics is derived from their understanding of the pervading power of sin.[77] Catholic theology can legitimately be criticized for not giving enough importance in the past to the reality of sin, although such a consideration was not always lacking in Catholic thought. Thomas Aquinas, for example, acknowledged the existence of the right to own private property not on the basis of the dignity and needs of the human person as was done by later Popes, but because of human sinfulness. Peace, order and the care of goods would be better provided for if each person owns his own property even though all property retains a relationship for all mankind so that one's use of his right to private property is limited by this communal consideration.[78]

---

[75] Paul Ramsey, *Basic Christian Ethics* (New York: Charles Scribner's Sons, 1950) ; Ramsey, *Christian Ethics and the Sit-In* (New York: Association Press, 1961) , pp. 40-98.

[76] See my *Catholic Moral Theology in Dialogue* (Notre Dame, Ind.: Fides, 1972) , Chap. iv.

[77] Helmut Thielicke, *Theological Ethics*, Vol. I: *Foundations,* ed. William H. Lazareth (Philadelphia: Fortress Press, 1966) , pp. 434-451. Practical implications of this teaching are developed in Thielicke, *Theological Ethics,* Vol. II: *Politics* (Philadelphia: Fortress Press, 1969) . A somewhat similar emphasis is found in Ramsey, *Christian Ethics and the Sit-In,* pp. 40-98.

[78] Thomas Aquinas, *Summa Theologiae,* IIa IIae, q. 66, a. 2.

Today Catholic theologians are trying to develop a better understanding of the reality and moral significance of sin. Böckle here presents a more adequate picture of the developments in Catholic theology than does Mehl, who is obviously writing from within a different theological tradition.[79] Catholic theology has learned especially in dialogue with Protestant theology to place more emphasis on sin and the sinner rather than on sins. Relying heavily on biblical theology and more personalist and existential themes, as well as a revival of older Thomistic notions, contemporary theology has developed the reality of sin in terms of the fundamental option.[80] Catholic theology has also tried to recover a way in which it can accept and incorporate the insights of the *simul justus et peccator* concept of the Reformation with the corresponding call for continual conversion on the part of the Christian.[81] Likewise, the natural order does not continue to exist as if it were unaffected by sin but rather the very fact that sin has not destroyed man and the human is the work of God's gracious love.[82]

The effect of sin in the moral life of man is seen in the attempts by some Catholic theologians to come to grips with conflict situations in the light of the presence of sin.[83] The overly rationalist approach of the manuals according to Nicholas Crotty denied the very existence of the possibility of a conflict of values in moral decision making. In the older

[79] Böckle, pp. 117-131.

[80] For complementary summaries and further bibliography, see Josef Fuchs, S.J., *Human Values and Christian Morality* (Dublin: Gill and Macmillan, 1970), pp. 92-111; John W. Glaser, "Transition Between Grace and Sin," *Theological Studies,* XXIX (1968), 260-274.

[81] Bernard Häring, C.SS.R., "Conversion," in *Pastoral Treatment of Sin* (New York: Desclée, 1968), pp. 87-176; Karl Rahner, "Justified and Sinner at the Same Time," in *Theological Investigations,* Vol. VI: *Concerning Vatican Council II* (Baltimore: Helicon, 1969), pp. 218-230.

[82] Böckle, pp. 122, 123.

[83] Norbert J. Rigali, "The Unity of the Moral Order," *Chicago Studies,* VIII (1969), 125-143.

approach there could be no conflict of values because there is a perfectly ordered plan for the world in which all things are arranged in proper relationships and order, and reason can perceive this order. In all situations including those which apparently involve conflicts there is an objectively valid moral decision which can simply be called good. Moral duties can never really conflict.[84]

Crotty points out that some Catholic theologians deny such a view of reality because there are true conflict situations which are brought about by the presence of sin. Some might still object that these are not real moral evils but only physical evils or pre-moral evils.[85] In some cases I would readily agree that the evil is pre-moral (e.g. contraception), but in other cases the social dimension of sin so affects reality that there is the necessity of recognizing that the conflict arises because of the presence of sin. Strictly speaking, the evil here is not moral in the sense of intended by one of the persons involved, but it results from the presence of sin incarnated in the structures of human existence and not just from human finitude and limitation. Crotty sees the Christian as weighing the good and the evil consequences of his action with the realization that his action will bring about some evil which must be recognized and deplored in true Christian repentance.[86] It seems to me that those who deny this fact or say the values involved in all cases are only pre-moral have too individualistic a view of sin and repentance. Above all in these days we must understand the very real existence of corporate guilt and repentance. Theories of this type in Catholic theology obviously owe much to the ongoing dialogue with Protestant ethicians.

---

84 Nicholas Crotty, C.P., "Conscience and Conflict," *Theological Studies*, XXXII (1971), 209-212.

85 Such objections are made by McCormick, *Theological Studies*, XXXIII (1972), 81.

86 Crotty, *Theological Studies*, XXXII (1971), 212-219.

Justification and sanctification have been a perennial source of debate among Catholics and Protestants, and different approaches to those theological questions can have important repercussions in the area of Christian ethics. Differing opinions about the possibility of growth or development in the Christian life depend upon one's understanding of the reality of justification and sanctification.[87] Recent Catholic scholarship has tried to show that there may not be that much difference on the question of justification between Protestant and Catholic position.[88]

In moral areas Catholic thought has underscored the importance of works, and the danger of pelagianism is ever present and sometimes succumbed to, at least in practice. The tendency in Protestantism is to highlight faith, and quietism and passivity have threatened such an approach.[89] Some Protestant and Catholic theologians seem to be more aware of the dichotomies in their older approaches to these questions and are now trying to do justice to both faith and the rightful place of works in the Christian life.

Another important theological difference between Protestant and Catholic thought centers on the concept of freedom. A few years ago it was a commonplace in the incipient ecumenical dialogue to show that Catholic thought exaggerated order at the expense of freedom, whereas Protestant thought overlooked order in their insistence on freedom.

---

[87] Compare on this particular point, the different approaches proposed by George T. Montague, S.M., *Maturing in Christ: Saint Paul's Program for Christian Growth* (Milwaukee: Bruce, 1964), esp. pp. 101-110, and Victor Paul Furnish, *Theology and Ethics in Paul* (Nashville: Abingdon, 1968), p. 176.

[88] Hans Küng, *Justification: The Doctrine of Karl Barth and a Catholic Reflection* (London: Nelson, 1964). For a sympathetic acceptance of Küng's thesis, see Karl Rahner, S.J., "Questions of Controversial Theology on Justification, *Theological Investigations*, Vol. IV: *More Recent Writings* (Baltimore: Helicon, 1966), pp. 189-218.

[89] James Sellers, *Theological Ethics* (New York: Macmillan, 1966), pp. 39-65.

There is obviously truth in this assertion, but there have also been some attempts to overcome such dichotomies.

Protestant theology highlights the transcendence and graciousness of God, who in his freedom has chosen to act in human history. God in his freedom acts in concrete ways with individual men which can never be totally determined in advance by any human calculations or laws, since the freedom of God is sovereign. Catholic theology traditionally understands God's acting with man through different mediations; whereas Protestant theology has insisted often on the immediate character of God's relationship with man. Catholic theology has developed these mediations of the divine action in terms of the Church, the sacraments, Church order and natural law. Some Protestant ethicians understand the divine transcendence, the freedom of God and the concreteness of his way of acting with man in the context of a soteriology which places an unbridgeable chasm between Christian ethics and any form of human or philosophical ethics.[90] This type of approach is quite foreign to the Catholic tradition with its acceptance of mediation and the role of the natural. Catholic theology, however, is beginning to recognize the importance of the transcendence and freedom of God as practically reflected in the whole dispute about absolute norms in the moral life.

Correlatively, Protestant ethics recognizes the fundamental importance of the freedom of the believer, whereas Catholic theology has traditionally had difficulty with the concept of freedom. Catholic insistence on the objective and on the ordered structure of human existence left little room for creative freedom and the subjective. Recall the tortuous development in Catholic thinking on the question of reli-

---

[90] E.g., Paul Lehmann, *Ethics in a Christian Context* (New York: Harper and Row, 1963), pp. 165-284.

gious liberty.[91] The recent change of emphasis is evident in a development in Pope John's teaching. In 1963 he insisted that a just and Christian social order should be based on truth, justice, charity and freedom,[92] but two years earlier in *Mater et Magistra* he had not mentioned freedom.[93] Today some Catholics are calling for a morality based on freedom with the consequent importance of responsibility which fits in with the move away from an understanding of an essential structure of man and human community as presupposed in the older natural law approach.[94]

IMPLICATIONS

This chapter has attempted to survey the present state of Roman Catholic theology under the limited perspective of the ongoing dialogue with Protestant ethics. There still do exist some differences based primarily on theological presuppositions which are especially evident in discussions with Orthodox and neo-Orthodox Protestants. In general there has been a remarkable breaking down of the barriers and differences between Catholic and Protestant ethics so that often there is agreement across denominational lines on both methodological and content questions. The factor contributing the most to this change is the breakdown of a monolithic, Roman Catholic moral theology. Whatever value judgments one might want to make about the present situation, the fact seems to be that there is no monolithic, Cath-

---

91 Pius Augustin, *Religious Freedom in Church and State* (Baltimore: Helicon, 1966) ; Richard J. Regan, S.J., *Conflict and Consensus: Religious Freedom and the Second Vatican Council* (New York: Macmillan, 1967) .

92 *Pacem in terris,* n. 35; *A.A.S.,* LV (1963) , 265-266.

93 *Mater et Magistra,* n. 226; *A.A.S.,* LIII (1961) , 454.

94 Antoine, *Projet,* XLII (1970) , 131-141. On the centrality of responsibility, see Albert R. Jonsen, *Responsibility in Modern Religious Ethics* (Washington/Cleveland: Corpus Books, 1968) .

olic moral theology and no such thing as *the* Catholic position on specific, complex moral questions.

What are the implications of this description of the factual situation of Catholic moral theology today? I think that many Catholic moral theologians actively working in the field and teaching today would be in general accord with the situation of pluralism as described here. However, the rapidity of the change and the somewhat radical nature of the change have contributed to the fact that the vast majority of people outside the field of Catholic moral theology are unaware of this new situation. Obviously this situation with so many possibilities for tension and misunderstanding is difficult. The Catholic moral theologian has the responsibility of making other interested people aware of the actual situation in his field as it exists today, even though there would be a number of Catholic ethicians, perhaps a minority, who would not agree with this description. The Catholic theologian has a responsibility to communicate this situation to many publics, but this discussion will just concentrate on three different groups.

First, Protestant ethicians. As exemplified in the case of Mehl the rapidity of the changing situation in Catholic ethics has caught some Protestant theologians unaware. Many Protestant ethicians are quite familiar with the present state of Catholic moral theology, probably more so in this country than elsewhere. A realization of the breakup of a monolithic methodology or a detailed monolithic code will prevent Protestants from speaking about *the* Roman Catholic ethics or *the* Roman Catholic solution to a particular problem without further nuances.

Secondly, the Catholic community generally. Roman Catholics on the whole are unaware of the present state of Roman Catholic theology. In any science there is always an educational lag between what the theoreticians are saying and what the ordinary person knows. This gap is even more pronounced now because of the suddenness and the radical-ness of the change. Such a change has obviously been very difficult and traumatic for people who were in the field of moral theology. One of the many problems with Catholic moral theology in this country and even abroad today is the fact that most of the people actively engaged in the field today have been in the field for less than 15 years.

The gap between the actual state of Catholic moral theology and the understanding of the Catholic in the street is enormous. There is need for a real educational effort on the part of all, including theologians. Fears of subjectivity, relativism and individualism must be put aside. Likewise such people also have to be shown how the discipline arrived at the present state and continuities as well as the discontinuities with the past teaching. One can appreciate the anxiety and fears of many Catholics, but this only underlines the need for education.

Thirdly, the bishops and the hierarchical teaching office in the Church. The Catholic Church has experienced many painful shocks in the last few years. The easiest solution at times is to blame the Pope and the bishops. As an ethician who believes in the theoretical and practical importance of complexity, I tend to reject overly simplistic solutions which really fail to respond to the realities of the situation. The Pope and the bishops have enormous concerns and many groups asking for their attention and consideration. More than anyone else, they experience and know the tensions of the rapid changes which have taken place in Catholic life and theology in the past few years.

There has not been a relationship of dialogue and trust between bishops and theologians in the past few years. This is true not only of the United States but also exists in countries such as Germany. Obviously there is fault on both sides contributing to this lack of dialogue.

However, the simple fact of the matter is that the bishops of the Roman Catholic Church in general and the bishops of the United States in particular are unwilling to admit the present state of Roman Catholic moral theology and apparently feel unable to enter into dialogue about this. Again I realize that different perspectives exist between theologians and bishops and that there will always be such a tension between them; but the existing differences are actually quite destructive for the life of the Church as a whole. Nor would I merely reduce the teaching office of the bishops to repeating a theological consensus, but there must be increased dialogue and understanding.

In a sense the bishops were forced by the quality and quantity of the dissent to *Humanae Vitae* to try to live with such a reality. However, they obviously thought that it was an isolated phenomenon which would quickly disappear or that would be forgotten about if they just stayed around long enough. What they have not realized is that the dissent to *Humanae Vitae* was symptomatic of changes occurring in moral theology and these symptoms are bound to appear ever more increasingly. Much more was involved than just speculative dissent from one specific teaching of the hierarchical magisterium. This historical episode signified a new understanding of Catholic moral theology and the way in which the hierarchical magisterium should carry out its teaching function in the area of morality.

Perhaps the most blatant sign of the gap between bishops and theologians was the issuance by the bishops of the United States of "The Ethical and Religious Directives for Catholic Health Facilities," which was approved by the American bishops at their November 1971 meeting by an overwhelming vote. This document in the words of the chairman of the bishops "Committee on Doctrine" amounts to a mere updating of the 1955 directives. In such things there can never be essential changes but only accidental changes.[95]

---

95 Whealon, *Hospital Progress,* LII (October, 1971), 75.

In the light of the present state of Roman Catholic moral theology, especially the discussions on absolute norms and medical ethics, it seems preposterous that the American bishops could issue medical directives substantially the same as those issued in 1955. The bishops by their action show that they do not understand the present state of Catholic moral theology and consequently are trying to exercise their teaching function in a way that is totally incompatible with the concept of our search for moral truth.

The preamble of these directives speaks about the prohibited procedures as recognized to be clearly wrong according to present knowledge. The document goes on to talk about the basic moral absolutes in a way that completely ignores the developments of the past few years. The reference to Catholic moral teaching is to a "code," although it is precisely such an approach that is questioned by many Catholic theologians today.[96] This document fails to recognize three important realities stressed in this paper: the pluralism of ethical methodologies in Roman Catholic moral theology; the possibility of dissent on specific questions and the more positive formulation admitting of some pluralism; the particular moral conclusions which have been seriously questioned by Catholic scholarship in the last few years.

I personally and many other Catholic theologians would object to the following specifics of this code: the condemnations of contraception, direct sterilization, masturbation for seminal analysis, artificial insemination with the husband's seed; some aspects of the teaching on abortion and euthanasia; the processes forbidden in the handling of extrauterine pregnancies; the distinction between direct and indirect which is stated in terms of the physical structure of the act

---

[96] Preamble, "Ethical and Religious Directives for Catholic Health Facilities." These directives may be obtained from the Department of Health Affairs, United States Catholic Conference, 1312 Massachusetts Avenue, NW, Washington, D.C. 20005.

itself ("Any deliberate medical procedure, the purpose of which is to deprive a fetus or an embryo of its life"; "Every procedure whose sole immediate effect is the termination of pregnancy before viability is an abortion."[97]—Notice here the failure to adopt the traditional terminology of direct and indirect abortion and the effort to redefine abortion in terms of direct abortion so that the absoluteness of the prohibition may be strengthened) ; the solution of conflict situations involving life by the application of the principle of double effect.

Perhaps even more disturbing is the attitude proposed by one bishop who was influential in the work of the directives because of his position as chairman of the "Committee on Doctrine" of the American bishops. In a commentary on the proposed hospital directives the bishop took up the question of possible dissent from the norms of such a code.

All this is risky business—this following of personal conscience in any issue on which the moral law holds otherwise. It is possible to find these days a Catholic writer on speculative moral theology advancing in nearly every subject a theory contrary to traditional Catholic doctrine. You cannot "follow" him, because he is not an authorized leader of the People of God. Accept his theories and you are on your own, crossing Niagara Falls on a tightrope with the abyss beneath, rather than using the bridge which the Church has constructed for your safety and direction in reaching the opposite shore.[98]

This paragraph contains a very poor and I believe harmfully erroneous notion of the teaching authority in the Church and how it is exercised. The bishop acknowledges there is existing a plurality of theological opinions in nearly every subject.[99] In the midst of this moral complexity the

---

[97] "Ethical and Religious Directives for Catholic Health Facilities," n. 11, 12.

[98] Whealon, *Hospital Progress*, LII (October, 1971) , 75.

[99] *Ibid.*

problem can be solved in a juridical and authoritarian way by the teaching authority of the Church. This is the worst kind of juridical and voluntaristic notion of a true teacher. Perhaps some of the problem arises from the too frequent juxtaposition in the Catholic tradition of those two words— teaching authority. The teaching office thus easily becomes understood in a juridical and authoritative way. The possibility and the right to dissent are not specified in a way that a true teacher should explain these realities. One sees in these hospital directives and in this interpretation that monolithic natural law theory based on the nature of things, a legalistic code approach to complex specific questions, and an authoritarianism which are the precise points of contention and dispute in contemporary Catholic moral theology.

Obviously we are living in changing and confusing times. The American bishops felt many pressures urging them to give some hospital directives. There are good points contained in these directives as well as in the older directives. I am not sure how I would proceed in trying to draw up such directives in the light of the changing theological scene, the possibility and even the right to dissent acknowledged to exist in the Church, the changing understanding of the Catholic health facility in terms of its funding and its service, the principle of religious liberty and the rights of people to act in accord with their conscience provided public order and the rights of other innocent people are not disproportionately affected. The problem is very complex, and no perfect solution can ever be arrived at; but the directives as issued by the American bishops are in my judgment theologically inaccurate and pastorally harmful in the long run.

The issuance of the hospital directives by the American bishops is just another indication of the tension existing in the Roman Catholic Church today. Obviously one does not want to exacerbate such tensions, but at times it is necessary to speak forthrightly in the hope of bringing about greater good. Obviously theologians are also at fault for not having done more in this area. If Catholic theologians had taken the initiative and come out with their own set of directives, perhaps they could have avoided some problems.

The implications of the state of Catholic moral theology have thus far concentrated only on the present. What are the implications for the future? This essay has in general followed an approach showing the importance of both continuity and discontinuity in moral theology. A revision and restudy of past teachings has brought about almost radical reinterpretations. At the same time newer approaches have also greatly contributed to the changing reality of moral theology. Any valid approach in the future must appreciate the significance of both continuity and discontinuity, but it seems that discontinuity will need a greater emphasis both because of the rapidly changing conditions of human existence and also because of the fact that an artificial, monolithic approach backed by an overly juridical teaching authority was able to preserve in existence what was really an historically and culturally limited reality.

The future development of Catholic moral theology can well profit from some of the traditional emphases—the ability of human reason to arrive at good ethical decisions, a basic goodness in man which despite sinfulness remains in some continuity, as well as some discontinuity, with grace and redemption. Likewise the traditional Catholic emphasis on the structure of man and human existence can be of help if interpreted in a way to appreciate the web of relationships in which man finds himself so that he cannot be defined primarily in terms of an unrestricted freedom which does not take into account the relationships which both limit and perfect him.

However, the future will continue to develop the discontinuities especially in terms of the understanding of man and the ethical methodologies proposed for decision-making. The incipient pluralism described above will only become more evident in the years to come. Dialogue with contemporary scientific and philosophical approaches will result in newer approaches in Catholic moral theology. In the area of personal ethics, if one can make a distinction between personal and social ethics, this dialogue has already begun. But in the area of social ethics Catholic theology must begin to develop different approaches. The natural law approach of the papal encyclicals of the past is no longer sufficient. A suitable methodology must be constructed which will incorporate a critical dialogue with the sciences in trying to deal with questions of social morality. One can notice the lack of any such methodology among Roman Catholic ethicians at the present time. The great social problems of our day obviously involve the question of means to bring about the values to be incorporated into our society. Perhaps in the area of social ethics there is the greatest need for newer approaches and methodologies.

The fact that there will be discontinuities with the past and perhaps very noticeable discontinuities in the area of approaches to social ethics should not be discomforting to one who deeply appreciates the Catholic tradition. The greatness of Thomas Aquinas comes from his boldness and creativity in trying to express the Christian message in the thought patterns which were then current in his world. Thomas was not content merely to cite the authorities of the past, but rather he creatively attempted to express the Christian message in terms of the Aristotelian thought which was then coming into the University world of Europe. The Catholic tradition with its rightful appreciation of human reason must always be willing to enter into rational dialogue and discover newer approaches and understandings.

Ironically, Thomas Aquinas in the last two centuries has been used by the hierarchical magisterium for the exact opposite purpose of what he tried to accomplish in his own times. The hierarchical magisterium has employed Thomas as a means of prohibiting any dialogue with the modern world and of preserving a monolithic philosophical system often referred to as the perennial philosophy.[100] If Catholic theology had been allowed to develop normally in the last two centuries there would not be the traumatic experience of so abrupt and sudden a change as the Roman Catholic Church is experiencing today. Future developments will only accent and bring to the fullest development the changes already mentioned as occurring in Roman Catholic moral theology. But the willingness to accept the ability of man to arrive at moral truth, together with an historical world view, implies the need for a continuing dialogue ever incorporating contemporary human wisdom with the critical realization that such wisdom must always be put to the test.

Obviously the present state of Catholic moral theology and my understanding of its future development will also create problems for the discipline of moral theology as well as for the life of the Catholic Church. I have expressed my personal disagreement with some aspects of these new developments although I generally favor such a pluralistic understanding. However, whether one likes it or not, it will be impossible to change the present directions in Catholic moral theology.

---

[100] Chapter Two will discuss this use of Thomas Aquinas at greater length.

2

The Stance of Moral Theology

This chapter concerns the most fundamental question in moral theology—the stance which serves as the starting point of moral theology by forming the perspective with which Christian ethics or moral theology reflects on man's life and actions in the world. The same stance or horizon plays a similarly important role in the practical life of the Christian so that the question pursued here has both theoretical and practical importance.

SOME PROPOSED STANCES

In his *Theological Ethics,* James Sellers raises the question of the stance of Christian ethics as logically the first consideration.[1] Sellers admits that one does not necessarily have to begin his ethics with this question, as is exemplified in the case of Reinhold Niebuhr, who began with temporal actions and especially the injustices existing in the life of society.

---

[1] James Sellers, *Theological Ethics* (New York: Macmillan, 1968), pp. 31-68.

Not only is stance the most fundamental question in Christian ethics, but it serves as a source of other ethical criteria. Sellers, however, would not maintain that the other criteria are merely deduced from the stance. Sellers also describes the stance as the servant of the gospel although it can never be adequate to the whole gospel. Finally, the stance is always subject to revision in the light of the gospel and of the changing times.[2]

Sellers rejects the more traditional approach by Orthodox Protestantism which made faith the stance for Christian ethics. *Sola fide* (Faith alone) was a most fundamental consideration even in Protestant ethics. Faith as a stance is rejected by Sellers for two reasons: 1) *Sola fide* implies an altogether passive view of man who merely receives the gift of God, but it does not pay enough attention to the active and creative role man is called upon to play in our ageric society. 2) Faith as a stance introduces a cleavage between faith and the cultural and the social life of man. Man today places more stress on the worldly and temporal aspects of his life in the world.[3]

The standard alternative to faith as a stance in Protestant ethics has been love, but Sellers also rejects love as the stance. The word love has been battered and poorly understood on the one hand by the biblical theologians who have made love something almost humanly impossible and, on the other hand, by the sentimentalists who have reduced love to trivialities. The ultimate reality in the Christian life is not love but redemption, and love is the qualitatively highest mode of attaining the goal of redemption.[4]

Love continues to be proposed very often as the stance for Christian ethics, but there are also other problems connected

2 *Ibid.*, pp. 31-38.
3 *Ibid.*, pp. 39-53.
4 *Ibid.*, pp. 54, 55.

with love as the stance for moral theology. No one can deny the high priority which Christian ethics should give to love, but love as the fundamental stance is another question. One aspect of the problem is the nature of the stance itself. As the logical starting point for ethical reflection the stance must be comprehensive enough to include all the aspects of Christian ethics and yet limited enough to serve as a foundational point and a source of further criteria. One wonders if any content aspect of the Christian experience, whether it be love, hope, humility, or any particular virtue can ever serve as the stance for moral theology. H. Richard Niebuhr realized the difficulty of finding any one virtue which gives the key to the life of Jesus and his followers. Niebuhr sees the uniqueness of Jesus in terms not of any one virtue but in terms of his unique relationship with the Father. Thus Niebuhr disagrees with much of Protestant liberalism which had equivalently made love the stance for Christian ethics.[5]

The question of love as stance has been raised in the more contemporary literature in the light of the situation ethics debate especially as centered on the ethics proposed by Joseph Fletcher. On a popular level there is an untested assumption that love is the stance for moral theology, but again there remains here the danger of not understanding precisely what is the meaning and function of stance. Fletcher unhesitatingly makes love the starting point, the boss principle, and the only thing that ultimately counts in his ethics. He succinctly summarized his approach in six propositions.[6] The debate on situation ethics occasioned by Fletcher's book has brought to light some problems and

---

[5] H. Richard Niebuhr, *Christ and Culture* (New York: Harper Torchbook, 1956), pp. 14-19.

[6] Joseph Fletcher, *Situation Ethics* (Philadelphia: Westminster Press, 1966). Also see Fletcher, *Moral Responsibility: Situation Ethics at Work* (Philadelphia: Westminster Press, 1967).

difficulties with love as the fundamental stance for moral theology.[7]

If love is to have such an all encompassing role, then it seems to take on many different and even contradictory meanings. Donald Evans, who is basically sympathetic to a situational approach to morality, claims that Fletcher gives four conflicting accounts of love. The one moral test of an action is whether it increases love. Secondly, love is an attitude of good will. Thirdly, love is what the agent does. Fourthly, love is a faculty by means of which the agent discerns what he is to do.[8] Basil Mitchell argues that in ethics love is not enough. Love requires thought, and specifically moral thought; but also love requires some decision as to what human ends are or are not worth seeking.[9] Mitchell begins his essay with the common sense observation, illustrated by a parlor game, that one is faced with two possible alternatives neither of which is helpful to the ethicist who wants to enshrine love as the stance for Christian ethics—either there are some sorts of actions that cannot be performed lovingly or there are no actions that cannot be performed lovingly.[10]

These comments generally work from the same basic assumption that love, or for that matter any one virtue, cannot encompass all the things that go into ethical considerations. It is too simplistic to reduce all morality to love. Evans and Mitchell are not speaking specifically about love as the

---

[7] For a variety of reactions to Fletcher, see John C. Bennett *et al., Storm Over Ethics* (n.p.: United Church Press, 1967) ; *The Situation Ethics Debate,* ed. Harvey Cox (Philadelphia: Westminster Press, 1968) .

[8] Donald Evans, "Love, Situations and Rules," in *Norm and Context in Christian Ethics,* ed. Gene H. Outka and Paul Ramsey (New York: Charles Scribner's Sons, 1968) , pp. 369-375.

[9] Basil Mitchell, "Ideals, Roles and Rules," in *Norm and Context in Christian Ethics,* p. 363.

[10] *Ibid.,* p. 353.

stance understood in our exact sense, but their criticisms stem from the fact that it is too simplistic to reduce everything to love. I cannot accept love as the stance for Christian ethics precisely for the same basic reason—the stance really cannot be equated with any one aspect or any one attitude of the Christian life no matter how important it is.

Another set of problems arises from the fact that there is great disagreement about the exact meaning of love and the different elements involved in love. Fletcher, for example, claims that he is talking about love as *agape* and not love as *philia* (friendship love) or *eros,* (romantic love) .[11] I would argue that love must contain all three of these aspects and cannot be just pure *agape* as separated from and distinguished from any concept of reciprocity and self-fulfillment. Although in his description Fletcher draws a very exalted concept of *agape,* in practice it does not seem to be all that different from other forms of human wisdom.

The fact remains that love is a very complicated reality and includes many different aspects. Some theories of love appear inadequate precisely because they do not include certain elements that cannot be excluded. There has been a long debate in the history of Christian ethics about the exact relationship of human love and Christian love which shares in the *agape* of God. The Catholic tradition following in the footsteps of Augustine has always seen Christian love as incorporating the best of human love.[12] In the strict position of Lutheran Protestantism, Anders Nygren sees Christian love as altogether different from human love.[13] One can also ask if love of God and love of neighbor are the same

---

11 Fletcher, *Situation Ethics,* p. 79.

12 M. C. D'Arcy, S.J., *The Mind and Heart of Love* (New York: Meridian Books, 1956) ; Jules Toner, *The Experience of Love* (Washington/Cleveland: Corpus Books, 1968) .

13 Anders Nygren, *Agape and Eros* (New York: Harper Torchbook, 1969) .

thing. The seemingly simple reality of Christian love raises a number of significant and important questions about its precise meaning and the elements it includes.

After rejecting love as the stance, Sellers proposes his own stance. Salvation or redemption for contemporary man is best understood in terms of wholeness, but man as yet does not fully possess this wholeness and is searching for it. Man's way to wholeness has been presented in the Scriptures as a pilgrimage. "The Judaeo-Christian faith, then, offers a distinctive understanding of what is happening to man: he is moving from promise to fulfillment."[14] The stance for Christian ethics is thus promise and fulfillment.

I have difficulty accepting the stance proposed by Sellers for the precise reason that he gives too great a role to fulfillment in Christian ethics. Perhaps the ultimate reason for the difference lies in two different views of eschatology and the possibility of fulfillment in this world. Sellers insists in a number of places that this fulfillment will take place in finitude, temporality and spatiality—in the world.[15] At times Sellers is willing to admit that there might be something beyond this life in terms of fulfillment, but he is interested in fulfillment only in this world.[16] I would hold for fulfillment only outside time and beyond history. In this world there seems to be more promise than fulfillment both in terms of the biblical witness and in the light of human experience.

One could interpret the biblical message as being opposed to the stance proposed by Sellers. Paul Ramsey, for example, on the basis of biblical considerations refuses to accept any ethical methodology that depends on the Christian's attain-

14 Sellers, p. 63.
15 *Ibid.*, pp. 62-64.
16 *Ibid.*, pp. 55, 63.

ing certain goals or ends. Ramsey is opposed to any teleological basis for Christian ethics. "Eschatology has at least
this significance for Christian ethics in all ages: that reliance
on producing *teloi,* or on doing good consequences, or on
goal seeking has been decisively set aside. The meaning of
obligation or of right action is not to be derived from any of
these ends-in-view in an age that is fast being liquidated."[17]
Ramsey also understands the biblical concept of covenant as
emphasizing the aspect of promise and fidelity much more
than the note of fulfillment.[18]

I would interpret both these eschatologies as somewhat
extreme. With Sellers I would give more importance than
Ramsey to this world, its continuity with the future and
man's vocation to work for building the new heaven and the
new earth. But I think Sellers has wrongly collapsed the
eschatological tension into a realized eschatology, for man's
fulfillment lies ultimately outside time, history and space.
There is also discontinuity between this world and the next.
Sellers has too optimistic a view of the possibility of true
human fulfillment in this world, and thus his proposed stance
seems inadequate.

James M. Gustafson raises the same basic question in
terms of the perspective or the posture as the fundamental
angle of vision which the Christian gospel requires. The
words perspective and posture each refer to something
which is basic. Perspective, drawn from the visual experience, ultimately refers to the state of the viewing subject.
Posture has developed from its use in describing the arrangement of the parts of the body to now suggest the basic characteristic of a person, his fundamental state or frame of

[17] Paul Ramsey, *Deeds and Rules in Christian Ethics* (New York: Charles
Scribner's Sons, 1967) , p. 108.
[18] Paul Ramsey, *Basic Christian Ethics* (New York: Charles Scribner's Sons,
1950) , pp. 2-24.

mind.[19] The perspective or posture for the Christian is Jesus Christ. Jesus Christ as the revealer of the Father is the One through whom the ultimate meaning of life is known and understood. Jesus Christ is the focal point of the Christian community, and he remains the common object of loyalty of all Christians.[20]

I have some difficulties in accepting Jesus Christ as the basic stance, posture or perspective of Christian ethics. Some Protestant theologians (not Gustafson) employing, at least implicitly, Jesus Christ as the stance of Christian ethics adopt an unacceptable Christological monism. A Christological monism so emphasizes the centrality and importance of Jesus Christ that it does not give enough importance to other aspects of the moral perspective of the Christian. If Jesus Christ becomes the only way into the ethical question not enough importance is given to the reality of creation and all those things that have some meaning and intelligibility even apart from the explicit redemption in Jesus Christ. Some Christian ethics thus rule out any other source of ethical wisdom and knowledge for the Christian except Jesus Christ. Such a vision (which, I repeat, is not Gustafson's) is too narrow and exclusive.

There is no doubt that in a certain sense Jesus Christ is what is most distinctive about Christian life and ethics, but there is a danger that too exclusive an emphasis on what is distinctive in Christian ethics will not do justice to what the Christian shares with all mankind. Especially with the realization that Christians constitute a minority of mankind, one might be somewhat hesitant to take as the perspective of Christian ethics what could be construed in so exclusive a

---

19 James M. Gustafson, *Christ and the Moral Life* (New York: Harper and Row, 1968) , p. 242.
20 *Ibid.,* p. 241.

way as to neglect the elements which Christians share with all men.

The fact that there can be different ways of understanding Jesus Christ as the stance or posture of Christian ethics points to a problem which is even true with regard to Gustafson's use of Jesus Christ. One has to unpack the meaning of Jesus Christ. As such, Jesus Christ as stance needs some further elaboration and development. Obviously any stance would need such elaboration, but one wonders if this stance says both too much and too little.

In reflecting on this whole question of stance it might seem quite unusual that faith, love and Jesus Christ have all been rejected as the proper stance for Christian ethics. In no way does this deny the importance of all these realities, but the stance has some specific functions to fulfill. It is the logically prior first question in ethics which is comprehensive enough to include all that should be included and yet gives some direction and guidance in terms of developing other ethical criteria. There will never be the perfect stance, but some seem more adequate than others in terms of the function the stance should fulfill in moral theology. To adequately judge any stance it is necessary to see precisely how it does function in practice, but the ones proposed thus far do not seem to fulfill the role of stance as well as the one about to be proposed.

In talking about the stance, posture or perspective of moral theology, I would add the term horizon to try to further clarify the meaning and function of what is being discussed. Bernard Lonergan understands horizon as a maximum field of vision from a determinate viewpoint. Horizon thus includes both an objective pole and a subjective pole.[21]

---

[21] David W. Tracy, "Horizon Analysis and Eschatology," *Continuum*, VI (1968), 166-172.

The use of the term horizon allows one to emphasize the importance of the subject as well as the object in the question of stance. The horizon forms the way in which the subject looks at reality and structures his own understanding of the world and reality. Horizon indicates that what we are talking about is not necessarily in terms primarily of content or of object, but rather a formal structuring of the way in which the individual views reality. Christian ethics and the Christian in my judgment must view reality in terms of the Christian mysteries of creation, sin, incarnation, redemption and resurrection destiny.

The stance or horizon must be comprehensive enough to include all the elements which enter into the way in which the Christian understands reality and the world in which he lives. Problems arise whenever one adopts a stance which does not include all the elements which should enter into the Christian perspective on man and his life in this world. These five mysteries point to the five aspects which together form the proper stance or horizon for Christian ethics and for the individual Christian in his life. This chapter will explicate and develop the horizon of Christian ethics in terms of this five-fold aspect of creation, sin, incarnation, redemption and resurrection destiny. This stance must serve as a critique of ethical approaches and as a criterion for developing more adequate approaches in moral theology. The stance is not the only question to be considered in the methodology of moral theology, but it is logically the first and primary consideration. One must judge the ultimate adequacy of the stance in terms of how it does fulfill its function. Obviously there are many theological and ethical presuppositions which also influence the stance which one employs, but the following description and application of the stance should bring to light many of the presuppositions involved in the proposed stance.

The five aspects taken together form the horizon for moral theology. This essay will proceed by investigating each of the aspects and showing the insufficiency of those approaches which have forgotten one of the aspects or have given proportionately too much importance to what is only one aspect of the total horizon. Thus in the course of the development the way in which the five aspects are related to one another should become clarified.

CREATION

The Christian believes that God has created this world and that creation is good. The work of creation then serves as a basis for ethical wisdom and knowledge for the Christian. All men share the same humanity and world created by God, and by reflecting on the work of God they can arrive at some ethical wisdom and knowledge. The Christian who accepts the basic goodness of creation and its continuing validity has a source of ethical wisdom which exists outside the pale of explicit Christianity and which he thus shares with all mankind. In Roman Catholic theology, the theological presuppositions of the natural law theory accepted such an understanding of creation. The natural law is the participation of the eternal law in the rational creature. God has implanted and written his law in the hearts of all men.[22] The terminology appears to me to be too deontological in tone, but it points to the basic understanding of a common ground morality based on creation. In such a generic approach the Scriptures are not the only source of ethical wisdom for the Christian.

The realization that on the basis of creation the Christian shares ethical wisdom and insights with non-Christians has important ramifications both theoretically and practically.

___

[22] Josef Fuchs, S.J., *Natural Law: A Theological Investigation* (New York: Sheed and Ward, 1965). Fuchs rightly points out that the natural does not correspond with creation as it exists today, but rather the natural refers to what would be true of man in all possible states of existence in salvation history.

Theoretically such an approach affects the basic methodology of moral theology, for the Scriptures or Jesus Christ are not the only way into the ethical questions for the Christian. Catholic teaching and theology have followed such a generic approach in using the ethical wisdom and knowledge common to all men because of their human nature. Many of the recent papal encyclicals especially in the area of social justice have been addressed to all men of good will.[23] The methodological tone of these teachings is such that non-Christians could find them congenial, and even if they might not agree they could argue on human and rational grounds with the teaching proposed by the Popes. In *Pacem in Terris* John XXIII explicitly explains the methodological approach of the encyclical in terms of the law which the creator has written in the hearts of all men.[24] Such an ethical methodology does not usually begin with the Scriptures or Jesus Christ, even though these may be used in a confirming and supplemental way.

The Declaration on Religious Freedom of the Second Vatican Council well illustrates this type of methodology. The teaching on religious liberty is based on the dignity of the human person existing in civil society. The first chapter of the document proves the right to religious liberty on the basis of reason and does not invoke revelation or the Scriptures. The second and final chapter tries to show that the teaching on religious liberty has its roots in divine revelation, and for that reason Christians are bound to respect it all the more conscientiously.

---

23 E.g., *Pacem in Terris, Acta Apostolicae Sedis*, LV (1963) 257. *Populorum Progressio, A.A.S.*, LIX (1967) 257. *The Pastoral Constitution on the Church in the Modern World*, n.2, follows the same approach. References to the documents of the Second Vatican Council are from *The Documents of Vatican II*, ed. Walter M. Abbott, S.J., trans. ed. Joseph Gallagher (New York: Guild Press, 1966) .

24 *Pacem in Terris*, n. 1-7, *A.A.S.*, LV (1963) , 257-259.

The methodology of Vatican II differs from the approach of the documents of the World Council of Churches which treat of religious liberty. The World Council of Churches teaching antedates the Vatican Council teaching by many years, but also employs a different approach. The "Declaration on Religious Liberty" of the Amsterdam Assembly of 1948 sees religious liberty as an implication of the Christian faith and of the world-wide nature of Christianity. The rights which Christian discipleship demands are such as are good for all men. Religious freedom is required as an outward protection and an expression of that freedom by which Christ has set us free.[25] The "Statement on Religious Liberty" issued at New Delhi in 1961 holds a distinctive Christian basis for religious liberty which is still regarded as a fundamental right for men existing everywhere. The Christian basis is the fact that God's redemptive dealing with man is not coercive. The freedom given us by God in Christ Jesus implies a free response on our part.[26]

Interestingly, in the course of Vatican II a number of bishops wanted to change the proposed draft on religious freedom so that it would be more firmly rooted in the Scriptures and in revelation. These bishops were committed to the newer approach to religious liberty, but they wanted a methodology which would be more expressly Christian and biblical. These bishops were unsuccessful in their attempt.[27] The approaches of Vatican II and the World Council of Churches with their different starting points on religious liberty well illustrate the two different approaches, but there could be some convergence depending on the way in which

---

[25] A. F. Carillo de Albornoz, *The Basis of Religious Liberty* (New York: Association Press, 1963), p. 157. The author has an appendix containing the main ecumenical statements on religious liberty.

[26] *Ibid.*, p. 159.

[27] Richard J. Regan, S.J., *Conflict and Consensus: Religious Freedom and the Second Vatican Council* (New York: Macmillan, 1967), pp. 117-119.

the other source of ethical wisdom is employed. Some Protestant theologians, for example, would add no arguments or reasons based on things common to all men, whereas others would be willing to introduce these arguments, but usually in a more secondary role.

The practical implications of the recognition that Christians share ethical wisdom and knowledge with all men because they share the same human nature involve the recognition that Christians do not have a monopoly on ethical insights and wisdom, but rather Christians must constantly be in dialogue with their fellow men. The acceptance of the goodness of creation and the possibility of deriving ethical knowledge from God's creation gives to moral theology a universalism. At times in practice the Roman Catholic Church has forgotten this basic insight implied in its theological methodology. An authoritarian approach to natural law coupled with an overemphasis on the rights of the Church as the authentic interpreter of the natural law prevented the type of dialogue and discussion with science, philosophy, art and culture which in principle was accepted by the ethical methodology proposed in the Catholic tradition. If one takes seriously the fact that all men share the same humanity and can arrive at some true ethical conclusions, then dialogue becomes an absolutely necessary aspect of our existence as Christians. Of course, this does not imply that one blindly accepts what others or a majority of people are doing.

I maintain that Roman Catholic theology was correct in asserting that Christians share a great deal of ethical wisdom with all mankind on the basis of creation, but unfortunately the Catholic tradition has not always satisfactorily solved the problem of the relationship between this ethical wisdom and the knowledge which is derived from the specifically Christian source of revelation. Too often the natural was distinguished from the supernatural as the bottom layer common to all men, on top of which is now added a layer of the supernatural. This poor concept of the relationship between the two contributed to the fact that man's life in the world and society was seen primarily in terms of the natural law but did not appear to have much bearing on man's supernatural destiny. The somewhat rigid separation of the past between the natural and the supernatural has had disastrous effects both in theory and in practice in the life of the Roman Church. There are many attempts being made today to develop a better understanding of this relationship in general and specifically the relationship between the ethical wisdom and knowledge which is common to all men and that which is specifically Christian.

Those theologians who deny the existence for the Christian of a source of ethical wisdom and knowledge which the Christian shares with all men have proposed different reasons. Three of the more fundamental reasons will be considered here.

The first reason stems from the overinsistence in Protestant theology on the famous axiom *Scriptura sola,* Scripture alone. There is an obvious connection between the insistence on Scripture alone and the insistence on faith alone as the stance for moral theology. Sellers recognizes such a connection and rejects both of them.[28] Some Protestant theologians have so interpreted the Scripture alone axiom as to deny the possibility of any true ethical wisdom being derived from a non-Scriptural source. It seems that to a certain extent Martin Luther, but especially John Calvin, did not entirely reject the idea of a natural law, but in both scientific and popular expression Protestant thought has in some cases denied the existence of any ethical wisdom which does not come from the Scripture.[29] Roman Catholic theology, with

---

[28] Sellers, pp. 85-92.
[29] Ernst Troeltsch, *The Social Teaching of the Christian Churches* (New York: Harper Torchbook, 1960), II, 528-544, 602-616; Arthur C. Cochrane, "Natural Law in the Teachings of John Calvin," in *Church-State Relations in Ecumenical Perspective,* ed. Elwyn A. Smith (Pittsburgh: Duquesne University

its emphasis on faith and reason, Scripture and tradition, has never in theory denied the existence of ethical wisdom outside the Scriptures. The major problem in Roman Catholic ethics has been the failure to give enough importance to the scriptural aspect in its reflection on the Christian life.

A second reason for denying a source of ethical wisdom based on the creation which all men share stems from a theology of sin. Sin has affected man's world and his reason. Christian theology readily acknowledges that creation no longer exists in its state of goodness but has been affected by sin. Even our everyday experience reminds us how sin continues to affect our reason so that often our prejudices and biases are rationalized away. Some theologians in the Protestant tradition, especially the Lutheran tradition, claim that sin has so affected creation and man's reason that these can no longer serve as a source of positive ethical knowledge for the Christian. "In this whole problem of the natural, and specifically in the question of the possibility or the impossibility of a recognizable order of being, I see a basic difference between Roman Catholic and Reformation theology. For the possibility or impossibility of working back to the eternal order depends upon the understanding of sin, upon the degree to which we think the being of our world is altered and impaired by the rest of the fall."[30]

Thielicke here expresses quite succinctly the difference between Roman Catholic and some forms of Protestant theology, but there would be many other Protestants who would not accept Thielicke's approach. For Thielicke the natural law is not the participation of the eternal law in the rational creature so that creation is a source of positive ethical in-

---

Press, 1966), pp. 176-217; David Little, "Calvin and the Prospects for a Christian Theory of Natural Law, "in *Norm and Context in Christian Ethics*, pp. 175-197.

30 Helmut Thielicke, *Theological Ethics*, Vol. I: *Foundations*, ed. William H. Lazareth (Philadelphia: Fortress Press, 1966), p. 398.

formation even for the Christian, but rather in the *sinful* world in which we live we can at least negatively learn what we should not do if we want to preserve our existence in the fallen world. What Catholic theology calls the natural law, Thielicke would call the orders of preservation in this sinful world.[31] In my judgment Thielicke overemphasizes the reality of sin so that it completely takes away the basic goodness and positive meaning of creation. Roman Catholic theology, as will be explained later, has distorted reality by not giving enough importance to sin and its effects in our world.

A third theological reason for denying the existence of true moral wisdom which the Christian shares with all men on the basis of creation derives from a fundamental presupposition of Barthian theology and ethics. Paul Lehmann also advocates such an approach to Christian ethics. Lehmann summarizes the Barthian position that the difference between Christian and philosophical ethics is unbridgeable not because Christian ethics rejects philosophical ethics but because philosophical ethics rejects Christian ethics. The grace of God protests against every humanly established ethic as such. For Barth, a theological ethic must include all ethical truth under the rubric of the grace of God.[32] The later Barth, however, does not see this grace of God as denying and condemning the human but rather as affirming and saying yes to man.[33]

The position that includes all ethical wisdom under Christ and the grace of God in Christ Jesus is in keeping with a basic Barthian assumption that one must begin theology with

[31] *Ibid.*, pp. 420-451.

[32] Paul L. Lehmann, *Ethics in a Christian Context* (New York: Harper and Row, 1963), pp. 269-277.

[33] Will Herberg, "The Social Philosophy of Karl Barth," in Karl Barth, *Community, State and Church* (Garden City: Doubleday Anchor Books, 1960), pp. 17-18.

God and not with man. Barth staunchly maintains that one cannot go from man to God, but rather must begin with God and God's Word to us. Barth is thus opposed to natural law, natural theology and even religion. In the Barthian understanding religion is the creation of man's own wants, needs, hopes, and desires. Religion, by beginning with man, commits the great blasphemy of ultimately making God into the image and likeness of man. Once Barthian theology refuses to go from man to God, the only possible procedure is to start with God and his revelation to obtain a proper understanding of man and his world.[34]

Again, there is some truth in the fact that distortions do occasionally arise in going from man to God if one forgets the discontinuity that exists between the human and the divine. Think for example of how we usually think of God in terms of our own culture, our own sex and our own racial color. Barthian theology, however, goes too far in denying the possibility of any valid moral truth that can be derived from man and his nature and by insisting that we arrive at ethical wisdom only by hearing the Word and command of God.

In recent theology especially in the United States there appears to be a growing convergence even among Protestant theologians on the existence of a common ground morality which the Christian shares with all mankind.[35] This also indicates a similarity in the ethical methodology employed by both Protestant and Catholic theologians thus overcoming some of the differences of the past. The Christian horizon with its acceptance of creation recognizes the basic goodness of creation and its continuing validity because of which it

---

[34] For a concise summary of Barth's moral thought in these matters see Gustafson, pp. 13-60.

[35] John C. Bennett, "Issues for the Ecumenical Dialogue," in *Christian Social Ethics in a Changing World*, ed. John C. Bennett (New York: Association Press, 1966) , pp. 377-378.

can serve as a source of moral wisdom, but at the same time such a vision must also realize the imperfections, limitations and sinfulness of the creation as it exists today.

SIN

The second aspect of the stance for Christian ethics concerns the reality of sin and its effects on man and the world in which we live. The Christian faith has pointed out the sinful condition of man which serves as the backdrop for the redeeming act of God. Even after redemption the Christian fails to live in accord with the fullness of the new life he has received. Protestant theology has constantly reminded us of the sinful condition of man even after he has responded in faith to God's loving gift. In the more Orthodox forms of Protestantism the stress on the sinfulness of man and his inability to perform good deeds cohered with its *sola fide* and *sola Scriptura* approach. The emphasis was on the transcendence and power of God while man was considered to be incapable of good works on his own. Whatever good works he performed were the gift of God and from God's grace. By exalting the transcendence of God, a much less positive role was given to man. Even after baptism man was viewed as *simul justus et peccator* (at the same time sinner and justified) who is saved by faith and not by works.[36]

The Roman Catholic theology of justification has argued for a transformation and change of man so that he now becomes a new creature. Contemporary Catholic scholars realize, however, that there is truth in the realization that the Christian remains *simul justus et peccator,* and they are striving to understand this in a way which is compatible

---

[36] John Dillenberger and Claude Welch, *Protestant Christianity* (New York: Charles Scribner's Sons, 1954), pp. 255-283.

with the Roman Catholic tradition and belief.[37] In general, one might summarize the theological approaches to the reality of sin by noting that while some forms of Orthodox Protestantism have overstressed the totality and effects of sin, Catholic theology has generally not given enough importance to sin. This essay will now illustrate how Catholic theology, together with some aspects of Protestant theology, and Catholic life especially in the decade of the 1960's failed to give enough importance to the reality of sin.

The encyclical *Pacem in Terris* well illustrates the failure of Roman Catholic theology to realize the existence of sin in the world. A theology which does not come to grips with the existence of sin will tend to be dangerously naive and romantically optimistic—dangers which are to some extent present in *Pacem in Terris*. The very title of the encyclical indicates the penchant for a too one-sidedly optimistic understanding. I do not think there will ever be perfect peace on earth. History reminds us that humanity has constantly known the lack of peace, and our own experience of the last few years shows that peace on earth is still far distant from the world in which we live. The Christian vision with its understanding of eschatology and the realization that sin will always be part of our human existence will never hope to find the fullness of peace within history.

For one who acknowledges the continuing reality of sin in our world, there is need to recognize that the existence of sin can never become an excuse for an easy acceptance of the situation as we know it. Christians are called upon to continue to struggle against sin and in the Power of the Risen Lord to overcome the reality of sin if at all possible. Christians can never use the existence of sin as an excuse for

---

37 Karl Rahner, S.J., "Justified and Sinner at the Same Time," *Theological Investigations* (Baltimore: Helicon, 1969), VI, 218-230; Bernard Häring, C.SS.R., "Conversion," in P. Delhayee *et al., Pastoral Treatment of Sin* (New York; Desclée, 1968), pp. 90-92.

acquiescing in the injustices and ills that afflict our contemporary world. As human beings and Christians we are called upon to work for peace, and can and should do much more than is now being done. The fullness of peace in all its remifications, however, will always elude our grasp. The very title of Pope John's encyclical thus appears somewhat distorted in the light of the full Christian vision of reality.

In the Introduction Pope John explains the methodology which he will employ in the encyclical. The creator of the world has imprinted in man's heart an order which conscience reveals to him and enjoins him to obey. The laws governing the relationships between men and states are to be found in the nature of man where the Father of all things wrote them.[38] In the final introductory paragraph the Pope explains that these laws teach citizens how to conduct their mutual dealings, show how the relationships between citizens and public authority should be regulated, indicate how states should deal with one another, and finally manifest how individual men, states and the community of all people should act towards each other.[39] These four considerations are the skeleton outline of the encyclical which then develops the teaching on each of these points in the four main parts of the encyclical.

In a certain sense what Pope John says is true, but there is something else in the heart of man—disorder or what Christians have called sin. A glance at the world around us only too easily confirms the existence of these disorders even in the four areas in which the encyclical stresses the existence of order. The vision of the papal teaching is somewhat unreal if it does not take into account this sinful aspect of reality. There is definitely order and the possibility for a greater order in the world, but there remains the obstacle of

---

[38] *Pacem in Terris,* n. 1-6, *A.A.S.,* LV (1963) 257-258.
[39] *Ibid.,* n. 7, *A.A.S.,* LV (1963) , 259.

sin which any realistic ethic must consider. One perhaps could argue that Pope John was talking about the ideal and urging people to live up to that ideal without descending into the very concrete ways in which this is to be accomplished. Perhaps there is some validity in such a defense of *Pacem in Terris*, but if the encyclical is to serve as a realistic guide for life in our society, then it must at least recognize the persistent reality of sin and how sin will affect our world and our actions. One must always talk about the ideal towards which men must strive, but a realistic assessment of the obstacles is necessary for the completeness of the teaching.

Whereas some forms of Protestant theology have over-emphasized the reality of sin, Catholic theology generally has not given enough importance to sin. In ethics the natural law theory tended to forget sin. A poor understanding of nature and supernature understood sin as depriving man of his supernature, but leaving his nature intact. Thus sin did not really affect man in his nature. In parts of the Catholic theological tradition it was constantly maintained that through sin man was wounded in things pertaining to his nature (*vulneratus in naturalibus*), but this did not completely destroy his humanity.[40] However, in moral theology this wounded nature was not given enough attention.

The better part of the Catholic theological tradition realized that nature did not refer to what is historically existing at the present time after the fall, but rather to that metaphysical understanding of what man is in all possible states of salvation history. This basic nature was then modified by the historical circumstances of the state in which it exists; for example, the state of fallen nature or the state of redeemed nature.[41] Even in such an understanding it appears that not

---

40 Severinus Gonzalez, S.I., *Sacrae Theologiae Summa* (3rd ed.; Madrid: Biblioteca de Autores Cristianos, 1956), III, 521-542.

41 Fuchs, pp. 42-52.

enough importance is given to the realities of sin and grace in the history of salvation. In the more popular understanding, which was generally presupposed in the manuals of moral theology, the effects of sin on man were definitely underdeveloped. Such a theology was poorly equipped for coming to grips with the presence of sin and the surd in our human life.

There have been aspects of Protestant theology which have also forgotten the reality of sin. Twice in the present century trends in Protestant theology have ignored to their own peril the reality of sin. Protestant liberal theology arose in the nineteenth century in reaction to the somewhat negative approach of Orthodox Protestantism with its stress on the transcendence of God and the sinfulness of man.[42] A very popular form of liberal theology was the social gospel movement which reached its zenith in the United States in the early decades of the twentieth century.[43] Liberalism stressed the humanity of Jesus and understood him primarily in ethical terms. The individual Christian is no longer thought of as a sinner who passively receives the gift of salvation but rather as a free person with responsibility to build the kingdom of God on earth. The notions of evolution and progressive development fit in with the liberal conception of an optimistic eschatology which inclined towards a progressivistic view of history. The kingdom of God and its progress readily become identified with human and scientific progress. Liberal theology looked to the prophets and Jesus as the great biblical figures who call man to work for bringing about the kingdom of God in history.[44]

In general this teaching with its emphasis on immanence, progressivism and man's moral effort and responsibility for-

---

[42] Dillenberger and Welch, pp. 179-254.

[43] *The Social Gospel In America 1870-1920,* ed. Robert T. Handy (New York: Oxford University Press, 1966).

[44] Lloyd J. Averill, *American Theology in the Liberal Tradition* (Philadelphia: Westminster Press, 1967).

got the reality of sin. H. Richard Niebuhr in a somewhat exaggerated way pointed out the one-sidedness of liberal Protestant theology. "In its one-sided view of progress which saw the growth of the wheat but not that of the tares, the gathering of the grain but not the burning of the chaff, this liberalism was indeed naively optimistic. A God without wrath brought men without sin into a kingdom without judgment through the ministrations of a Christ without a cross."[45]

The omissions of liberal theology became even more glaring in the light of the historical circumstances of the day. The First World War burst the bubble of any progressivistic dream of a world that was becoming better and better in every way and every day. The war was the sign of man's inhumanity, his greed, selfishness and inability to live in peace with others. It was no mere accident that in Europe Karl Barth reacted against the liberal theology in his commentary on the Epistle to the Romans which was first published in 1919. The naively optimistic theology of liberal Protestantism was not all that convincing in the aftermath of World War I. The early Barth reemphasized the transcendence of God and saw the Word of God as a negative judgment on man. A short time later while still holding on to transcendence Barth saw the Word of God not so much as judging man but rather affirming and saying "Yes" to the human.[46]

In the United States the major theological attack against Liberalism and the social gospel was launched by Reinhold Niebuhr in his *Moral Man and Immoral Society* published in 1932. "Insofar as this treatise has a polemic interest it is directed against the moralists, both religious and secular, who imagine that the egoism of individuals is being progres-

---

45 H. Richard Niebuhr, *The Kingdom of God in America* (New York: Harper Torchbook, 1959) , p. 193.

46 Herberg, pp. 13-21.

sively checked by the development of rationality or the growth of a religiously inspired goodwill and that nothing but the continuance of this process is necessary to establish social harmony between all the human societies and collectivities."[47] Niebuhr castigates this liberal theology for its failure to realize the brutal character of human behavior especially in terms of class egoism.[48]

The tendency within liberal Protestant theology to forget the reality of sin became evident again in the 1960's. In some versions of a theology of the secular and in the death of God movement there was a denial or at least a downplaying of the role of sin with the resulting overly optimistic view of reality and the world, as well as man's capabilities for bringing about quick and radical change. Harvey Cox, for example, did not deny the fact of sin, but he interpreted it in such a way that sin was viewed primarily in terms of apathy or failure to take responsibility for the world. Sloth is the traditional name for this sin.[49] This remains one aspect of sin, but one must also recognize that human beings too often use their power for the exploitation of others and for their own aggrandizement. Pride is the traditional name for such an understanding of sin.

Others went much further than Cox in reducing the emphasis on sin. Perhaps the most illustrative example of this approach is William Hamilton's essay, "The New Optimism —from Prufrock to Ringo." Hamilton believes that pessimism does not persuade anymore, for there is an increased sense of the possibilities of human action, human happiness, human decency in this life. Hamilton wants to establish a new mood of optimism based not on grace but on a worldly

---

[47] Reinhold Niebuhr, *Moral Man and Immoral Society* (New York: Charles Scribner's Sons, 1960) , p. xii.

[48] *Ibid.*, p. xx.

[49] Harvey G. Cox *On Not Leaving It to the Snake* (New York: Macmillan 1967) , pp. ix-xix.

optimism that believes it can change the human conditions that bring about fear and despair.[50] Hamilton sees the "State of the Union" address of President Lyndon B. Johnson in January 1965 as an example of this new optimism and the new possibilities open to man. Allowing for political rhetoric, Hamilton still claims that Johnson's invitation to accept revolutionary changes in the world was believable.[51] A few intervening years have apparently decimated Hamilton's thesis. Theologians such as John Macquarrie[52] and Roger Shinn[53] have called attention to the failure of secular theology to give enough attention to human sinfulness.

Not only Catholic theology and some trends in Protestant theology but also Catholic life especially in the last decade has tended to deny in practice sin and its effects. A naive optimism has often characterized Catholic life in the 1960's. The encouraging reforms of Vatican II seemingly provided an impetus for the possibilities of massive reform and renewal both within and outside the Church. Disillusionment, however, quickly followed as this reform movement was not able to accomplish such grandiose schemes. The whole process of reform and growth is much more complicated and difficult to attain than many had realized in the warm afterglow of Vatican II.

A romantic understanding of reality with its over optimism tends to idealize and easily forgets about the harsh and difficult side of reality. Romanticism frequently has a tendency to idealize the past as the perfect time in which there was no tension, frustration or division. In Christianity this

50 William Hamilton, "The New Optimism—from Prufrock to Ringo," in Thomas J. J. Altizer and William Hamilton, *Radical Theology and The Death of God* (Indianapolis: Bobbs-Merrill Co., 1966), pp. 157-169.

51 *Ibid.*, pp. 159-160.

52 John Macquarrie, *God and Secularity* ("New Directions In Theology Today," III; Philadelphia: Westminster Press, 1967), pp. 81-85.

53 Roger Lincoln Shinn, *Man: The New Humanism* ("New Directions in Theology Today," V; Philadelphia: Westminster Press, 1968), pp. 145-164.

romanticization often takes the form of an uncritical under-standing of the circumstances of the primitive Church.

A few years ago I was asked to criticize a paper which set forth the plans and rationale for the senate of priests in one of the large archdioceses of the United States. The document began with a consideration of the Church as found in the Acts of the Apostles with the implication that this should be somehow normative for the way in which the Church functions today. The priests' senate is a vehicle for the bishop in union with his priests to serve the people of God. The Acts of the Apostles bears witness to the great unity and community existing in the early Church. Christians were known by their service of others and by their love. They gathered together for the breaking of the bread as the sign of that unity of love which they lived out in their daily existence. So too the Church today on the local level must be this community of love and service united around the bishop and characterized by their mutual sharing and service which is symbolically represented in their breaking the bread together.

Again there is some truth in such a picture, but it is not the whole story even as this is recorded for us in the literature of the primitive Church community. Also such a naively romantic view of the past can too easily occasion disillusionment when the reality of the present falls so far short of such a picture. The primitive Church obviously knew the struggles and tensions which the Church community will always experience.

Paul felt the need to stand up to Peter and rebuke him for his attitude towards the Gentile converts (Gal. 2:11-21). Ananias and Sapphira are reported as lying to Peter and holding back some of their funds for themselves, all the while giving others the impression that they were sharing their goods with the community (Acts 5:1-11). Paul and Barnabas were unable to agree on whom they wanted to accompany them on their missionary journeys so they were forced to split up (Acts 15:36-41). Apparently at times there also arose problems at the meetings of the early community in terms of some members not being willing to share with others and thus seemingly acting against the real meaning of *agape* (1 Cor. 11:20-22). One must avoid a naive romanticism that enshrines the past as as ideal time, when in reality the past, like the present and the future, will always know the problems and tensions of life in the Christian community, which Christian tradition sees as affected by human sinfulness.

To acknowledge the reality and effects of sin does not demand a negative, pessimistic and despairing worldview. By no means. Sin is not so total in its effects that it destroys the goodness of creation. Some forms of Orthodox Protestant theology, especially in the Lutheran tradition, have over-emphasized the reality of sin so that it pervades and even destroys the goodness of creation. Creation remains as a true but limited source of ethical wisdom for the Christian existing today. Sin can never be the last word or the ultimate or the most influential word for the Christian who believes that the redemptive love of Jesus Christ has conquered and overcome sin. Even now by our participation in the Paschal Mystery we are called upon to share in Christ's struggle with sin but also in this world to some extent we can also partially share in Christ's triumph over sin. The fullness of redemption will only come outside history, but in the meantime we are called to share in the fellowship of his sufferings and in the power of his resurrection. Sin thus has an important but somewhat limited place in the Christian view of reality.

The failure of Roman Catholic theology and life to give enough importance to sin not only produces at times an overly simplistic view of progress and development with a corresponding failure to consider all the elements and obstacles which are present, but also has influenced the way

in which Catholic moral theology deals with certain concrete
ethical problems. Elsewhere I have developed a theory of
compromise theology precisely because of inadequacy of
Catholic ethics to come to grips with sin-filled situations.
Sometimes the presence of sin in the world will force one to
do something which, if there were no sin present, should not
be done.[54] This is just another illustration of the fact that in
Roman Catholic theology there has been a built-in tendency
not to give enough importance to the reality of sin.

INCARNATION

The third aspect of the stance for moral theology is furnished by the Christian mystery of the incarnation. The incarnation by proclaiming that God has united himself to
humanity in the person of Jesus Christ gives a value and an
importance to all that is human and material in this world.
The very fact that God has joined himself to humanity
argues against any depreciation of the material, the corporeal
and the worldly. The sacramental celebration of the Christian mysteries is a constant reminder of the incarnational
principle, for the common elements of human existence—
wine, water, bread and oil—are part and parcel of the sacramental celebration and have their meaning transformed in
this mystery of faith.

In our contemporary world there seems to be no danger
of forgetting this aspect of the basic goodness of the material
and the worldly and its incorporation into the whole mystery
of God's union with man, but the history of Christian
thought reveals the various forms of dualism which have

---

[54] Charles E. Curran, *A New Look at Christian Morality* (Notre Dame, Indiana: Fides Publishers, 1968), pp. 169-173, 232-233; *Catholic Moral Theology
in Dialogue* (Notre Dame, Indiana: Fides Publisher, 1972), pp. 209-219.

existed in the Church and have exerted their influence on theology and practical life. Any attempt to belittle or condemn the material or earthly as being evil or a total obstacle to the higher calling of man fails to appreciate the reality and meaning of the incarnation.

In Roman Catholic spirituality even in the decades immediately preceding the Second Vatical Council there were two different schools of spirituality—the one called the incarnational and the other, the eschatological.[55] The incarnational approach emphasized the responsibility of the Christian to make incarnate in his daily life the Christian gospel and to take seriously his earthly existence with his vocation to transform the human into the divine. The eschatological approach tended to think more of the future life and deemphasized the importance and place of life in this world. The incarnational approach marked the attempt of recent theology to try to develop a spirituality for Christians living in the world which had been a lacuna in Christian thinking until the time of Vatican II. Even the spirituality proposed for diocesan priests was modeled on a monastic spirituality and unadapted to the needs of ministering the Word and Work of Jesus in the world.[56] These decades before Vatican II also saw the increase of theological literature on the value and meaning of earthly realities.[57]

Time has now bypassed this historical discussion although the basic question of a Christian spirituality for the con-

[55] Bernard Besret, S.O. Cist., *Incarnation ou Eschatologie?* (Paris: Éditions du Cerf, 1964).

[56] Eugene Masure, *Parish Priest* (Nortre Dame, Indiana: Fides Publishers, 1955); Gustave Thils, *The Diocesan Priest* (Notre Dame, Indiana: Fides Publishers, 1964).

[57] Gustave Thils, *Théologie des réalités terrestres, I. Préludes. II. Théologie de l'histoire* (Bruges: Desclée de Brouwer, 1946, 1949); Thils, *Théologie et réalité sociale* (Tournai: Casterman, 1952): John Courtney Murray, S.J., "Is It Basketweaving?" in *We Hold These Truths* (New York: Sheed and Ward, 1960), pp. 175-196.

temporary man has not been solved. The dangers in the older discussion were an either-or approach which tended to exclude one aspect and the poor understanding of eschatology which viewed eschatology as referring only to the last things and not really present in any way here and now. The entire horizon as described in this essay can serve for the development of a more adequate spirituality which will avoid some of the shortcomings of the past debate especially by seeing the incarnation also in terms of the other important realities and by not opposing incarnational and eschatological reflections.

The failure of Catholic theology to develop a spirituality for Christians living in the world does indicate the fact that such a theology did not give enough importance to the earthly aspects of our existence. In earlier periods in Church history the failure was even more noticeable in terms of the various forms of dualism which tended to look down upon the earthly, the material and the corporeal as being evil. Such a dualistic mentality often, for example, misinterpreted the Pauline dichotomy between spirit and flesh as if Paul were referring to the spiritual part of man in opposition to the material or lower part of his being. Such an understanding was far from the mind of Paul who understood spirit to refer to the whole man insofar as he is under the Spirit and flesh to refer to the whole man insofar as he under the power of sin. The Pauline dichotomy did not refer to the body-soul relationship in man. A theologically unacceptable dualism paved the way for such a misinterpretation of Paul.[58] Today, however, there does not seem to be a pressing problem resulting from a failure to accept the implications of the incarnation. If anything, the problem is a failure to recognize the reality of transcendence in our human existence.

---

[58] A. Humbert, C.SS.R., "La morale de saint Paul," *Mélanges de Science Religieuse*, XV (1958), 12-13.

REDEMPTION AND RESURRECTION DESTINY

The Christian ethical horizon is also formed by the mysteries of redemption and resurrection destiny. In a sense one can and should speak of two different realities in this case, but both can be considered together with the realization that the resurrection destiny of all brings to fulfillment the work of redemption. There would be a problem in considering the two together if redemption were so identified with resurrection destiny that there would be no tension between the now and the future.

Redemption and resurrection destiny in the Christian ethical horizon serve to point to the danger of absolutizing any present structures, institutions or ideals. Resurrection destiny and the future serve as a negative critique on everything existing at the present time. The presence of sin and the limited aspects of creation reinforce the same relativizing tendency. As a result the Christian can never absolutize the present, but his critical assessment calls to mind the need for constant change and development with the realization that the eschatological perfection will never be arrived at in this world, and it will always be necessary to live with imperfections and limitations.[59]

Too often in the past Catholic theology tended to absolutize what was only a very limited and historically conditioned reality. The accepted natural law theory spoke in terms of the immutable order of God and the unchanging essences of things. Thus existing social arrangements or structures could very easily be mistaken for the eternally willed order of God. The tendency of such a vision was conservative in the bad sense of failing to see any need for change and development.

---

[59] Edward Schillebeeckx, *God The Future of Man* (New York: Sheed and Ward, 1968) , pp. 169-207.

One specific example concerns the outlook of the Church on the whole area of new developments arising in the nineteenth century. Here there were new developments in philosophy, science, politics, forms of government and understanding of the freedom and rights of citizens. In all these areas the reaction of the Catholic Church tended to be one of fear of these newer developments and an effort to turn back the clock to an older historical period with the assumption that this was the order willed by God.[60]

The nineteenth century witnessed an explosion of new philosophical ideas and major developments in science such as the theory of evolution. There was a stirring in some segments of the Catholic Church to bring Catholic theology and thought abreast of these modern developments. A congress for this purpose was organized by Döllinger in Munich in 1863, but the reaction of Rome to such an approach was negative.[61] The Pope, in a letter to the Archbishop of Munich, stressed the need to continue to follow the traditional and accepted theologians and writers, who for centuries have shown the true way of explaining and defending the faith. At the same time, Pius IX insisted on the need for all Catholics to obey the papal magisterium and also the decisions of the Roman congregations. The general tone of the letter was negative to any real dialogue with the contemporary world and urged a return to the safe teaching of the past.[62]

In this context of the nineteenth century Thomas Aquinas was declared to be the patron of Catholic theology and philosophy which was to be taught in Catholic schools according to the plan, the principles and the teaching of

---

[60] For the best historical description of this period see Roger Aubert, *Le pontificat de Pie IX* (Histoire de l'Église depuis les origines jusqu'a nos jours, XXI; Paris: Bloud & Gay, 1952) .

[61] Aubert, pp. 240-242.

[62] *Acta Sanctae Sedis*, VIII (1874/5) , 438 ff.

Thomas Aquinas.[63] One cannot deny that many benefits have accrued to the Catholic church and to mankind through the Thomistic renewal sparked by Leo XIII and his successors, but there were also harmful effects. Ironically the nineteenth and twentieth century popes used Thomas Aquinas for exactly the opposite of what Thomas himself had accomplished in his own lifetime. The return to Thomas was an obvious attempt to cut off dialogue with the contemporary world of philosophy and science, but the genius of Aquinas consisted in his successfully trying to express the Christian message in the thought patterns of Greek philosophy which had just been entering the university world of the Europe of his day. Thomas was not content merely with repeating and handing down what had been said in the past, but in a very creative way he tried to use the contemporary philosophical insights for a more profound understanding of the Christian faith. This tendency to turn back the clock and to avoid dialogue with the contemporary world characterized much of Catholic life and thought until Vatican II.

Perhaps the most significant expression of the condemnation of the thought of the nineteenth century is found in the "Syllabus of Errors" which Pius IX published in 1864 and which collected some of the more important condemnations which the Pope had earlier made about various new trends in the philosophical and political worlds. The severity of the

---

63 *Ibid*, III (1867/8), 168ff. Leo XIII in his encyclical letter, *Aeterni Patris* of August 4, 1879, *Acta Sanctae Sedis*, XI (1878-9), 98 ff., prescribed the restoration in Catholic schools of Christian philosophy in the spirit of St. Thomas Aquinas. For subsequent papal directives on following the philosophy and theology of St. Thomas, see Pius X, *Doctoris Angelici, Acta Apostolicae Sedis*, VI (1914), 384 ff; Pius XI, *Officiorum Omnium, A.A.S.*, XIV (1922), 449 ff; Pius XI, *Studiorum Ducem, A.A.S.* XV (1923), 323 ff; various allocutions of Pius XII; *A.A.S.*, XXXI (1939), 246 ff.; XXXVIII (1946), 387 ff.; XLV (1953), 684 ff. According to Canon 1366 of the Code of Canon Law promulgated in 1917, rational philosophy and theology should be taught *"ad Angelici Doctoris rationem, doctrinan, et principia. . . ."*

document was somewhat modified by Dupanloup's famous interpretation based on the difference between thesis and hypothesis. The Pope condemned all these things in thesis; i.e., what roughly corresponds to the ideal world. But in hypothesis, or in what corresponds roughly to the actual historical world in which we live, some of these things may be tolerated. In theory things should be different, but we can tolerate and live with the real situation.[64]

Specifically in the area of social ethics the hierarchical magisterium in the nineteenth century continued to argue for the union of Church and State as the immutable order willed by God and at the same time rejected the emphasis on freedom which was manifesting itself in many different areas of concern including of course political freedom, freedom of conscience and freedom of religion.[65] New political forms of government based on freedom were being espoused. I do not think that the Catholic Church should have uncritically accepted the new political thought, for there were many shortcomings in such new theories as was pointed out from a different perspective by Karl Marx.

The general problem was that Catholic theology looked upon the union of Church and State as the eternal plan of God when in reality as later changes made clear it was only a very historically and culturally conditioned reality. This furnishes an example of that unacceptable conservatism in Catholic social ethics which proceeds from the basic error of identifying an historically limited and conditioned reality with the eternal and immutable order willed by God. In fairness to Catholic social ethics there was also a great willingness, especially in the area of economic ethics, to point out the failures and injustices of the existing order although

---

[64] Aubert, pp. 254-261.

[65] Heinrich A. Rommen, *The State in Catholic Thought* (St. Louis: B. Herder, 1945), pp. 507-612.

here too the impression also persisted among some Catholics that a solution could be found by returning to an older social form such as the guild system.[66]

The danger of a false conservatism arising from absolutizing existing or previously existing structures is even greater in the rapidly changing circumstances of contemporary existence. A law and order mentality tends to absolutize the present structures and fails to notice the imperfections and even the positive sinfulness and injustice present in the existing social order. The individual Christian looking forward to the fullness of resurrection destiny can never be content with the present. This realization calls for the necessity of growth and constant conversion in the life of the individual Christian who can never be smug or content about his response to the good news of God's loving call. In the light of resurrection destiny the Christian realizes his own sinfulness and lack of response, the hardness of his heart and the Christian imperative of growth and change.

In the area of social ethics the fullness of resurrection destiny likewise emphasizes the imperfections of the present and the need for change and growth. The Christian can never be content with the status quo and can never identify the existing order or structure as the perfect reflection of the eternal plan of God. This does not mean that every proposed change is necessarily good and to be embraced, for this would be the most naive of approaches and in its own way be against the horizon of Christian ethics which tends to point out the ambiguities of all existing and proposed orders and structures. In the light of redemption and resurrection destiny social change and the constant improvement of existing structures remains an imperative for the Christian.

---

[66] Richard L. Camp, *The Papal Ideology of Social Reform* (Leiden: E. J. Brill, 1969), pp. 26-27, 38-40.

There is another important function which redemption and resurrection destiny serve as part of the horizon of moral theology. This aspect exists in tension with the function of resurrection destiny serving as a negative critique on all orders and structures and a spur for growth and change. Resurrection destiny also reminds us that the eschatological fullness will never be present until the end of history. The Christian always lives in the tension between the imperfections of the now and the perfection of the future. One can wrongly destroy that tension either by absolutizing the present and seeing no need for change or by thinking that the fullness of resurrection destiny will come easily and quickly. The danger in the past decade both in theory and in practice has resided in collapsing the eschaton and thinking that the fullness of resurrection destiny will arrive shortly.

The question of redemption and resurrection destiny entails a theory of eschatology. In general I would adopt a theory of eschatology in the process of realization. This argues for continuity between the present world and the next but also for discontinuity. Man by his efforts must try to cooperate in bringing about the new heaven and the new earth, but our efforts will always fall short. The naive optimism seen in the failure to appreciate the fact of sin also tends to think of human progress in an evolving way that progressively and somewhat easily becomes better and better. Some of the frustration and malaise both in the world and in the Church at the present time appears due to the fact that people naively expected progress and fulfillment to come too easily and too quickly. When the social structures do not change overnight, there is a tendency to abandon the effort and commitment needed to bring about such change in the real order.

It is helpful to see progress and growth in the social order according to the paradigm of growth and progress in our individual lives. Christians must honestly admit their own sinfulness and failure to fully respond to the gift of God and the needs of our neighbor. The eschatological fullness of the gospel challenges us to continual conversion and growth. However, the process of growth and change is a constant struggle that seems at times not to progress at all. In honesty, we willingly confess how slow we are at changing our hearts and responding more fully to God and neighbor. Growth and progress in the social order will likewise be a slow and painful process. One might argue that growth in the social order will be even more difficult than in the personal realm because of the greater complexity involved in social relationships.

Such a realistic view of progress and development will not place primary emphasis on fulfillment and accomplishment but rather sees the reality of struggle and the consequent Christian emphasis on hope which comes from the promise God has made to us and not primarily from our own deeds and accomplishments. The paschal mystery as another paradigm of growth reminds us of the need to suffer and die in order to live. The Christian with the proper horizon avoids a naive expectation that change will be rapid and easy. The Christian struggles for growth and progress because of his hope in the power and presence of the living God and does not ultimately base his hope on his own accomplishments and deeds although these do retain a secondary but still important role in the Christian understanding of ethics.

The life of the individual person and the paschal mystery as paradigms for social progress also remind us that there is no perfect continuity between this world and the next. Death is an important reality which too often has been pushed to the background in modern life and theology. Death for the Christian does not constitute a reason for despair or a denial of all that has gone before. There certainly is an aspect of death as break between the past and the future, and a sorrowful break that on the surface appears to deny any continuity between past and future. But death for the Christian is also a transformation which ultimately does transform the past and the present into the fullness of resurrection destiny.[67] The ultimate work of transformation at the end of life serves as a reminder of the discontinuity between this world and the next and the fact that it is the power of God that will usher in the fullness of resurrection destiny.

Redemption and resurrection destiny thus serve to create the proper tension by which the Christian is constantly reminded of the need for change and growth in his individual life and in the life of society, but at the same time realizes that the fullness of growth and progress will only come at the end of time and in some discontinuity with the present. In the times in between the comings of Jesus, the Christian lives in hope and struggle as he cooperates in the joyful work of redemption and resurrection destiny.

One final word of explanation is necessary. The stance proposed in this chapter presupposes an explicitly Christian understanding of reality and is based on what the believer properly calls five Christian mysteries. A very important problem concerns the relationship of Christian ethics to other ethics. Chapter Four will summarize my position on this question. For now, it is sufficient to note that I believe the realities referred to as redemption and resurrection destiny are also in some way available to those who are not Christian. In the same context it should be noted that contemporary theology realizes there is no longer in actuality a clear distinction between creation and redemption. In the last few years Roman Catholic theology has rightly tried to overcome the older distinction and even dichotomy between the natural and the supernatural. But in so doing there is

---

[67] Ladislaus Boros, S.J., *The Mystery of Death* (New York: Herder and Herder, 1965); Karl Rahner, S.J., *On the Theology of Death* New York: Herder and Herder, 1961); Roger Troisfontaines, S.J., *I Do Not Die* (New York: Desclee, 1963).

the danger of seeing everything as supernatural, grace or the kingdom. Catholic and Protestant theology in the 1960's too easily forgot the limitations and finitude of creation, the fallenness of sin and the future aspect of resurrection destiny.

This completes the analysis of the various elements which make up the horizon or stance for moral theology. One ultimately has to judge the adequacy of this or any other model by the way in which it accomplishes its function. I have tried to indicate that a stance for moral theology involving the aspects of creation, sin, incarnation, redemption and resurrection destiny adequately serves as the first logical consideration in moral theology and is a standard or criterion which can be effectively employed to criticize other ethical approaches and thus contribute to a more adequate methodology for moral theology.

3

The Radical Catholic
Social Ethics of Paul Hanly Furfey

One of the most noteworthy happenings in Roman Catholicism in the United States in the last few years has been the emergence into broad public view of a radical Catholic social movement. Catholic radicalism did not begin only in the last few years, but has claimed a comparatively small but staunch number of adherents and coalesced especially in the 1930's.

Aaron I. Abell in his historical account of Catholic social teaching and action describes the last decades of the nineteenth century and the beginning of the twentieth century as the coming to the fore of Catholic social liberalism. This approach became the dominant theme of the American Church including especially the hierarchical Church. Under the leadership of Cardinal Gibbons and others this movement was characterized by a crusade for social justice, cooperation with non-Catholics, and rapid Americanization of immigrants. There was always some opposition from conservative elements, but this approach formed the mainstream of Catholic social thought in the United States.[1]

The best exponent of Catholic social liberalism in the first half of the twentieth century was John A. Ryan, whose name, because of his teaching at The Catholic University of America, his many publications, and his role as Director of the Social Action Department of the National Catholic Welfare Conference, became synonymous with Catholic social ethics for nearly five decades. Ryan's works well illustrate the approach of social liberalism. He continued the basic thrust of Gibbons and others that one could be both Catholic and American, for there was no irreconcilable gap between the two. The realization that in social matters Catholics have much that they share both in theory and in practice with many others in society has been a hallmark of Catholic social liberalism. Ryan's theories were derived primarily from reason which is common to all men. Especially in his later writings there are frequent appeals to papal teachings, but these too are primarily based on reason. The strategy was cooperation with others in society, for Catholics had to enter into the mainstream of American life and cooperate to achieve justice. The goal was a reform of the structures of society so that justice could be more present in society. The title of Ryan's biography by Francis Broderick is most revealing—*Right Reverend New Dealer: John A. Ryan.*[2]

Differing from the social liberalism championed by Ryan and others were conservatives, on the one hand, and radicals

---

[1] *American Catholic Thought on Social Questions,* ed. Aaron I. Abell (Indianapolis: Bobbs-Merrill Company, 1968), pp. xxiii-xxvi; Abell, *American Catholicism and Social Action: A Search for Justice, 1865-1950,* (Garden City, New York: Hanover House, 1960), pp. 90-188.

[2] Francis Broderick, *Right Reverend New Dealer: John A. Ryan* (New York: Macmillan, 1963). Most representative of Ryan's publications are his doctoral thesis *A Living Wage: Its Ethical and Economic Aspects* (New York: Macmillan, 1906) and *Distributive Justice* (New York: Macmillan, 1916).

on the other. The best known name among the Catholic radicals is Dorothy Day whose Catholic Worker Movement has exerted great influence on American Catholicism. However, in many ways the primary theoretician and writer of American Catholic radicalism as it developed in the 1930's is Paul Hanly Furfey. Abell in his historical overviews of American Catholic social thought and action does not generally give much importance to the Catholic radical movement and apparently does not even mention Furfey in tracing the historical development.

David J. O'Brien in *American Catholics and Social Reform* devotes one chapter to radical Catholicism and succinctly summarizes the writings of Furfey:

> Furfey's sociology was a self-conscious tool for a Christian reform that was more radical than anything advocated by his Catholic University colleague, John A. Ryan. Furfey charges that exponents of moderation in Catholic social action bargained and compromised with the world, overlooked the need for fundamental change and acquiesced in materialism, racial discrimination and injustice. In return they were allowed to sit on the boards of community chests, their charities received large grants from millionaires, their schools were objects of philanthropic favor and their religious liberty was respected. Furfey regarded himself as an extremist, who interpreted gospel teachings literally. He purposely set impossibly high standards that he knew could not be reached without God's help; he relied on grace and example rather than politics as methods of reform, and he regarded social work as a "poor substitute for charity."[3]

---

[3] David J. O'Brien, *American Catholics and Social Reform* (New York: Oxford University Press, 1968), pp. 185-186.

Paul Hanly Furfey came to his radical Catholicism in the course of his life. After studying at the Sulpician seminary at Catholic University he was ordained a priest in 1922. He did graduate work and received his degree in sociology from Catholic University in 1926, and the year before he began his lifelong teaching career at that University. His early academic interests were in the areas of sociology and psychology where he published widely. He shared the belief that the social sciences could provide the empirical tools which would enable Catholics to change society in the direction of the Christian ideal.

Furfey spent the academic year 1931-32 on sabbatical in universities in Germany doing research; here he apparently began questioning his whole approach to bring about changes in society. By that time he had acquired a scholarly reputation both in psychology and in sociology, but he realized that psychology and sociology were not sufficient to bring about the necessary changes in society. The only thing that would change society was the gospel, if people would truly live in accord with it. Returning to this country he came into contact with Dorothy Day, Peter Maurin and the Catholic Worker movement. His ideas continued to develop along the same lines.[4]

In 1936 he published his *Fire on the Earth* which set out the basic theory of radical Catholicism which he espoused as the way for bringing about social reform.[5] This influential book has gone through numerous printings and has exerted a great influence on the lives of many Catholics in the 1930's and later who were thrilled by its message and sought to live in accord with its thesis.

---

[4] Paul Hanly Furfey, *The Morality Gap* (New York: Macmillan, 1968), pp. 99-102. Msgr. Furfey has also talked with me about this early period in his life.

[5] Paul Hanly Furfey, *Fire on the Earth* (New York: Macmillan, 1936).

FURFEY'S GENERAL THEORY

Furfey has remained faithful over the years to the general theory he first laid down in *Fire on the Earth* and expanded in his writings ever since. *Fire on the Earth* began with a call for a "supernatural sociology." Only the gospel, and not scientific theories or methods, would bring about true social reform. Catholic social action in the United States, despite its marvelous organization, its social workers, its efficient youth movements, its up-to-date financing and its large banquets to aid charity, is inadequate. It is at best a mediocre approach which does not dare take the risk of the heroic based on the supernatural means we have at our disposal. In the field of social theory worldly prudence tells us to rely on the best, modern, tested, scientific methods. Faith tells us that the facts of revelation are more important, but too often we are afraid of the folly of the cross.[6]

Furfey did not advocate that one should completely forget about political and legislative reform, for the citizen cannot totally abandon his civil duties. But these political reforms are very imperfect and always doomed at least to partial failure. They can never truly change the heart of men which is only the reform of divine grace. Legislation and political activity are at best a very minor part of social reform.[7]

In *Three Theories of Society* published a year later Furfey indicates the failures of both the positivistic and the noetic approaches to society. The positivistic approach, with its rejection of deeper knowledge, accepts the success goal or ideal which is so much in accord with contemporary mores. The noetic approach strives for that deeper truth which is so essential. But the noetic approach is not enough in the light of the sinfulness of men, for the majority of men will not

---

[6] *Ibid.*, pp. 1-21.
[7] *Ibid.*, pp. 90-95.

accept this deeper wisdom with its downplaying of worldly and materialistic success and will not have the courage to live in accord with such wisdom. Only a pistic theory of society based on revelation, faith and grace can truly bring about social reform.[8]

Here the pistic society merely becomes another name for the supernatural sociology of *Fire on the Earth*. "It follows that whoever wishes to improve human society should place his reliance ultimately on the truths of faith and not on human wisdom. Given the transcendent quality of revealed truth, it is sheer folly to try to base a society purely on science or philosophy. This is particularly inexcusable in a Catholic. To accept the truths of faith in theory, and then to disregard them as aids in the practical task of social reform, is to neglect what is incomparably the best means to the desired end."[9]

Such a supernatural sociology presupposes a radical incompatibility between the gospel and the accepted mores of society. The great temptation for Catholics comes from their desire to be acceptable. They fear to be different, but in the process they merely choose the unacceptable mores of the day which are in direct opposition to the gospel. This theme runs through all of Furfey's writings. His 1966 book *The Respectable Murderers* deals with four great crimes perpetrated by organized society under the leadership of respectable citizens.[10] Such crimes are possible only because there exists a strong delusion that attempts to justify these things in terms of respectability and what other people are doing. Such beliefs constitute a delusion which directly contradicts the gospel ethic.[11]

---

8 Paul Hanly Furfey, *Three Theories of Society* (New York: Macmillan, 1937).

9 *Ibid.*, p. 179.

10 Paul Hanly Furfey, *The Respectable Murderers* (New York: Herder and Herder, 1966), pp. 17-111.

11 *Ibid.*, pp. 140-162.

Fire on the Earth constantly insists on this radical incompatibility. A thorough-going social Christianity must be an opposition movement. Although the antagonism at times may relax into indifference, the respected classes will always be antagonistic. There can be no peace or even desire for peace with the world which has crucified Our Leader.[12] Furfey stresses that Jesus was a social agitator. The chapter on the New Testament in his *A History of Social Thought* begins with a section entitled: "Our Lord as a Social Agitator."[13] Elsewhere, he has a chapter on the fact that Jesus was not a conformist.[14]

Furfey's own words on the subject are eloquent:

When we preach caution and counsel moderation, we are not following Christ. We are following the world, and we are following the world because we are secretly afraid of the world's contempt. We are afraid to be called radicals and extremists. But this world which calls us extremists is not afraid to demand extreme heroism when its own selfish aims are to be served. The world takes it for granted that our young men must die in the next useless war, as young men died in the mud of Ethiopia. . . . Let us have done with this hypocrisy! Christ asked for heroism. Christ showed heroism in his own life. . . . Let us, also, be heroic if we dare. But if we are too cowardly, let us at least not borrow excuses from the hypocritical world. Let us humbly acknowledge our own weakness. Let us ask Christ for strength, and let us beg Him for His grace, that perchance we too may gain some spark of that heroism which makes saints.[15]

---

[12] *Fire on the Earth*, p. 76.
[13] Paul Hanly Furfey, *A History of Social Thought* (New York: Macmillan, 1942), pp. 133-135.
[14] Paul Hanly Furfey, *The Mystery of Iniquity* (Milwaukee: Bruce, 1944), pp. 55-67.
[15] *Fire on the Earth*, p. 136.

The theme of the radical incompatibility between the gospel and the accepted mores of the times, especially in the matter ot social morality, stands as the central theme of Furfey's book *The Mystery of Iniquity* published in 1944. The book begins with the assertion that Catholics have their own distinctive doctrine about the ills which plague society and their possible remedies. Unbelieving social scientists and the modern world have a doctrine of their own, but the two viewpoints are completely and utterly different. Catholic social thought explains the ills of society in terms of the mystery of iniquity which is overlooked by the nonbeliever, but which remains the only adequate explanation of the social evils that plague our society. The conclusions of his opening chapter are obvious: "Since there is a radical antithesis between the Catholic viewpoint on the root cause of social problems and the current materialistic viewpoint, Catholic social action must be fundamentally different from the type of social action which is current in the modern world."[16]

The theme of *The Mystery of Iniquity* stands out in the chapter titles which consistently warn of the danger of conformism and call for Catholics to be dissidents and dissenters. Catholics must hold uncompromisingly and put into practice the basic truths which Christ brought into the world without conforming in the slightest way to the spirit of this world.

What is the proper Catholic response to the social problems of the day? Furfey has rejected the responses proposed by most social reformers because they do not go to the root of the problem and they always involve some type of compromise with the mystery of iniquity. Furfey's response centers on a Catholic or Christian personalism. He finishes his *A History of Social Thought* with a call to Christian personal-

---

16 *The Mystery of Iniquity*, p. 30

ism based on the supreme duty of an all-embracing charity. Gross materialism leads to the malign hatred which separates class from class, race from race and nation from nation. Christian charity remains the one remedy "which can save and reconstruct society in our own discouraged and disillusioned generation."[17]

Christian personalism stems from love and calls for the renovation of the individual person in the light of the gospel and God's grace so that he now begins to live the life of supernatural charity. Its gentle influence spreads imperceptibly until the whole mass of people are changed. Personalist action is effective through the influence it will have on others. Even if Christians are not effective in changing social institutions they will not despair, because they believe in the power of Christ which is always present. Jesus himself worked in a personalist fashion with just a few followers.[18] The theme of Christian personalism remains the primary response of the Christian in the writings of Furfey down to his last book *The Morality Gap*.[19]

He proposes no precise blueprint for reform, but insists on the fundamental principle of personal responsibility whether its peculiar type of organization is in small groups or in an individual's own life. The Christian merits heaven when he feeds the hungry, clothes the naked and practices the other works of mercy. When this form of loving service becomes much more widely diffused among Christians, then will the face of the earth be renewed.[20]

Catholic personalism thus gives primary attention to spiritual and moral reform as the basis for Catholic social action. Catholic liberalism paid more attention to the need to change the institutions of society so that they could better

---

17 *A History of Social Thought*, p. 405.
18 *Fire on the Earth*, pp. 92-97.
19 *The Morality Gap*, pp. 89-113.
20 *Ibid.*, pp. 97-98.

serve people in the light of the natural law teaching laid down in the papal encyclicals. The bulk of Catholic writers, in disagreement with Furfey's Christian personalism, try to find natural causes and cures for the social ills of our society. The natural law and human reason can instruct man how to bring his institutional structures more into line with the true needs of all mankind. All men of good will can and should work together to bring about a more humane, rational and ordered political, cultural and economic life for men. Note that both sides in this debate tried to find support for their position in the papal encyclicals.[21]

What are the means for carrying out this program of Christian personalism? Obviously they are the supernatural means which God has given to his Church. God's grace gives man the strength to live in accord with the perfectionist ethic. Furfey sees grace as incorporating us into the Mystical Body of Christ. Furfey, long before the papal encyclical *Mystici Corporis* of Pius XII in 1943, adopted this idea of the Mystical Body. Grace unites us not only to God but also to all other persons and to the social whole through the Mystical Body.

This concept became an important device for understanding the social mission of the Christian who can never exist as an isolated individual but because of membership in the Mystical Body is called upon to love and serve his neighbor. United more closely with Christ we must also become united with our neighbor especially the poor, the oppressed and the powerless.[22] Catholic moral theology has been too individualistic in its concerns and has not paid enough attention to the Christian's relationship to his neighbor. The older code morality must give way to a more charity-centered morality with concern for the neighbor stemming from our incorporation by grace into the Mystical Body of Christ.[23]

---

21 O'Brien, pp. 22-24.
22 *Fire on the Earth*, pp. 39-59.
23 *The Morality Gap*, pp. 34-45.

The greatest source of grace is the Mass, but even thirty-five years ago Furfey insisted on the Mass as "the supreme social act which the Kingdom of God performs."[24] If Catholics would daily participate and fully participate in the Mass as Christians conscious of our unity within the Mystical Body, our common life would truly become the light of the world and the salt of the earth. The success and the strength of capitalism, Fascism and Communism are really our fault because we as Catholics have the power to build a new world based on man's common purpose of attaining his ultimate end which calls for a love that embraces all the family of God.[25]

The emphasis on grace also involves the importance of prayer, contemplation and Christian asceticism by which we can and should resist the spirit of the world with its horrendous materialism. Prayer and contemplation are necessary for the Christian to constantly evaluate reality in the light of faith. Otherwise, he too easily conforms to the attitudes and spirit of the world. Prayer and meditation not only serve the intellect, but affective prayer moves the will to the love of God and neighbor, thus providing the impetus for the Christian life.[26] Voluntary poverty and the willingness to share with others become most vital aspects of the Christian life lived in accord with the grace of God which unites us in the Mystical Body and comes to us especially in and through the Sacraments, but primarily the Mass.[27]

Faith also supplies the Catholic with the knowledge and wisdom he needs to put into practice his Christian personalism. Furfey, in a somewhat overly simplistic manner, calls for an acceptance by an act of faith of the Church's whole social doctrine. By this he means not only the gospels but also tradition and the teaching of the Popes as found in the

---

24 *Three Theories of Society*, p. 222.
25 *Ibid.*, pp. 222-227.
26 *Ibid.*, pp. 177-191.
27 *The Mystery of Iniquity*, pp. 99ff.

encyclicals. Whoever wishes to improve society must place his reliance on faith and not on mere human wisdom. The scholar can make his contribution by bringing to light and making explicit the aspects of social doctrine connected with revelation. Then the Church can explicitly teach the entire body of social doctrine found in the Scripture and tradition. Thus theologians and scholars can aid the process of the development of dogma, which Furfey understands in a way consonant with the Catholic theology of the time.[28] Throughout his writings Furfey frequently invokes the Scriptures and the papal encyclicals as the basis for Christian action in the world. He also criticizes other approaches in the light of this faith teaching.

CHRISTIAN STRATEGIES

What are the particular strategies which should mark the life of the Christian striving to improve the life of society? In keeping with his basic understanding of Christian personalism Furfey frequently mentions three related types of what might be called strategies of the Christian life—separation, nonparticipation and bearing witness.

Separation arises because of the irreconcilable differences between Catholic social teaching and worldly sociologists. There is no common ground on which these two opposing ideas can meet. The moral corollary of this irreconcilability forms the command: "Come out from among them, be separated." Furfey employs this citation from 2 Corinthians 6:17 as the title of the last chapter of *The Mystery of Iniquity*.[29] Conformism remains the greatest evil for those who are called to be different and live in accord with faith and revelation. "Catholics must recognize that their social doc-

---

28 *Three Theories of Society*, pp. 179-182.
29 *The Mystery of Iniquity*, pp. 168-179.

trine is completely distinctive and completely irreconcilable with the perverse contemporary spirit. We must stand by ourselves in honorable isolation. We must break sharply and clearly with the modern world."[30] His last book, *The Morality Gap*, contains a similar chapter entitled, "Be Ye Separate."[31]

Nonparticipation constantly appears as a very important technique for the Christian in Furfey's understanding of the Christian life. The Christian not only rejects the mores of society but he refuses to participate in the observance of the mores that he condemns.[32] Voluntary poverty refuses to participate with avarice. Voluntary simplicity refuses to participate with luxury; voluntary renunciation of social class argues against class discrimination; voluntary abstention from certain business practices stands as a strong condemnation of those practices.[33]

Fire on the Earth describes a number of different forms such nonparticipation might take, especially for Catholic laity. An attractive possibility is the establishment of Catholic village communities, which would be able to cut themselves off from the contemporary world. But there are also forms of nonparticipation for those who feel bound to remain in the world because of certain obligations. Obviously one can choose his vocation with Christian criteria and not just for success and money. Even within honorable vocations such as law there are many possible forms of nonparticipation. Voluntary poverty remains a most appealing form of nonparticipation in this consumer oriented society.[34]

In contemporary times Furfey praises the nonparticipation of Catholic radicals. David Miller, Tom Cornell and others

---

[30] *Ibid.*, p. 171.
[31] *The Morality Gap*, pp. 114-124.
[32] *Ibid.*, p. 119.
[33] *Fire on the Earth*, p. 123.
[34] *Ibid.*, pp. 117-136.

were willing to set themselves apart from the American system and the great number of American youths who merely accept the draft system. By burning their draft cards and refusing to participate in this system, they gave eloquent testimony to their beliefs. Furfey realizes that the nonparticipation of the Christian actionist is not always well received by his fellows or superiors. Furfey lauds the action of Father Philip Berrigan and others who spilled blood on draft records in Baltimore in 1967. He wonders if the response of the Baltimore Archdiocesan Chancery office condemning their action as "disorderly, aggressive and extreme" might also have been the response of the same Chancery office to the action of Jesus in driving the money changers out of the temple.[35]

Nonparticipation follows from the irreconcilable gap between Catholic social life and the accepted mores of the times. The heroic Catholic must expect to find himself in opposition with the respectable society and its leaders. A later emphasis in Furfey's thought, as illustrated in *The Morality Gap,* describes the technique of nonviolence as a development in the line of nonparticipation. Nonviolence takes different forms such as simple nonresistance, passive resistance, and nonviolent direct action. There are many practical matters (e.g., organization) which must be settled before nonviolence can be used successfully; but by demanding self-sacrifice for the sake of others, nonviolence is a very active and pure form of Christian charity. It can be very effective in eliminating social evils and building a holy society.[36]

A third strategy which is closely connected with the other two but emphasizes more the positive aspect of Christian personalism is bearing witness. The Christian must be a martyr; that is, one who bears witness for his faith. The

---

35 *The Morality Gap,* pp. 122-124.
36 *Ibid.,* pp. 137-147.

concept of bearing witness assumed a large place in the lives of John the Baptist, Jesus and the Apostles in the early Church. The most effective witness was to give one's life for his belief so that martyr came to signify those who had died for their faith. Here again Furfey illustrates this bearing witness in the lives of the saints. Throughout his works he frequently refers to the saints and their lives because he wants to inculcate the need for heroism in the Christian life which the saints showed so abundantly in their lives. Witness bearing, above all, calls for us to use means and methods, not because they seem sufficient to us but because God has pointed them out to us. Then we too can come to learn with Paul the Apostle that when we are weak, we are powerful, for the power of God is made perfect in infirmity. This is the hard path of Our Lord and the saints which involves great renunciation on our part, but such work will be blessed with the marvelous and supernatural significance which characterized the lives of the great saints.[37]

Bearing witness can take many different forms. Bearing witness is illustrated by the Christian who voluntarily lives among the poor to share with them, thereby acquiring a true empathy for their condition. Such a person proves by his life that he takes seriously the gospel ethic of Jesus. By actions such as this other people are then forced to ask themselves questions about their way of life and their response to the gospel which is so often only nominal. The hearts of others must be touched by such witness so that they too begin to share their wealth with the poor.[38]

The Christian witness proclaims the message of Jesus in season and out of season. If Christianity is to be socially effective, there must be witnesses who are willing to speak up "out of season" and incur the alienation, suspicion and wrath of many others especially those in high places. In this

---

37 *Fire on the Earth,* pp. 98-116.
38 *Ibid.,* pp. 92-95.

connection Furfey praises the Anglican Rector in Williamsburg, Virginia, who boldly challenged the morality of the war in Vietnam when Lyndon Johnson was in the congregation.[39]

Such are the strategies or techniques of a radical Christian personalism. Furfey knows that such an approach runs counter to the generally accepted approach of Catholics as individuals and of the American Catholic Church in general. Conciliation has been the policy and the strategy of the American Catholic Church under a succession of leaders—England, Hughes, Gibbons, Ireland, Spellman. There seem to be many signs of success connected with such an approach—the prosperous state of the Church in this country, the lack of prejudice, the fact that a Catholic could become president. "Conciliation as a strategy, however, has one overwhelming disadvantage. It makes impossible the construction of a new society according to the guidelines of Jesus Christ, for, in order to change the current society one must be free to criticize it."[40]

THE ISSUES

What are the issues with which Furfey has been involved in the last forty years? Consistently he has been concerned with the same basic problems—the problems which still exist today and are the rallying points for contemporary radicals of all kinds—the treatment of minority groups, especially the blacks in our society, the inequalities of our society and especially the lot of the poor, the question of peace. *The Respectable Murderers* begins with four chapters pointing out four concrete instances of paramoral societies and of the crimes of these societies in which the decent and the "God-fearing" cooperated: American Negro slavery, the

---

[39] *The Morality Gap*, pp. 134, 135.
[40] *Ibid.*, p. 121.

slaughter of European Jews, the bombing of noncombatants, the subproletariat.[41]

Furfey, both in his writings and in his actions, has condemned American society for its treatment of blacks. *The Mystery of Iniquity* includes a chapter on conformism and race. The obligation of showing our love for the Jew, the Oriental, the Mexican, the Indian and the Negro is a matter of eternal life or death for the true Christian. His discussion centers on the black question, but even in 1944 he was conscious that the problem extended to many others in our society.[42]

His analysis of the problem almost twenty years ago shows the penetrating understanding of the trained social scientist but above all the empathetic understanding of the committed Christian. The economic plight of the blacks in comparison to whites is a scandal. Jobs are closed to the black; even job training opportunities are closed to him. The housing problem is especially galling for the black worker, for here discrimination constantly raises its ugly head. Inferior educational opportunities and the denial of basic civil rights to blacks merely add to the indignities heaped upon the blacks by a white majority. Unfortunately, this discrimination even exists in the Catholic Church which has become too conformed to the mores of the contemporary society. The progress of the Church in America will be gravely handicapped until the average Catholic can put into practice concerning all men, but especially minority groups, the love command of Jesus.[43]

Furfey's Christian empathy and concern for the blacks is illustrated in the research he has been doing in the past few years. To improve and help the situation of the blacks in

---

[41] *The Respectable Murderers*, pp. 17-111.
[42] *The Mystery of Iniquity*, pp. 138-151.
[43] *Ibid.*

Washington he has been devoting his scholarship to learning about the culture of the ghetto, but always within the context of the empathy generated by a Christian personalism. His latest publication *The Subculture of the Washington Ghetto* indicates again how his Christian, ministerial and scholarly life have been integrated in the service of the causes which he has deemed so important in the area of social reform.[44]

A second issue of constant concern has been the question of peace. Furfey has consistently worked for the gospel ideal of peace even while his country has often been following the path of war. In 1935 Paul Furfey wrote the first article in the *Catholic Worker* on pacificism.[45] In the last few years he has established Emmaus House in Washington as a center for the Catholic Peace Fellowship and has been the father figure in the Catholic peace movement in the Washington area. There have been peace groups centered at many universities in this country, but no other group has centered around a 75 year old man who remains today a dedicated gospel radical.

In the *Mystery of Iniquity,* written in the course of the Second World War, Furfey courageously called attention to the dangers of an exaggerated nationalism. He cited papal texts to show the evils of a system that set up the national will to power in place of the law of God. He asserted even in the midst of that war the fact that the morality of a particular war is always subject to review by the individual conscience.[46] Furfey maintained that in the course of history the spirit of iniquity was probably nowhere more visibly at

---

44 Paul Hanly Furfey, *The Subculture of the Washington Ghetto* (Washington: Bureau of Social Research, The Catholic University of America, 1972) .

45 Letter of Dorothy Day and Tom Cornell to the Banquet Committee for the celebration of Paul Hanly Furfey's fiftieth ordination anniversary.

46 *The Mystery of Iniquity,* p. 161.

work than in the spirit of nationalism.[47] He carefully distinguished between patriotism and nationalism and admitted that historically the United States had been saved from some of the excesses of nationalism. However, then during the World War there were unfortunate indications and indices that nationalism was affecting America and American Catholics specifically on the question of war.

The crucial test arises when the loyal Catholic is confronted with nationalistic propaganda in favor of courses of action which are immoral. Here Furfey expounds the teaching that an individual must judge the justice of a particular war. Then he expressly brings up the immoral actions sanctioned by the American government which run counter to the teaching of the gospels and of the popes. The stated policy of the allies in World War II included the demand for unconditional surrender. The Pope had asked for a negotiated peace if possible, but this fell on deaf ears in the American Catholic community. Ironically, non-Catholic organizations were arguing against the policy of unconditional surrender, but Catholics generally followed the policies of their government.[48]

The second government policy which Furfey condemned during the Second World War was the practice of the Allies of indiscriminate bombing which meant direct attacks on noncombatants. Paul Furfey spoke out against such immoral bombing even before Hiroshima and indicated that such a policy was contrary to the teaching of the Popes.[49] Furfey obviously recognized the excesses of nationalism in Germany, but as a radical Christian he pointed out the errors of

---

47 *Ibid.*, p. 157.

48 *Ibid.*, pp. 163-165.

49 Paul Hanly Furfey, "Bombing of Noncombatants is Murder," *The Catholic C.O.*, II (July-September 1945), pp. 3-4; *The Mystery of Iniquity*, pp. 165-166; *The Respectable Murderers*, pp. 69-85.

nationalism in our own country especially in the midst of war.

In writing, in speaking and in acting Paul Hanly Furfey has been dedicated to the cause of peace and has warned about the dangers of war. During the Second World War he assisted Catholic conscientious objectors, was active in anti-war organizations, and served on the board of the National Council for the Prevention of War.[50] When war came to South Vietnam Paul Furfey again spoke out against it and actively worked with the Catholic Peace Fellowship in opposition to it even in the early 1960's. His radical Christianity always made him aware of the excesses of nationalism especially in times of war and gave him the courage to take unpopular stands because he believed they were in accord with the gospel which always claimed his primary loyalty. Consistently in his writings he refutes the often quoted cliché, "My country, right or wrong."[51]

The third issue which perhaps constitutes his main concern is the economic situation and the plight of the poor. Obviously Christianity has much to say about the poor and the way in which Christians should treat the poor with love. Likewise any observer of the human scene recognizes the enormity of the problem of poverty existing even in our own society. The exploitations in society generally are at the expense of the poor so that the poor stand as the symbol of all the oppression in society and of all that is wrong with society. Thus one would expect Furfey with his all consuming interest in the gospel and in social problems to concentrate on the question of poverty.

Furfey flatly condemns the economic systems of the present whether they are communistic, fascistic or capitalistic. Since he sees sin and the mystery of iniquity as the root cause

51 E.g., *The Mystery of Iniquity*, p. 160; *The Respectable Murderers*, p. 84.
50 *The Respectable Murderers*, p. 83.

of all problems in society, the economic system obviously reflects such sinfulness. "To take an example, all Christians must acknowledge that capitalism in its modern form is evil. That is to say that our modern economic system is shot through with injustice."[52]

Furfey the sociologist produces the figures to show the inadequacies of our economic system. In the United States in 1929 there were 42% (11,653,000) of the total number of families in the nation earning less than fifteen hundred dollars, while 36,000 families or one tenth of one per cent of the total averaged $272,000.00 per year. The aggregate income of the upper one tenth of one per cent of the families in the United States was only slightly less than the aggregate income of the lower forty-two percent.[53] Statistics issued by the government in March of 1965 indicated that 34.1 million or 18% per cent of the total noninstitutionalized population in the United States was living in poverty.[54] Statistics thus bear out Furfey's condemnation of the current economic system.

What is wrong with the present economic system? Furfey indicates a number of contributing factors but concentrates especially on its basis in the success ideal, its competitiveness, its materialism and its individualism. He finds a root cause in the success ideal stemming from positivistic sociology. Others have also condemned the success ideal, but Furfey's own condemnation remains most eloquent.

The ideal of the success-class is then essentially a compromise, and herein lies its real weakness. It is an ideal which preaches decency and respectability but it is not an ideal to make moral heroes. It is an ideal rooted funda-

---

[52] *Fire on the Earth,* p. 119.
[53] *Three Theories of Society,* p. 43.
[54] *The Respectable Murderers,* p. 89.

mentally in the obvious. For it seeks what is obviously pleasant for self, such things as comfort, security and respectability. At the same time it seeks also what is obviously good for others and therefore encourages popular education, political democracy, and organized philanthropy. But the success-ideal implies no quests for vague and distant ideals, ineffable truths, half-realized beauties. The success-ideal is a philosophy of life for middle-aged shopkeepers, but it is not an ideal to fire the heart of youth with dreams of a suffering which transcends joy. The success ideal is sane and moderate and common sense, but is it the ideal in which man finds his deepest fulfillment? Is it the best we have to offer?[55]

In the success ideal man strives for those objects which bring him pleasure. Materialism restricts those objects to the crass and material at the expense of the intellectual and the spiritual. Money, power, prominence and respectability will never bring true satisfaction. Obviously the Scriptures point this out, but even human experience bears witness to the same truth.[56]

Competitive individualism forms the basis for our present economic system, but this again is a failure both in terms of the gospel and in terms of accomplishing its own purpose. Competition often costs the consumer because of the nonproductive costs such as advertising. More importantly, such a system concentrates wealth in the hands of just a few, and it seems to reduce both worker and capitalist to the level of the machine.[57] Furfey summarizes the attitudes behind the American economic ethos with the concept of the bourgeoise. He even translates the biblical Greek work

---

55 *Three Theories of Society*, p. 34.
56 *Ibid.*, pp. 51, 52.
57 *Fire on the Earth*, pp. 143, 144.

plousios not as the wealthy but the bourgeoisie. The bourgeoisie are the class which is interested in, and totally engaged in, the pursuit of money. The bourgeois spirit influences all of our economic life and becomes most difficult to expel.[58]

Furfey does not merely condemn the existing economic system, but he proposes another approach based on the doctrine of the Mystical Body rather than on the doctrine of competitive individualism. The papal encyclicals, especially *Rerum Novarum* and *Quadragesimo Anno* propose an economic system which is corporative and not competitive. While not destroying private property, it would seek the good of all rather than the profit of a few. The assurance of a living wage to all would involve a gigantic reorganization of our economic system. Such an approach would ease the strain of competition and permit each man, worker or industrialist to be first of all a person.[59]

Such a system obviously could not be put into practice right away, but Christians right away can begin trying to bring it about. Christians must take seriously and act upon the Christian love ethic with its insistence on the practice of the spiritual and corporal works of mercy.[60] But above all Furfey sees the proper Christian response in terms of a voluntary poverty. Voluntary poverty does not call for an extreme giving up of everything that one possesses. Furfey, interestingly enough, calls for a voluntary poverty which is reasonable. People should spend money on themselves and their families to provide decent clothing, adequate shelter, wholesome food, moderate recreation and proper medical attention; but then what is not needed for these legitimate purposes should be given to the poor. The approach of

<hr>

[58] *The Mystery of Iniquity*, pp. 87-101; "PLOUSIOS and Cognates in the New Testament," *Catholic Biblical Quarterly*, V (1943), 243-263.
[59] *Fire on the Earth*, p. 145.
[60] *Ibid.*, p. 147.

voluntary poverty realizes man's need for the basics but
willingly gives to others anything above and beyond these
needs. Such an approach is diametrically opposed to the
bourgeoise spirit influencing the contemporary ethos.[61]

Paul Hanly Furfey has been grappling with the important
issues of discrimination against minorities, peace, poverty
and the unfair economic system for over thirty-five years.
Both the gospel insights and his acute observations of our
society brought him to see long before most of his contem-
poraries that these are the crucial problems facing our society. Today such radical proposals and radical solutions are
heard more frequently, but years ago Paul Furfey was bearing witness like John the Baptist crying out in the wilderness
to make ready the way of the Lord.

PERSONAL INVOLVEMENT AND ASSOCIATIONS

The gospel forms the integrating center not only of Paul
Furfey's theory but also of his life. The remarkable characteristic of his life remains that integration of Christian
life, priestly ministry and scholarship around the centrality
of the radical acceptance of the ethical teaching of Jesus.
Furfey's life bears witness to his own theory, for he has been
associated with the movements, the institutions and the
persons who have been in the forefront of the radical Catholic movement in this country. His associations of this type
fully related his personal life to the theory he proposed.

His association with the Catholic Worker movement and
its guiding lights, Dorothy Day and Peter Maurin, dates back
to the very beginnings of that movement. Its paper *The
Catholic Worker* first appeared in 1933. There is no doubt
that the Catholic Worker is the most influential group in
the short history of American Catholic radicalism. Furfey's

---

[61] *Ibid.*, pp. 130-134; *The Mystery of Iniquity*, pp. 99-101.

important writings grew out of discussions in this context, and he also enflamed the zeal of many others to join and participate in this movement. For years he frequently gave retreats and conducted discussions with the Worker people.[62]

Furfey did have one important disagreement with the Catholic Worker people over what he termed the romantic and utopian agrarianism which thought the answer to the social problem could be solved only by a return to the land.[63] Furfey had earlier insisted that his system did not oppose technical advance or machines as such. There is no need for a literal return to the Middle Ages.[64]

Relationships with people in the Catholic Worker spun off other apostolates and movements in which he was intimately involved. A group had been meeting every Sunday at Catholic University, and one of this group, Gladys Sellew, purchased a house in a very poor section of Washington in which the members tried to share the poverty of those around them. One of the purposes of Il Poverello House, as it was called, was to have black and white people live together to show that Christian charity knew no distinctions based on race, but this was obviously not respectable in Washington in the 1930's.[65]

In 1940 Mary Elizabeth Walsh, who had been living at Il Poverello House, started a similar house of her own called Fides House. Throughout her life Dr. Walsh has been associated with Msgr. Furfey in both his theoretical and practical concerns, as is evidenced by their long association together at Catholic University and in practical areas of the apostolate. Fides House grew and expanded gradually in the

[62] *The Morality Gap,* pp. 100-103.
[63] O'Brien, p. 200. See, Furfey, "There are Two Kinds of Agrarianism," *Catholic Worker,* VII (December 1939), 7, 8.
[64] *Fire on the Earth,* pp. 144, 145.
[65] *The Morality Gap,* pp. 107-110.

direction of a settlement house, but the idea was for the staff to live there and associate themselves with the people of the neighborhood. The Archbishop of Washington, Patrick O'Boyle, took a great interest in this work and helped them to expand. In 1958 Walsh and Furfey, because of other pressing commitments and the growing activities of the Fides House, were no longer able to continue their active leadership in it.

Furfey was also associated with the Friendship House Movement begun by the Baroness de Hueck, who came to New York City in 1938 and opened a house in Harlem. The movement gradually spread to other cities in the United States.[66] Here again a group of dedicated Catholics came together in voluntary poverty to serve the needs of the poor by living in their midst and sharing their lot. The twin interests of concern for racial equality and of care for the poor characterized all these movements with which Furfey was associated. His books often served as the guide and the inspiration for many who became involved in these movements. In addition his scholarly expertise brought a sociological sophistication to these endeavors.[67]

Paul Furfey was also influential in the development of the liturgical movement which was spearheaded by the Benedictine monk, Virgil Michel. A program of social renewal through Christian personalism would obviously find its source in the Mass and in the liturgy. The liturgy, according to Furfey, is the perfect expression of the new social Catholicism.[68] Furfey in the 1930's dwelt on the social implications of the Mass which had usually been seen only in individualistic terms. The Mass is the social celebration of those joined together by charity in the Mystical Body. The Mass calls for

---

[66] *Ibid.*, pp. 110-111.
[67] *The Respectable Murderers*, fn. 33, pp. 180-181.
[68] O'Brien, p. 189.

the active participation of the whole community and not just the priest. Furfey asserted that the Mass, celebrated properly, is the chief means of Catholic social action.[69] Furfey's insistence on the role of the saints and the great example they give for heroism in the Christian life was shared by the liturgical movement which thus tried to bring together the liturgy and the daily life of Catholics.

Throughout his last forty years Paul Furfey has been actively involved in the cause of peace and associated with many of the radical movements connected with it. He defended Catholic conscientious objectors in World War II and condemned as immoral some of the actions of the United States government. He has been actively engaged in the Catholic Peace Fellowship especially in Washington. His Emmaus House founded in 1968 became a center for the Catholic antiwar movement in the Washington area.

Paul Furfey was not only the theorist of American Catholic radicalism, but he actively participated in the movements which have been identified with that valiant minority of American Catholics. The same radical gospel spirit, with the call to be separated from the respectable mores of the day, appears just as burning in his later books as in those written over thirty years before. Obviously age has not mellowed his spirit, for his radicalism owes its source not to idealism and the dreams of youth but to his faith commitment to the gospel and to the Church.

Paul Hanly Furfey as the theorist of American Catholic radicalism was both a Catholic and a radical because of his Catholicism. The theology behind his approach was very much orthodox Catholicism, which accepted the Catholic doctrines and the generally proposed Catholic theology of the times. His theological innovations were in seeing the social importance of some aspects of Catholicism which had

---

[69] *Three Theories of Society,* pp. 222-227.

unfortunately been downplayed. Thus he used the newly developed notion of the Mystical Body as the basis for social reform and understood the Mass in terms of more active participation on the part of all and the source of the social mission of the Church.

Furfey's supernatural sociology was based on faith and a very self-conscious Catholicism which constantly appealed to the papal teachings in the encyclicals as the basis for Catholic involvement in social reform. One might say that this radical Catholicism had quite conservative theological roots. However, it would be wrong to judge this movement in the light of later theological developments. Furfey accepted the ecclesiology which made the Catholic Church the one, true Church of Jesus Christ and gave great weight to the directives and teachings of the papal office. The whole movement of radical American Catholicism, as it grew up in the 1930's, generally shared this same basic approach built on a strong commitment to the Catholic Church as the one, true Church of Jesus Christ.

According to Furfey the Catholic accepts the whole social doctrine of the Church by an act of faith. This maximalist interpretation of faith and revelation includes in some way the papal social teaching to which frequent reference is made throughout his writings.[70] The Church as the supernatural society obviously is of prime importance. There is room for other types of subordinate societies which must exist, but their activity should always be subordinate to the dominant purpose of the pistic society which contains them.[71] His earlier writings for all practical purposes identified the kingdom of God, the Mystical Body of Christ and the Catholic Church.[72] Consequently other people are saved

---

[70] *Ibid.*, pp. 180-182.
[71] *Ibid.*, p. 212.
[72] *Ibid.*, p. 221.

only because invincible ignorance keeps them from finding the true Church of Christ.

Since this radical approach had its foundation in the supernatural sociology which sprang from the Catholic Church and it emphasized the differences with all others, this movement had to be very consciously Catholic. The radical is opposed to the liberal not only in social theory but also to a certain extent in ecclesiology. It is one of the signs of those times that Furfey's earlier writings show no familiarity with similar movements among Protestants in this country.

In this context it is interesting to note Furfey's differences in the 1940's with John Courtney Murray over the possibilities of intercredal cooperation. The liberals read the social encyclicals to propose concrete proposals such as collective bargaining or specific types of legislation. But Furfey insisted that the liberals often forget as concrete proposals the papal stress on the Eucharist, children's prayers and a crusade of prayer and penance. The mind of the Roman documents and the mind of the Church is that every true and lasting reform has proceeded from the sanctuary. "By all means let us continue our collaboration with non-Catholics, but until we put an enormously greater emphasis than we do now on the supernatural and distinctively Catholic elements in our social program we shall not be doing our full duty in the struggle against the evils of society."[73]

Paul Furfey based his supernatural sociology on his belief in the gospel and in the Church. His sociology helped him to know and examine the actual conditions. But the gospel and the Church held out the only radical remedies for the situation brought about by the mystery of iniquity. He was quite familiar with the Catholic theology of the time and

---

[73] Paul Hanly Furfey, "Intercredal Co-Operation: Its Limitations," *American Ecclesiastical Review*, CXI (1944), p. 175. See also, Furfey, "Why Does Rome Discourage Socio-Religious Intercredalism?" *American Ecclesiastical Review*, CXII (1945), 364-374.

with Thomistic philosophy. Likewise, he had a proficiency in biblical studies and biblical languages which he used in his efforts to understand the gospel and apply it to the problems of society.

Furfey's strong belief in the gospel and in the Catholic Church made him not a liberal but a radical. One could interestingly compare his approach with that often proposed today by contemporary radicals of the new left. He concentrated on the issues that have been of most importance in radical movements—peace, poverty and discrimination. For him there is a great gap between the existing social structures and what should exist, so that the proper response is not conciliation but opposition and nonparticipation. His nonparticipation even supported small communities that would withdraw from the contemporary society in which it is difficult for men to live while being true to their own principles. Furfey likewise did not put much hope in any efforts to change the system from within, for the problems are too radical to be solved by such an approach. Of course the great difference between Furfey and some other radicals remains his basis in a radical commitment to the gospel and to the Church.

CRITIQUE AND EVALUATION

A believing Christian must be moved in reading the works of Paul Hanly Furfey. Furfey is not a theorist in an abstract reflexive way who gradually tries to draw the reader deeper into the profundities of his thought. Furfey begins with the gospel and then tries to apply the radical gospel message with much the same simplicity as the gospel itself to the problems of Christian living in our society. The attractive power of his writing seems to come from the attractive power of the gospel itself spelled out in greater detail in the light of contemporary society. The power and attractiveness of his message certainly differentiate it from an ethic for middle age shopkeepers.

The stance of the radical provides an acute vision of the problems and troubles of society. Precisely because of his radical stance and insistence on the gospel, Furfey clearly recognized the ills in our society long before many others. Those who emphasize cooperation, common bonds with others and what we share in common too often fail to see the real sores of society. The issues which Furfey pinpointed almost three decades ago still remain the fundamental social issues of our times even though other new issues have also emerged.

Furfey is not as absolute a radical as his rhetoric would lead one to believe. It seems to me that in this world between the two comings of Jesus everyone must make some accommodation in the radical ethic of Jesus. Furfey, for example, does not espouse absolute pacifism, but he holds to a just war theory although in practice he sees very few cases where war would be justified. Perhaps his firm allegiance to papal teaching influenced his acceptance of the just war theory which he then severely limited in practice.

Even in the matter of poverty Furfey does not demand absolute poverty, but realizes that people need a sufficiency of food, clothing and shelter. A reasonable poverty should characterize the Christian life. His nonparticipation does not require the Christian to totally withdraw from the world, for he even recommends that people take up professions such as law and business but try to change them by living in accord with the gospel and Catholic teaching. In his own life Furfey has continued his scholarly and academic work and not abandoned all to take upon himself the lot of the poor and the uneducated. Furfey does accept some accommodation with life in this world and at times softens the radical ethical demands of Jesus. Perhaps the difference then between his radicalism and liberalism cannot be seen only in terms of a difference in kind but to some extent is a difference in degree. Thus there is some doubt about the consistency of any radical ethic including Furfey's.

The attractive force of gospel simplicity shines through Furfey's writings, but occasionally he does blunt the edge of that radical gospel simplicity. Nonetheless I would still criticize his theory at times because of its overly simplistic approach. Furfey's oversimplistic distinction between Catholics with all truth and grace on their side and others has already been mentioned and must be understood in the light of that aggressively self-conscious and self-assured Roman Catholicism of the 1930's. But even with this explanation there remains too clear-cut a distinction between the forces of good and the forces of evil. My view of reality sees more grey areas than the radical view of Furfey.

Too simplistic a methodology also appears in Furfey's literal acceptance of the gospel teaching. Nowhere does he show any appreciation of the theological debates about the eschatological influence on the Sermon on the Mount, but at times in practice he does water down some of the radical statements of Jesus as when he interprets wealth and riches as meaning the bourgeois spirit.

Christian personalism must be an important part of social reform, but one cannot simplistically avoid the need for the change of the structures of society even though this might require working with others and at times accepting some accommodations in terms of what is politically possible at a given time. The complexity of human existence is such that reform must include the reform of the structures of society and not just an overly individualistic approach. There is the tendency to forget the more fundamental conversion or change of heart that is required, but such a change of heart also has a social and cosmic dimension which calls for a change of the structures of society.

It is possible to test the adequacy of the stance proposed in Chapter Two by applying it to the writings of Paul Hanly Furfey. Furfey unlike many Catholics recognizes the presence of sin or the mystery of iniquity existing in this world so that he is quick to see the ramifications of sin in the social ills of society. Many followers of social liberalism could learn this emphasis from Furfey. Likewise there is no doubt that Furfey emphasizes the realities of the incarnation and redemption, for he constantly calls the Christian to follow the fullness of the gospel message and not to passively acquiesce in the *status quo.* In a sense Furfey also preserves the tension between redemption and resurrection destiny which many Christians today who insist on the fullness of the gospel teaching fail to do. Our author knows that the fullness of the kingdom will only come at the end of time and outside history. In this world the Christian and his efforts will often meet with opposition and not success, but the Christian places his hopes not in his own accomplishments but in the power of God.

From a negative viewpoint, I think Furfey does not give enough importance to the reality of creation which means all that we share on the basis of our common humanity with others. Also he overemphasizes sin so that at times the whole world is identified with sin. The Christian is warned not to be conformed with the world because the world is sinful. In one sense he does collapse the eschaton somewhat because he often calls on Christians, at least in theory, to live up to the fullness of the eschatological teaching of Jesus even though this goal can never be fully reached in this world.

One of the primary functions of the proposed stance is to highlight the various elements present in reality and the resultant complexity and tension arising from this fact. All these elements exist together so that it is impossible to speak of reality just in terms of any one of these aspects. Furfey often isolates one of these aspects at the expense of others, so that sin seems to be present in one particular area and redemption and resurrection destiny in another. My stance would feel more at home with the biblical parable of the wheat and the tares growing together. One cannot so readily or easily isolate either the reality of sin or the reality of redemption and resurrection destiny.

Within the Church and the Christian community there must always be room for the radical. In my judgment the radical position assumes a too simplistic view of reality and thus cannot and should not be accepted by the whole Church. But the very complexity of the reality in which we live argues for the fact that some should choose to bear witness to particular aspects of it, without saying that one form of bearing witness is better than others. Within the diverse gifts and vocations of the Christian community I hope and pray there will always be people inspired by the Spirit to bear witness to one particular aspect of the gospel (e.g. poverty, peace) in a radical way. Their lives help the whole Church show forth the fullness of the gospel teaching and at the same time serve the purpose of reminding us who see reality in a more complex way that we are always in danger of forgetting the gospel and conforming ourselves to the accepted and the customary.

Furfey rightly calls the Christian to gospel perfection and realizes that social problems cannot be changed without the conversion or radical change of heart which the Christian message demands. However, in the eschatological tension of the present times the Christian can only strive for the goal and ideal of the gospel teaching, which in its fullness will lie beyond his ability to respond. I agree that too often Christians just forget about the radical teaching of Jesus and acquiesce in the *status quo*. I view this teaching as a goal and ideal which always must spur us on and also as a reminder of our own sinfulness. We are pilgrim Christians always called to do more and yet at the same time made aware of our own creaturely limitations and sinfulness. The gospel ethic serves the threefold purpose of pointing out the goal towards which we strive, making us aware of our own continued sinfulness and reminding us of the mercy and forgiveness of God for a pilgrim people who will know the fullness of the kingdom only through his gracious gift.

4

Theological Reflections on the Social Mission and Teaching of the Church

A few decades ago this chapter would probably have been entitled: "A Theology of the Social Mission and Teaching of the Church." With the advent of the theologizing associated with Vatican II with its call for a greater dialogue and its appreciation of the dangers of triumphalism, a better title would be: "Toward a Theology of the Social Mission and Teaching of the Church." Today amidst a plurality of theologies even within Roman Catholicism, a more accurate title is: "Theological Reflections on the Social Mission and Teaching of the Church."

The first section comprises a critique of some theological approaches to this question using as an example "A Theology of Charity" as proposed by a special study cadre of the National Conference of Catholic Charities and published in *Toward a Renewed Catholic Charities Movement.*[1] The

---

[1] "A Theology of Charity," in *Toward a Renewed Catholic Charities Movement* (Washington: National Conference of Catholic Charities, 1971).

second section will discuss theological considerations emphasizing both the importance of the social mission of the Church and the limitations of the Church in its social mission. In the light of both the importance and limitations on the social mission of the Church the third section will discuss the more theoretical question of how the Church should speak on social questions and then suggest some criteria for the more practical question of structuring the social mission and function of the Church.

I   A CRITIQUE

The purpose of this study is to critique as sharply as possible the theological section of a self-study done by the National Conference of Catholic Charities. The Charities movement in the United States has long been identified as one of the major, if not the principal, instrumentality for the social mission of the Church. Catholic Charities people themselves realize the need for change and renewal in their own function and mission and have courageously begun the work of self-renewal which will call for many significant changes in their mode of operation, mission and apostolate.[2]

The tone of this part or critique is decidedly negative, but an explanation must be given. In preparing this study originally for the Catholic Charities group involved in their self-renewal my mandate was to point out as forcefully as possible the difficulties I find in their proposed "A Theology of Charity." I wholeheartedly believe in the new directions which these study groups are plotting for Catholic Charities. Catholic Charities, as at least the most visible national instrumentality of the social mission of the Catholic Church,

---

[2] The continuing progress of this renewal can probably best be followed in *The Catholic Charities Review* which is the official publication of the National Conference.

realizes that its concerns can no longer be only Catholics and only individuals. The social mission of the Church seeks to serve and help all the poor and those in need. Likewise, effective help is not primarily in terms of providing "band-aids" for the wounded but must call for a revision of the structures of society.

Another reason for the negative tone of what follows stems from the different perspectives of those who authored "A Theology of Charity" and my own optique. The framers of this document wanted to furnish theological reasons but also Christian motivations to support the new directions proposed for Catholic Charities. As an exhortation it accomplishes its purpose well, but as a reasoned theological justification there seem to be shortcomings. The first part of this study will concentrate on particular difficulties I find in this document.

The second and third parts of this study will develop what I believe are the most important aspects of the problem. In a sense "A Theology of Charity" does not go far enough or deep enough. The primary problem for people involved in Catholic Charities is undoubtedly the need to put into practice a broader and more comprehensive understanding of the social mission of the Church. My vision in the later parts of this paper accepts the absolute need for such a social mission of the Church, but the crucial problem arises in recognizing both the need for such a social mission and also the inherent limitations involved. The actual structuring of the social mission of the Church is more complex and difficult than appears at first sight.

Critique in the Light of the Proposed Stance

Most theological statements about the social mission of the Church correctly call for Christians and the Church to overcome the split between the faith which people profess and their daily lives.[3] In the process of overcoming that split there is the danger of seeing all earthly reality only in terms of the fullness of the kingdom. Here it is important to employ the critical stance proposed earlier. The Christian vision sees reality in terms of the fivefold mysteries of creation, sin, incarnation, redemption, and resurrection destiny.

The fullness of the kingdom belongs to resurrection destiny and will only come at the end of time. Meanwhile Christians must live in the tension of the times between the two comings of Jesus. The full Christian stance or vision refuses to collapse the tension either by canonizing the *status quo* and doing away with the future or by expecting the fullness of the kingdom to come too quickly or too easily. The Christian is called to strive to make the kingdom more present, but he will never totally succeed, for the kingdom remains God's gracious gift. Man's cooperation is absolutely essential but not sufficient for bringing about the new heaven and the new earth. Progress in the kingdom is probably, in my judgment, much less and slower than many people in the last few years have assumed. The Christian works for the greater presence of the kingdom but with the realization of the continuous struggle involved.

One example of such collapsed eschatology in "A Theology of Charity" concerns the mandate of Catholic Charities to "overcome the dichotomy between the good news of the gospel and the scandal of human suffering, for only in their blending will the mature and integrated life expected of the Christian community be forthcoming."[4]

To struggle to overcome the dichotomy—yes. To have this as a goal toward which we continuously strive but which we can never reach—yes. To overcome such a dichotomy—no.

---

[3] The Pastoral Constitution on the Church in the Modern World, n. 43.
[4] "A Theology of Charity," p. 5.

The scandal of human suffering in its manifold forms will always be a part of the pilgrim life of Christians in this world, but such an understanding does not mean a passive acceptance of the *status quo*.

The problem of reconciling the good news of the gospel and human suffering does not arise for the first time in the latter part of the twentieth century, for the question has perennially troubled the followers of Jesus. A different solution was proposed by what the Christian tradition accepts as the gospel of Luke. Luke knew of the beatitudes of Jesus which in their original form were probably a messianic pronouncement of the good news—Happy are you, for the Messiah has come. The problem for Luke centered on reconciling the proclamation of the good news with the actual state of the people to whom the good news is preached.[5]

Luke solved the dilemma by postponing the good news to the future. Happy are you who are hungry now, you shall be satisfied. Happy are you who weep now, you shall laugh. But alas for you who have your fill now or laugh now. Luke introduces the sapiential theme of the now and the then to show the good news refers to these people primarily in terms of the future.[6]

I personally cannot accept Luke's approach as the total Christian understanding. Too often similar approaches have furnished an excuse for a too easy acceptance of the *status quo* and a failure on the part of Christians to become involved in changing the conditions of society. Luke does point to one aspect of the total Christian approach—the fullness of the good news will never be here. In the meantime, however, Christians try to make the kingdom more present; but

---

[5] Jacques Dupont, *Les Béatitudes* (Bruges: Éditions de l'Abbaye de Saint-André, 1954) pp. 129-181. This section was amplified in a separate volume (as earlier the first two chapters were amplified in a separate volume) published as *Les Béatitudes*, Vol. II; *La Bonne Nouvelle* (Paris: Gabalda, 1969).

[6] *Ibid.*, pp. 193-246. An amplification of the last two chapters in a separate volume has been promised by the author, but has not yet appeared.

with the realization that they always fall short. Both those who think they can overcome the dichotomy and those who put off the good news until the future too easily collapse the tension that will always be part of the Christian life.

Another illustration. The Preamble of "A Theology of Charity" calls for a "deep respect for all reality as a medium through which a loving God makes himself available to men."[7] This is later explained as perceiving all reality as a medium of revelation of a good and merciful Being.[8]

Such an expanded notion of revelation rightly comes to prominence in contemporary theology. I agree with it, provided that one is prepared to admit other aspects present in reality—the imperfections of a limited creation and the evils resulting from human sinfulness. A collapsed eschaton tends to canonize too easily present reality as a revelation of God without furnishing a critical stance by which one can attempt to evaluate the present reality and the plans proposed to change it. There seems to be a temptation today of easily accepting and baptizing some activities as the certain action of God in our world. God is present and active in our world, but there are also other elements so that the Christian vision must develop critical tools for discerning what God is doing in the world. The consciousness of the future eschaton as judgment and a realistic appraisal of sin in the world should be joined with the assertion that all reality is a medium through which a loving God makes himself available to men. God is present and revealing not in a pure form but rather mixed together with many other elements, so that Christian theology needs to develop a critical process for determining God's revelation here and now.

The rhetoric of certain assertions in "A Theology of Charity" reflects the romantic utopianism coming from a collapsed eschaton. "Catholic Charities must commit itself

---

7 "A Theology of Charity," p. 3.
8 *Ibid.*, p. 6.

boldly to the complete liberation of man so that he can be the real artisan of his destiny, the free active builder of his future."[9]

Such a statement forms an interesting contrast with the one page introduction entitled "A Fable" which Paul Ramsey places at the beginning of his collection of essays, *The Just War: Force and Political Responsibility*. Eve, the mother of all the living is pictured with Adam after the fall. Her imagination looks forward to the future which will be a new age based on the sound platform of friendly competition, co-operation, mutual respect and universal responsibility. "Adam looked with downcast eyes at the shadow on their pathway cast from behind them by the angel's two flaming swords. He knew better than she the shape of the advancing generations. Yet his mind had no relish for this knowledge, and he too wished that this new age might be launched from some other platform than the No-Returning."[10]

Somewhere between these two positions there is a more balanced understanding of the life of man on earth which has potentialities for great growth and development but also retains many limitations, imperfections and even positive shortcomings attributable to sin. Obviously preambles tend to be heavy on rhetoric, but many problems result today from such a view of man and of human progress. In many ways the technological age was built on such an ideology of ever developing progress which enshrined the inevitability of progress and forgot human limitations and the ambiguities of all human progress.

Even a theologian of the future and of hope such as Jurgen Moltmann reminds us that the struggle for freedom is continuous because no sooner does man overcome one obstacle

---

9 *Ibid.*, p. 3.

10 Paul Ramsey, *The Just War: Force and Political Responsibility* (New York: Charles Scribner's Sons, 1968) p. XXI.

than other ones begin to appear.[11] There is much unfreedom in our own society which is in no way related to physical and material poverty. Again the fullness of freedom lies beyond the grasp of man in this world, but all must strive to become truly more free.

A third illustration comes from the fact that "A Theology of Charity" describes its own approach as incarnational theology. A few decades ago Catholic theologians were discussing the merits of an incarnational or eschatological spirituality. The eschatologists saw the kingdom primarily as future and thus downplayed the importance of human activity in this world. The incarnationalists emphasized the present aspect of the kingdom and the call for the Christian to cooperate in his daily life with the mystery of the incarnation.[12]

The theological picture has changed at the present time. Eschatology no longer refers merely to the four last things that will occur at the end of the present world. A newer approach to eschatology, as illustrated, for example, in theologies of the future, understands the eschatological as being already present but not totally present. The question of eschatology has assumed a much greater importance today and disputes center on the precise relationship of the present existence to the future kingdom. My understanding of eschatology calls for a tension between the present and the fullness of the kingdom which will only come at the end of time, but which men here and now try to make more present. Note the conversionist or transformationsit motif which is implied in such an understanding of eschatology. The incarnation is just one aspect of the total Christian mystery and does not give sufficient attention to the total Christian vision.

---

[11] Jurgen Moltmann, *Religion, Revolution, and the Future* (New York: Charles Scribner's Sons, 1969) , pp. 63-82.

[12] Bernard Besret, S.O. Cist., *Incarnation Ou Eschatologie?* (Paris: Éditions du Cerf, 1964) .

Insistence on the incarnation alone contributes to the same problem of identifying all of present reality with the fullness of God's activity in the world.

Failure to Recognize Complexity

A second danger frequently found in contemporary theologizing about the social mission of the Church, especially in the literary genre of preambles, concerns the failure to recognize complexity. The tendency to oversimplification results in an undue emphasis on one particular aspect to the exclusion of other important considerations. In many ways the problems mentioned above also bespeak a mentality that fails to appreciate all the aspects of the question.

The dominant note of the preamble of "A Theology of Charity" stresses a theology of liberation. Such an approach fosters individual freedom and independence as opposed to oppression, bondage and coercion. I personally agree with what the framers of this document want to emphasize; namely, the need for Catholic Charities and the Church to free poor people from the manifold bonds keeping them in their condition of poverty and powerlessness.

Lately there has been great theological interest in the question of liberation. I am in basic agreement with the exposition proposed by Gustavo Gutierrez, but I would add some friendly amendments.[13] As noted above, liberation will never be fully accomplished but is rather an on-going process so that here too one must avoid collapsing the eschaton. Some writings about liberation give the impression that it is just the poor people of the world who need liberation. Obviously they do need liberation from economic oppression, but one can never forget the lack of freedom existing in our own wealthy society. We are imprisoned by all types of con-

---

13 Gustavo Gutierrez, *A Theology of Liberation: History, Politics and Salvation* (Maryknoll, New York: Orbis Books, 1973).

formity, and even those who most stress freedom exhibit in their dress, for example, the utmost of conformity.

From a more theoretical perspective there are also other possible dangers. Liberation is a very important theme, but it is only one theme in the Christian life. Chapter Two rejected love or any one content virtue as supplying an adequate stance for Christian ethics. There are other aspects to moral theology and the Christian life than liberation.[14] The fact that there are other aspects means that in practice one cannot absolutize freedom or liberation or any one aspect. The history of our moral teaching reveals some of the problems when liberation or freedom has been absolutized. It has already been admitted in Chapter One that Roman Catholic theology has always had difficulty giving enough importance and value to freedom, yet freedom always exists together with other values.

Religious liberty is most important but there are limits that can and should rightly be placed on religious freedom even though there will always be difficulty in determining those limits both in practice and in theory.[15] Some adherents of feminine liberation assert that the woman should have complete freedom over her body and the fetus is only tissue in the womb of the mother, a position which I cannot accept because it does not give the proper value to the fetus.[16] Papal social teaching has rightly condemned *laissez-faire* capitalism with its theoretical justification in an individualistic notion of freedom.[17] The ecological crisis re-

---

[14] For a similar viewpoint, see H. Richard Niebuhr, *Christ and Culture* (New York: Harper Torchbook, 1956), pp. 11-29.

[15] This particular question will be developed later in Chapter Seven in the discussion about the role of law and the freedom of persons in society.

[16] For an exposition and refutation of this opinion, see Daniel Callahan, *Abortion: Law, Choice and Morality* (New York: Macmillan, 1970), pp. 462-465.

[17] E.G., J. Y. Calvez, S.J., and J. Perrin, S.J., *The Church and Social Justice* (Chicago: Henry Regnery Co., 1961).

minds us that man is not free to intervene in nature any way he wants.

Scriptural and Theological Shortcuts

A third defect in many theological statements about the social mission of the Church involves the temptation of using scriptural or theological warrants for positions that have been arrived at on other (perhaps valid) grounds. Such a defect often has affinities with a short cutting of the theological process so that one goes from a very general theological or scriptural premise to a very specific conclusion. Such a temptation obviously exists for the committed Christian who wants Christian warrants for his actions.

There is also a certain type of theologizing, which I call theological actualism, that leads to a similar approach. Theological actualism believes that God is present and working in our world in his individual actions which the Christian tries to discern. Such theologizing moves from a general statement to a very specific conclusion without any theological reasoning or development involving the steps from the more general to the less general and down to the more specific or without appreciating the complexity involved in the inductions necessary to come to specific conclusions.

I recall one example of such theological actualism in a paper that went from a general citation of Mt. 25 in paragraph one to a condemnation of multinational corporations in paragraph two. In general I do share the sentiments expressed in this paper, but no real theological reasoning was presented in support of such a conclusion. Theology by assertion remains a questionable enterprise.

Short statements obviously are prone to suffer from such an approach. The document "A Theology of Charity" in one paragraph asserts that since reality is a medium of revelation, the Christian should not attempt to manipulate or control it as its absolute master or allow himself to be controlled by it.

From this two conclusions are drawn. Catholic Charities
should not impose itself through any form of coercive restraint or constraint and conversely, "by acknowledging the
social and cultural causes of oppression, we stop attempting
to resolve the poverty and misery of the oppressed by individual acts of charity alone."[18] I agree with the two conclusions, but I do not see how they are really derived from
the fact that all reality is a medium of revelation, and the
Christian should neither manipulate reality nor be manipu-
lated by it.

The document "A Theology of Charity" definitely suffers
from such a theological defect which in a sense is under-
standable because the purpose of the document is to convince others of the need to adopt newer approaches in the
Catholic Charities apostolate. Personally I am in favor of
the major thrusts mentioned in the document—the need to
change structures and not just be involved in acts of individual charity which merely put "band-aids" on the victims
of unjust structures; the emphasis on social action as well as
social service; the need to respect those we serve so that all
paternalism is avoided and the poor are empowered to develop their own policies; the fact that those we serve also
serve us in many different ways which we too easily forget.
However, I have difficulty with the theological methodology
explicitly employed in the document.

This theology is described as vital, experiential and existential.[19] All too often this seems to mean that one occasionally uses a scriptural reference or a theological assertion to prove the point that has been arrived at through experience of other means. Experience can be a valid form of
learning in this area. Any good theology must always take
cognizance of the experience of people especially those im-

---

[18] "A Theology of Charity," p. 7.
[19] *Ibid.*, p. 6.

mediately involved. Theology tries to reflect systematically on the different data and experiences of reality. Such a reflective and systematic approach must also exercise a critical function. Theology must involve more than just assertions.

II IMPORTANCE AND LIMITATIONS OF THE SOCIAL MISSION

This section will strive to develop some important aspects that must be taken into consideration in reflecting theologically on the social mission and function of the Church today. I begin with a judgment based on the reading of the signs of the times that there is doubt and uncertainty about the social mission and function of the Church today.

In the United States the bishops have been criticized for not speaking out against the war. Contemporary events have made us all conscious of the deplorable conditions in prisons, but the American Catholic Church has not taken a stand. On the other hand some Catholics argue that the Church should not be involved in politics and should not speak out on the war issue. Some Catholics have been upset that Catholic funds have been given to projects sponsored by the Black Panthers. Many Catholics have supported the bishops in their attempt to prevent abortion on demand, while other Catholics seem to resent the intrusion of the bishops in this political matter of legislation. Some Catholics are still horrified at the thought of priests and sisters in picket lines and even in jail because of civil disobedience. Others see this as one of the roles of Christian ministry in the modern world.

The signs of the times seem to justify the recognition of a crisis in the social mission and function of the Church. Perhaps it will help to understand the conditions that bring about such crisis situations. In general crises arise when the older forms and structures are no longer viable but there is no agreement about what new forms should take their place.

Such a situation characterizes much of our society today. The complexity of the times, plus the plethora of possibilities, only accentuates the crisis. In the question of the social mission of the Church, this description appears accurate. The older understanding of the social mission of the Church and the apostolate of Catholic Charities are no longer meaningful today. There are many different possibilities but also limitations because of which the Church cannot become involved in every facet of the social apostolate. In the midst of both so many possibilities and so many limitations the Church must try to develop its social mission. The following theological reflections will try to situate the problem better and offer some guidelines for a more constructive approach to the social mission of the Church today.

Theology cannot be done in an abstract way. History, changing circumstances and personal experience influence one's approach. A few years ago the problem, especially in the Catholic Church, seemed to be the need to convince people of the social mission of the Church as a constitutive and integral part of the total mission and life of the Church. Today the problem at least for some seems to be shifting. Many are now aware of the importance of the social mission of the Church, but do not fully appreciate the limitations that inhere in the social mission of the Church. These two aspects must always be present for any adequate understanding of the social function of the Church.

The document, "A Theology of Charity," obviously comes out of a context in which it is necessary to emphasize the social mission of the Church, but unfortunately it does not seem to realize that the greater problem today is accepting the limitations of the Church in this area and still trying to work out what its social mission should be. No longer is it sufficient to talk about the need for the social mission of the Church. The problem today, in my judgment, centers on how the Church should carry out its social mission in the light of the limitations in this area and the plethora of forms that such a mission can take. This seems to be the real problem for the future even though among some Catholics there is still the need to convince them of the social mission of the Church.

Social Mission as Constitutive of the Church

First it will be necessary to briefly indicate that the social mission of the Church is a constitutive part of the mystery of the Church.[20] The Church is not truly such without a social mission. The gospel joins together the love of God and the love of neighbor in an indissoluble union. The love of neighbor becomes the sacrament or the criterion pointing to the existence of our love for God. There always has been a moral dimension to the Christian message. Contemporary theology reiterates that the kingdom of God embraces all reality so that the world and terrestrial reality are not outside the pale of redemption. The daily life of men in this world is under the gospel and pertains to the work of the kingdom.

While accepting the importance of the Church's social mission, it might be helpful to point out some overemphases that often appear. At times some advocates of the social mission overstress the social mission of Jesus himself and thus expose themselves to rebuttal especially on the part of those who do not want to admit any social aspect to the mission of the Church.[21] Walter Rauschenbusch appears to exaggerate the social aspects of the life of the Apostolic Church.[22] On

---

20 "Justice in the World," the document of the Second General Assembly of the Synod of Bishops, 1971, as printed in *The Catholic Mind*, LXX (March 1972), 52-64.

21 Catholic personalism and radicalism in the 1930's at times appear to have overstated the case. Paul Hanly Furfey has a section on "Our Lord as a Social Agitator" in his *A History of Social Thought* (New York: Macmillan, 1942), pp. 133-135.

22 Walter Rauschenbusch, *Christianity and the Social Crisis* (New York: Harper and Row Torchbook, 1964), pp. 139-142.

the other hand Rudolf Schnackenburg appears too one-sided in asserting that Jesus assumed no definite attitude on economic and social problems, for Jesus did nothing to change the social or the political order.[23] I would maintain that the social implications are at least implicit in the teaching of Jesus and have rightly been developed by the Church down through the centuries.

First Limitation: No Exclusive Knowledge

The first limit comes from the fact that Christians and the Church cannot claim a monopoly on social ethical wisdom and knowledge. The Catholic theological tradition has consistently maintained this fact, at least in theory. The famous social encyclicals which formed the backbone of Catholic social teaching through the first six decades of the twentieth century are grounded on natural law reasoning which does not explicitly depend on revelation.[24] Pope John XXIII in *Pacem in Terris* explicitly affirms that his teaching is based on the order that the Creator of the World has imprinted on the hearts of all men. The laws governing social relationships are to be found in the nature of man where the Father of all things wrote them.[25] In this context Pope John addressed his encyclicals not only to Catholics but to all men of good will.

There has been a development and change in the methodological approach of later statements of the hierarchical

---

[23] Rudolf Schnackenburg, *The Moral Teaching of the New Testament* (New York: Herder and Herder, 1965), p. 122.

[24] For the best commentaries on the approach of the papal encyclicals, see Calvez and Perrin, *The Church and Social Justice;* John F. Cronin, S.S., *Social Principles and Economic Life* (Milwaukee: Bruce, 1959). The encyclicals do generally refer to natural law and the gospel as the sources of their teaching, but the above commentaries representing the liberal interpretation stress the natural law aspects. A more radical approach with heavy emphasis on the gospel is illustrated in the writings of Paul Hanly Furfey which were examined in Chapter Three.

[25] *Pacem in Terris*, n. 5, 6; *A.A.S.*, LV (1963), 258-259.

magisterium on social questions as illustrated in the Pastoral Constitution on the Church in the Modern World, in Pope Paul's encyclical *Populorum progressio* and Paul's other writings such as his apostolic letter written on the occasion of the 80th anniversary of the encyclical *Rerum Novarum* of Leo XIII.

Catholic theology's traditional insistence on a natural law basis (understood now primarily in the theological aspect as a source of ethical wisdom and knowledge available to all men) for social ethics acknowledges that there is nothing specifically or explicitly Catholic or even Christian about this teaching. Catholic teaching mentioned both the gospel and reason, but as is evident in *Pacem in Terris* the natural law aspect served as the basis for the development of the teaching. Ethical wisdom in the realm of social ethics is available to all men. Obviously one of the problems with the Catholic approach in the past centered on the claim that the Catholic Church was the authoritative interpreter of the natural law.

The newer approach complained that the older approach based its teaching almost exclusively on the natural or what was common to all men and did not give enough importance to the influence of the supernatural, the gospel or the specifically Christian. The Pastoral Constitution on the Church in the Modern World proposes as its methodology an examination of the social, cultural and political realities in the light of the gospel and of human experience.[26]

More recent approaches explicitly affirm the specifically Christian element in dealing with social problems. As Catholic theology has explicitly affirmed the importance and the moral bearing of the gospel on social problems and not merely a natural law approach accessible to all men, there

---

26 *Pastoral Constitution on the Church in the Modern World*, n. 46; A.A.S., LVIII (1966) , 1066.

has been a practical development in the opposite direction. The experience of the last few years indicates the growing agreement in both theory and practice among Catholics, other Christians, Jews and other non-Christians, as well as nonbelievers, in the area of social justice. In practice Catholics and other Christians have realized that often they have more in common with nonbelievers than with fellow Christians on questions of the reform of society. In the light of this very frequent occurrence in the past few years the question naturally arises about what specifically the gospel contributes to political, social and cultural problems. Theologians have recently begun to study the question of determining if there is a specifically Christian social ethic and in what it consists if it does exist.

In this context some Catholic theologians developed the effect of Christian eschatology in terms of a negative critique of all existing human structures. The eschatological future functions as a negative critique on the sinfulness and imperfections of present social structures and impels the Christian to become involved in the process of changing society.[27]

In the past few years the debate has centered on what positive contribution Christian ethics brings to a consideration of social ethics which cannot be found elsewhere. Some theologians, such as Bernard Häring, say it would be incredible to think that the New Testament does not add any content to the natural law,[28] but there are a growing num-

---

[27] Johannes B. Metz, *Theology of the World* (New York: Herder and Herder, 1969), pp. 107-140; Edward Schillebeeckx, O.P., *God the Future of Man* (New York: Sheed and Ward, 1968), pp. 192 ff.

[28] Bernard Häring, *The Road to Relevance* (Staten Island: Alba House, 1970), p. 60. However, it is important to realize the way in which the question is framed. Since natural law excludes by definition the realm of faith, then one from my position might agree with Häring. But my contention is that what is available to the Christian is also available to the non-Christian, as will be explained later in the text.

ber of theologians arguing against any specifically Christian difference especially in the area of actions and plans for society. Josef Fuchs sees the specifically Christian affecting the area of transcendental behavior but not categorical virtues, values and norms that are operative in society.[29] Franz Böckle notes that elements of the Old Testament and New Testament morality are found in other religions so that Christianity is not bound to any specific and distinctive world order but only to Jesus Christ.[30] R. Simon suggests that the specificity of Christian ethics inheres in the being of the Christian and not in concrete norms and precepts.[31] Richard McCormick believes that human morality and Christian morality are materially identical.[32]

I have argued that "the explicitly Christian consciousness does affect the judgment of the Christian and the way in which he makes his ethical judgments, but non-Christians can and do arrive at the same ethical conclusions and also embrace and treasure even the loftiest of proximate motives, virtues and goals which Christians in the past have wrongly claimed only for themselves."[33] As might be expected Protestant theologians with a more Christocentric tradition tend to argue for more specific and unique Christian approaches.[34] There are a number of theological influences behind these newer theories including a greater knowledge coming from the study of comparative religions, a more in-

29 Josef Fuchs, S.J., "Gibt es eine spezifisch christliche Moral? *Stimmen der Zeit,* CLXXXV (1970), 99-112.

30 Franz Böckle, "Was ist das Proprium einer christlicher Ethik?" *Zeitschrift für evangelische Ethik,* XI (1967), 148-159.

31 R. Simon, "Spécificité de l'éthique chrétienne," *Le Supplément,* XXIII (1970), 74-104.

32 Richard A. McCormick, S.J., "Notes on Moral Theology," *Theological Studies,* XXXII (1971), 71-78.

33 See my *Catholic Moral Theology in Dialogue* (Notre Dame, Indiana: Fides, 1972), p. 20; also pp. 1-23; 55-64; 220-244.

34 E.g., James M. Gustafson, *Christ and the Moral Life* (New York: Harper and Row, 1968), pp. 238-240.

tense study of the Scriptures in comparison with other sacred books and non-sacred literature, and the theological recognition that God's gracious gift of himself to man (grace) is offered to all men and not just to Christians.

The conclusion derived from these newer approaches is not that Christians should have no concern for making a better world or that the Church should have no social mission. But Christians and the Church as such cannot claim any distinctive or exclusive ethical wisdom on the level of practical directives or even proximate virtues, goals and ideals for society. Thus all human beings have access to the wisdom and knowledge needed to cope with the social problems facing man today. The Christian or the Church cannot claim a unique competency in this area. Such a recognition in practice argues strongly against a triumphalism in social ethics which does not accept the fact that Christians and the Church cannot claim unique and distinctive proximate solutions to the moral problems facing society.

Second Limit: Nature of the Church and Its Relationship to Others

A second source of limitations comes from the inherent limitations involved in the reality of the Church as such. The social mission of the Church constitutes only one part of the whole function of the Church even though this is a constitutive aspect of the Church itself and must always be present if the Church is true to itself. The heart of the gospel message includes the preaching of the good news and the celebration of God's loving gift to man and not just the new life that the Christian should lead in the service of his fellow man.

Today there appears to be a danger of defining Christianity and especially the Church in terms of a specific moral stance or position or solely in terms of its mission to society. In my judgment this misinterprets the reality of the Church by collapsing the concept of Church into the social mission of the Church and not giving enough importance to the preaching and celebrating aspects. There are many groups interested in and working for the change of society, but the Church alone explicitly preaches and celebrates the Word and Work of Jesus. Often I may feel even closer bonds with nonbelievers with whom I am engaged in social action but this is not Church because it does not explicitly include the recognition of Jesus as Lord. Although a constitutive aspect of the Church, the social mission of the Church is not the only aspect of Church; and, in addition, the next paragraphs will develop the fact that in the area of social mission there are many other groups and individuals which have a competency and a role to play.

The Church as such forms only a small part of the total society. Most of the people who belong to the Church also claim membership in other societies and groups whose primary purpose concerns man and his life in society in this world. The Church must respect the autonomy and competencies of these other groupings within society. Triumphalism tends to inflate the role of the Church at the expense of those other autonomous groups in society. The Catholic proclivity to triumphalism wants to baptize and call Christian or even Church whatever is good that is happening in our society. More restraint and discipline would see that there are many good things happening in society which are not Church.

Many liberal Catholics appear horrified at the usurpation of Church power and dominance in the past, as for example in the Papal Bull *Unam Sanctam* issued by Boniface VIII in 1302.[35] However many of these same people today have

---

[35] Reference was made to *Unam Sanctam* in a somewhat similar context by Paul Ramsey, *Who Speaks for the Church?* (New York: Abingdon, 1967), p. 20.

just as triumphalistic a view of Church, inflate the role of the Church in society, and fail to respect the autonomy and integrity of other groups within society. These other groups in society interested in the reform of society can take on all sizes and shapes running the gamut from the state itself to political parties, to groups coalesced around a particular issue to all forms of voluntary societies—social, cultural, political, economic, educational. Every man, because of his humanity, shares in the vocation to work for a more just society for all mankind and to work with and cooperate with groups trying to bring this about.

The Church is only one grouping with an interest in the betterment of society. The Church obviously possesses its own unique resources in the light of all the other resources available, but the Church cannot act in practice as if there were no other individuals and groups with their own resources and competencies working for the betterment of human society.

The role of the Church and of its social mission in working for a more just social order is also limited by a proper internal understanding of the Church as such. Within the Church there are diverse functions, charismata and gifts. Very often the Church does not act in the social realm as Church but individual members of the Church work for the betterment of society as individual persons in their own jobs or in association with other people through groups and organizations. Not every involvement of members of the Church in striving for social justice, human development or the liberation of the oppressed should be the work of the whole Church as such.

Just as a triumphalistic spirit in Catholic thought not only wants the Church to play the dominant role in the reform of society and to take over the legitimate competencies of others in society, so too there is a tendency to absorb the proper function of individuals in the Church and of smaller voluntary societies within the Church itself. Perhaps an older Catholic understanding imposed too great a separation and distinction between the proper competence of the Church and the individual Catholic who was to apply Church teaching in his daily life in order to work for the betterment of society, but one cannot go to the opposite extreme and inflate the role of the Church as such to the extinction of the role of smaller groupings within the Church and the role of the individual Christian.

Third Limit: Changed Understandings

A third theological consideration also touches on the limitations of the Church in its social mission, but bears primarily on the changing self-understanding of the social mission of the Church. In many ways the structured social mission of the Church in the past is no longer adequate today. The social mission of the Catholic Church in the past, especially as measured by the work of Catholic Charities, rested heavily on an ecclesiology which understood the Church as a perfect society and had historical affinities to an older notion of Christendom, with distinct features brought about by the circumstances of an immigrant Church in the United States striving for survival and respectability. As a perfect society the Church has within itself everything necessary to achieve its purpose. The Church provides for its members much the same as the state provides for its members.

The Catholic Church in this country established Catholic schools to educate Catholic students; Catholic hospitals to provide for Catholics who were sick; Catholic orphanages to provide for its young who found themselves without a family; finally there were Catholic cemeteries in which Catholics were buried. Newer developments merely widened this already existing perspective to include new services; for example, counseling centers for married Catholics experiencing problems in their married life were made available; services were provided for Catholic couples to adopt Catholic babies.

In the United States one important breakthrough was made in this general pattern of approach. The papal social teaching proposed as the ideal the formation of Catholic labor unions in which Catholics would band together to work for their rights. Pope Leo XIII strongly favored Catholic unions founded on religion and looking primarily to God and man's relationship to God. Religious instruction would take place in these associations and men here would be taught to know and love the things of God and the Church.[36] Leo urged the formation of Catholic unions not so much on *a priori* grounds as on his reading of the signs of the times. He found much evidence to show that non-Catholic associations were controlled by secret leaders and based on principles opposed to the teachings of the Church. Obviously Leo here referred to the trends of socialism as he understood it. In the light of these circumstances Catholics should band together and form their own associations.[37]

In the United States Cardinal Gibbons gave strong support to the Knights of Labor, a nondenominational labor union, even though the Holy See had twice upheld the condemnation of the Knights of Labor by the Archbishop of Quebec.[38] This strong action by Cardinal Gibbons paved the way in the United States for Catholic participation in labor unions and the labor movement generally so that Catholic labor unions were always comparatively small in this country. This episode in many ways should be paradigmatic of

---

[36] Leo XIII, *Rerum Novarum*, n. 57. The reference is to the most available source for Leo's encyclicals in English: *The Church Speaks to the Modern World: The Social Teachings of Leo XIII*, ed. Etienne Gilson (New York: Doubleday Image Book, 1954) .

[37] *Ibid.*, n. 54.

[38] *American Catholic Thought on Social Questions*, ed. Aaron I. Abell (Indianapolis: Bobbs-Merrill, 1968) , 143-161.

the way in which the Church should respect the autonomy and competence of other groups existing within society.

The older understanding of the Church as a perfect society providing as best as possible for all its members remains no longer viable today—a fact admitted by all, at least in principle. From a practical viewpoint increasing costs indicate the lack of resources on the part of the Church to continue these programs across the board. The Catholic school crisis today stands as the obvious example of the crisis situation brought about by spiraling costs and limited, dwindling resources. Catholic hospitals continue to exist and function but only because of massive infusions of money from government and other sources. The problem of limited resources is now calling into question the older understanding of the social mission and function of the Church.

There are also important theological considerations arguing against the continuance of the older approach. The ghetto mentality restricted the social mission of the Church primarily to our own and especially to those in trouble. The concept of the Church as a perfect society somewhat paralleling the civil society and its functions in caring for its own is no longer acceptable today. The mission of the Church to the poor and the oppressed does not mean just Catholic poor and Catholic oppressed but all those who are truly poor and oppressed.

While praising and encouraging the move away from the older approach, one cannot forget the advantages connected with such an approach. There was a real acknowledgement of the limitations of what the Church can and should do. The Church was primarily interested in taking care of its own and did not bother, for the most part, with others who were non-Catholic. I would disagree with such an approach, but it does admit some principle of limitation even though the limited resources of the present are no longer sufficient to support such a system even if it were theoretically acceptable.

Another great advantage of the older approach concerned the unanimity of support given by Catholics to such programs. Nothing could be less controversial than trying to take care of Catholic orphans and Catholic widows. Catholic people readily agreed on the needs and rallied to make the necessary financial sacrifices. Such a social mission also enhanced and fostered the unity existing among Catholics. Today the situation has changed. Giving Catholic money to the Black Panthers or the Welfare Rights Organization will not find the same enthusiastic acceptance and support on the part of the Catholic community. Helping individuals in trouble, especially Catholics, is simple, straightforward and appealing; but efforts to change social structures involve complicated data, complex judgments and many possible areas of disagreement and dissension even within the Church. The unity of the Church will obviously be more threatened by such contemporary approaches. The solution does not lie in trying to turn back the clock to the more simplistic days of the past but in trying to reconcile the unity of the Church and possible disagreement on concrete ways of carrying out the social mission of the Church.

This second section has tried to establish the parameters for discussions about the structuring of the social mission of the Church. The social mission remains a constitutive aspect of the life of the Church, yet there are many limitations involved in the social mission of the Church. In addition the older approach is neither theoretically nor practically feasible. This understanding corresponds with the description of a general crisis situation in which the older forms and structures are no longer viable and it is most difficult amid a plethora of possibilities to determine what forms should be adopted.

III TOWARD A SOLUTION

The question of limitation in the social mission of the Church remains a very important and controlling concept in trying to structure the social mission and role of the Catholic Church. Obviously, a theologian alone can never draw up an adequate model of the social mission of the Church; but he can enter into dialogue with others about such a mission. The moral theologian, however, realizes that the problem created by the existence of the social mission of the Church and the need for its acceptance of limitations has similarities with a problem indigenous to his own field. The problem of Christian social ethics today, especially when seen in terms of how the Christian Church should address the problems of the contemporary world, again hinges on the existence of such an ethic and yet the recognition of limitations.[39]

The problem of actually structuring the social mission of the Church in the light of such limitations obviously involves more difficulties than the more theoretical question of determining how the Church should speak out on the social problems of the day. The fact that there is disagreement today on the theoretical level augurs for the fact that there will probably also be disagreement on the practical level of structuring the social mission of the Church. However, the important thing remains to face up to the existence of the acute question and try to respond to it. This section will consider first of all the theoretical question of how the Church should speak to the social problems of today in the light of its social teaching and its inherent limitations. Then the second section will offer, much more hesitantly and in the spirit of initiating a dialogue, some approaches to the vexing practi-

---

[39] For practical purposes, this essay will consider Christian social ethics in terms of the way in which the Church should address itself to social questions.

cal question of how the Church should structure its social mission.

The More Theoretical Question:
The Teaching of The Church

The problem of Christian social ethics or, more specifically, how the Church should speak to the social problems of our day, arises within the context of the demand on the part of many Christians that the Church should be relevant to the problems of modern society. Churchmen today recognize the prophetic aspect of the Church's mission. Churchmen and Church groups have been asked to make statements about particular problems confronting our society—the war in Southeast Asia, amnesty for those who have fled the country to avoid the draft, the rights of welfare recipients, ecology, nuclear deterrence, the population explosion, busing as a means of desegregating schools. These questions trouble many of the Church's members. Such questions have occasioned the need for serious theological reflections on the methodology and competency of Christian social ethics and the Church to speak to problems of society. Christian ethics and the Church obviously possess a competency in this area, but there are also important limitations.

Paul Ramsey has argued strenuously against the role which the churches have assumed in making specific pronouncements on major political issues such as the war in Southeast Asia, busing, admission of Red China to the United Nations and other disputed questions.[40] Ramsey claims that in these particular pronouncements the Church has overstepped its boundaries and its competencies. The Church must respect the "magistrates" (the duly elected

---

[40] Ramsey, *Who Speaks for the Church?* He refers to this question also in Paul Ramsey, *Christian Ethics and the Sit-In* (New York: Association Press, 1961) ; *The Just War: Force and Political Responsibility* (New York: Charles Scribner's Sons, 1968) .

officials and citizens of the state) and their competence. The Church cannot try to assume these roles which belong to others. Judgments of political prudence involving the good and evil consequences to come from particular courses of action belong to the competency of the magistrate and not to the Church. The Church neither does have nor should have a State Department. There is no specifically Christian perception of these fact judgments.[41]

What then is the competency of the Church and wherein lie the boundaries of its limited competency? The Church can and should speak only on the basis of specifically Christian warrants, and not on the basis of those things which do not belong to the specifically Christian. Ramsey generally understands the specifically Christian warrants in terms of in-principled love, so that the Church can become only as specific as in-principled love will go. This obviously means that perceptions and judgments of fact are excluded from the competency of the Church speaking. Ramsey argues strenuously against the penchant in the Church for making pronouncements on specific issues, but that does not mean that the Church can only speak in terms of generalities and platitudes. There is a middle ground in which on the basis of specifically Christian warrants the Church can give some directives for actions to guide the magistrate without illegitimately usurping the role of policy making. Such directives would not involve judgments of facts or judgments involving other competencies (e.g., the validity of the domino theory in international relations), for these lie outside the competency of the Church as such. In response to a critic Ramsey claims that the "no" the Confessional Church in Germany said to Hitler is the exception which proves the rule.[42]

---

41 *The Just War*, pp. 455-458.
42 *Who Speaks for the Church?*, pp. 47-57.

I agree with some of the criticisms made by Ramsey especially his underlining of some limitations on Church statements; but I disagree with his proposed solutions, for he seems to misunderstand the implications of the limitations of the Church in this area. Ramsey argues against a truncated Barthianism, which I would describe as a theological actualism, which operates on the acceptable premise that God is working in the world. But God works in individual actions, and the Christian as well as the Church try to discern the particular action of God. This approach shares many of the theological defects criticized in the first part of this paper. This theological methodology deals almost exclusively in the particular and the individual and implies that the Christian and the Church can affirm with certitude precisely what God is doing in the world to make and keep human life more human.[43]

Ramsey, in my judgment goes to the opposite extreme and asserts that not every decision is a moral decision and not every moral decision is a Christian decision.[44] There is not a Christian shape or style to every decision. "Concerning a great many choices it has to be said that only a deliberately or inflexibly imprudent decision would be wrong or an uncharitable exercise of prudence. The principle of prudence refers the matter in question to the magistrate or to the political process for decision and lies outside the competency of the Church."[45]

Human acts, in my judgment, should be described differently. Every truly human judgment is a moral judgment. Human judgments are distinguished from mere technical decisions such as how to fly an airplane, solve mathematical problems, or other purely technical skills. Some truly human

[43] *Ibid.*, pp. 73-80.
[44] *Ibid.*, pp. 53; 135 ff.
[45] *Ibid.*, p. 136.

judgments do involve much technical data and expertise, but they are still important human decisions. In so many areas of life today society recognizes the narrowness of the expert—military men should not run the defense department; school boards need members other than educators; hospital boards should not be composed only of doctors.

If one can speak of a crisis in contemporary society, it is the crisis of the human or the crisis of human meaning. In the midst of an overwhelming amount of data and complicated facts the individual must find meaning and make human decisions. Every human person needs to make important decisions, but often one is awed by all the elements that must go into the final decision and one's apparent inability to be able to come to a decision.[46] These truly human decisions can often call for great technical expertise and data, but they include more than just data collecting.

For the Christian human decisions are both moral and Christian. The truly human and hence moral judgment comes about after an appraisal of all the relevant data. Particular aspects of the question, be they purely economic, sociological, pedagogical or whatever, are relative in terms of the fully human perspective in the light of which the final decision is made. The truly human and moral decision is made in the light of such a universal human perspective and not just in terms of the narrower horizons of a particular science or art. The great difficulty today arises from the need for truly human decisions in the midst of complexity and so many particular perspectives. The Christian believes that all his truly human judgments and actions take on meaning and importance from the Christian perspective. There are no truly human actions which exist outside the pale of his Christianity, for the Christian mysteries remind him that the

---

46 Bernard Lonergan, S.J., *Collection*, ed. F. E. Crowe, S.J. (New York: Herder and Herder, 1967), pp. 252-267.

Christian embraces the human and gives it a fullness and perfection.

One cannot relegate truly human, moral and Christian judgments to the realms of a particular science or expertise. Likewise, one cannot exclude the realms of prudential judgments from the moral and the Christian. Naturally in some philosophies there is a different understanding of the prudential judgment, which deals with the particular and the individual. But prudential judgments involve more than just the perception of facts. Such judgments involve values and the relative priorities assigned to different values. Yes, such judgments do include much factual data, but they are truly human and Christian judgments because they all bring to bear one's understanding of values on the data and are more then mere technical decisions.

Ramsey firmly asserts the limitations of Christian ethics, but in my judgment he overrestricts the field of such Church teaching only to the specifically Christian warrants of in-principled love. Ramsey appears to have a disincarnate idea of love that does not really include all human reality but rather is derived deontologically from the biblical concept of love. Thus love and the Christian judgment are too restricted to those things which are specifically Christian and do not include any other elements belonging to other fields or disciplines. Here I would disagree with Ramsey, for Christian love or the specifically Christian aspect includes all the other aspects of the question. Catholic theology has traditionally seen Christian love as mediated in and through all aspects of creation and the human and not merely restricted to the specifically revealed or Christian.[47]

Despite my recognition of important limitations, I would still assert that every truly human decision is for the Chris-

---

[47] Gerard Gilleman, S.J., *The Primacy of Charity in Moral Theology* (Westminster, Md.: Newman Press, 1959), especially pp. 161-187.

tian both a moral and a Christian decision. There are many factors involved in such a decision or judgment—values, attitudes, goals, as well as a great amount of factual and technical data. One has a greater amount of certitude in talking about more general values, goals and dispositions, while in the matter of the more specific conclusions there will be less certitude. The more specific one becomes, the greater is the possibility of error and difference. Note that such an understanding obviously fits in well with a deductive theological approach; but it is in no way tied to such an approach, for even an inductive approach realizes there is greater agreement and certitude about the more general aspects and greater room for disagreement in the more specific aspects. The more specific judgments require great technical expertise as well as factual data, but such judgments are not exhausted just by the technical or factual component even though it might be quite large.

In the light of this understanding of the human and Christian act, what are the limitations on the way in which Christian social ethics and especially the Christian Church should speak to the world in the matter of contemporary social problems? First, the Church can and does speak with a greater degree of certitude on the level of more general values, goals, attitudes, dispositions and norms. Obviously the Church should frequently speak out in this area trying to inculcate the broad Christian perspectives within which Christians should try to form their judgments. For example, in the area of welfare reform, Church teaching should stress the fact that the goods of creation exist for all mankind and not just for a few.

Should Church statements ever descend to the particular in talking about problems such as the war in Southeast Asia, busing, welfare reform, abortion legislation? At times I believe that the Church should make specific statements on these issues but with certain limitations in mind. First, obviously the Church cannot make such statements unless it is familiar with the technical and the factual data necessary for making such a specific judgment. Knowledge of all the relevant aspects entering into the final judgment remains a most important aspect of any good human decision. Too often churchmen can be accused of "do goodism" because they betray an ignorance of the technical and factual data involved. Expertise is absolutely essential before such a judgment can be made. Obviously such knowledge calls for an extensive dialogue within the Church with those who have this technical and factual data.

When Church pronouncements or statements concern specific issues, then the Church must realize that its statements cannot claim to have absolute certitude. As one becomes more involved with particulars, there is a greater room for disagreement and dissent. Such an understanding remains implicit in the right to dissent which has recently surfaced in Catholic life and theology.[48] On specific moral teachings there exists a right to dissent when there are sufficient reasons for so doing precisely because the specific matter in question does not admit of certitude excluding all possibility of error. Chapter One has pointed out that in the future the right to dissent will become even more prominent in the Catholic Church and be more positively formulated in terms of a theological pluralism not only on questions of theological method but also in terms of practical judgments on specific moral issues.

If the Church is going to relate the gospel message to our modern world, which I believe it must, then it will be necessary to free the teaching Church from the albatross of certitude that still hangs around its neck. On specific issues, even within the Catholic Church, there will be the growing

---

[48] Charles E. Curran, Robert E. Hunt et al., *Dissent In and For the Church* (New York: Sheed and Ward, 1969).

realization of possible disagreement and dissent. The Church must propose its teaching in these areas by exposing the different values and attitudes that must prevail, but then can descend to particulars provided the factual and technical data are mastered and with the realization that in this matter one cannot claim certitude.

The Church cannot speak out on all the particular questions facing society. However, the process of discernment should try to point out the more important moral issues. The greatest effort of the Church must be in the area of the general attitudes, dispositions and goals which should characterize Christian life. Even in discussing particular problems the Church should point out the applicable considerations that come to bear on the specific decision. But at times on some more important issues the Church should speak out after having acquired the necessary knowledge and expertise and with the realization that Christians might have reasons for dissenting from such specific judgments.

Such an approach indicates a way in which the Church on a more theoretical level can speak to the problems of the contemporary world. It recognizes the fact that the Christian mission does embrace all human reality, but at the same time it acknowledges the inherent limitations the Church experiences in speaking about the life of man in society.

The More Practical Question: The Social Mission of The Church

There is a connection but also an important jump between how the Church as such teaches in the matter of social justice and how the Church should structure its own social mission. The problem of limitation is still present and even more acute. Dissent in the area of teaching has been difficult enough to accept in the life of the Catholic Church, but dissent and disagreement in the area of action will occasion more bothersome problems. Another source of limitation peculiar to the social mission of the Church stems from the fact that the social mission of the Church itself, as distinguished from the social mission of individual Christian and of smaller voluntary groups within the Church, is less extensive than the social teaching of the Church. Thus there is even more need to appreciate the problems brought about by limitation.

A theologian has the obligation of pointing out the problem and helping to initiate the dialogue among all the members of the Church especially those most concerned with its social mission. The important first step is to recognize the problem, which is brought about by the fact that the Church does have a social mission and function, but there are limitations of a theoretical nature which have been discussed as well as of a practical nature (resources) which have been alluded to but not developed at length. Dialogue remains an important first step, but dialogue alone is not enough. From the dialogue must emerge some practical agreement on how the social mission of the Church should be structured. The following discussion remains necessarily inchoate and suggestive of some criteria which can be employed to evaluate how the social mission of the Church should be structured. Obviously the ensuing discussion must involve all in the Church.

First, whatever the Church does should be primarily in terms of the service of others in need and not for its own well being. Too often the Church succumbs to the overt or covert temptation of self-aggrandizement and self-preservation. The criterion of service to others must show forth if the mission of the Church is to be true to the gospel message.

Secondly, a primary task of the Church is educational and motivational, which follows from the nature of the Church and its constituency. Obviously such a function does not necessarily call for a Catholic school system, but it does demand a serious commitment in educating and motivating church people to participate in improving the social condition of men in this world. The contemporary Church in season and out of season must remind its adherents of the gospel message with its concern for the poor, the oppressed, the hungry, the prisoners, the outcasts.

Thirdly, if other groups or even the government are already involved in a particular field, the Church should not unnecessarily duplicate what these others are doing. Such a criterion can be modified somewhat in the light of possible values of alternate approaches even within the same area.

Fourthly, one possible advantage the Church can have both in terms of its prophetic mission and in terms of the fact that it is often less encumbered than other bureaucratic structures concerns the ability to spot new needs and respond to them. In the light of the gospel and under the promptings of the Spirit the Church should try to develop a sensitivity to such needs. It does not follow that the Church as prophet always forms the cutting edge of society in these matters, which would be a thinly veiled triumphalism; but the Church in theory should try to be sensitive in this area.

Fifthly, the Church must constantly reexamine its social mission in the light of changing circumstances, which follows from some of the criteria already mentioned. Since with limited resources only limited things can be done, perhaps the apostolates of the past should no longer have top priority today. In this category one can think of the heavy Catholic involvement in hospitals. Such a priority should be rigorously discussed, for this no longer seems to be a true service to the poor and the oppressed. Likewise such services are regularly provided by others in the society. One also has the impression that hospitals in many ways serve to enhance and even enrich the sponsoring institutions at least to a greater degree than other forms of service. Perhaps hospitals might help to finance other approaches such as community health programs in poor neighborhoods.

Sixthly, the limited competency of the Church in specific knowledge as well as limited resources argues for a greater emphasis on the role of enabler—an approach which also corresponds with the need for the people concerned to do their own organizing and acting. The Church often does possess resources in terms of buildings as well as personnel, some with important skills who can aid the poor and the powerless in their work of organizing. In this way the Church will avoid the danger of paternalism associated with triumphalism which implies that the Church and churchmen must have positions of leadership in these various movements.

Seventhly, the role of articulator and advocate of the needs of the poor, the oppressed and the powerless. Here too one must admit the built-in limitations on the role of the Church and the danger of usurping the role of others. At least the Church should enable others to articulate their own feelings. In addition the Church in its role as educator must prepare its own people to hear the legitimate cries of the oppressed and powerless. Here resides a function well within the role and the obligation of the Church as such. One of the deficiencies of Catholic education in the past lies in this particular area. Catholic people must become sensitized to the needs of the poor and of those who have not made it in our society. The danger of respectability and of acceptability too often makes members of the Church side with the existing mores of society against those who appear to be not in tune with that society. The Church can also assist in advocating the cause of the poor in the society as a whole and in the political processes.

Eighthly, there seems to be agreement that today the need is not only to provide services for individuals who in a sense are victims of the system, but one must work for a change of the structures of society. In supporting particular groups or in calling for specific changes in legislation or in working for the reform of social structures, one runs the dangers brought about by specificity in the midst of complexity. There might be other approaches and one might object to the particular approach taken, but at times it might be necessary to become involved with particular groups, programs and proposed legislation.

There are two problems that arise in these areas. The first recalls the critical function of the Church, which always requires the independent function of judging. In the past the Church has too often lost its critical sense and made alliance with the controlling powers so that it lost its independence and ability to criticize. So now the Church must be careful about becoming totally identified with particular movements or groups, for in every such movement or group, human limitations and sinfulness will always betray their presence.

Although this objection does contain some truth, there are important nuances and differences which must be pointed out. The all-pervasiveness of human limitations and of sinfulness will be felt in any human group, but Christian priorities must always include a bias or prejudice in favor of the poor, the oppressed and the powerless. If the Church reflects the gospel message of Jesus, then this bias and prejudice must become more evident. There remains the danger of total over-identification with any group or cause, but the Church will have to run the risk in this case because of its bias in favor of the poor.

Another problem concerns the ethical question of means which has always been of great import in Catholic ethics. Very often one can agree on the goals of a particular group but disagree with the means that they choose to employ in pursuit of that goal. If the Church becomes identified with particular groups or specific movements, it might find itself in disagreement over some of the means employed. Here again a risk must be taken, but with open eyes to the possible problems involved. Especially in a situation where one must respect the rights of the individuals themselves to determine their own course of action, the problem is even heightened. However if the Church or churchmen have truly shown themselves sympathetic to the needs of the poor and oppressed, then their voices will command greater respect when they might object to certain means.

In this area of supporting particular groups or specific changes in the structure of society all the limitations mentioned in the theoretical question of how the Church should speak to the problems of the modern world come to the fore. Obviously the Church cannot be involved in all these movements or specific proposals for a change of structure. But at times this might be deemed a necessary approach in trying to fulfill the social mission of the Church. Obviously such approaches should constitute only a part of the total social mission of the Church.

Thus far the discussion has centered on somewhat formal criteria, but a specific example might clarify the approach that should be taken. We live among staggering problems of social import—rights of minorities, prison reform, educational reform, rights of the poor, oppression of people at home and abroad, the developing nations of the third world, war and violence. In many ways individual members of the Church can be involved in these different questions, but the whole Church as institution cannot and really should not be particularly involved in all these areas.

I would suggest that every year the Church in this country concentrate its efforts on a particular area which seems to be of importance and in which the Church can offer assistance, with the realization that perhaps other even more pressing problems will arise in the course of changing circumstances and have to be addressed by the Church. The Church could, for example, next year concentrate its social mission (not exclusively) on the question of the treatment of the poor in our society. Especially Catholic Charities could make this its own project. Resources and efforts could be concentrated on this question so that it has primacy in allocating the resources of the Church in terms of education, advocacy and legislation reform. This would be one practical way of acknowledging the reality of limitations but still trying to live out the social mission of the Church.

There is an obvious need to rethink and restructure the social mission of the Church at the present time. The older approaches no longer seem viable both for theoretical and practical reasons. However, in addressing this question one must take into consideration not only the fact that the social mission is a constitutive part of the life of the Church but also the realization of the limitations present in the social mission of the Church. This is the challenge for those involved in restructuring the social mission of the Church. Above all, the Church must continue to reexamine its own life and preaching in the light of the gospel which calls for that basic change of heart involving dying to self and rising in the newness of life which is manifested in care and concern for the poor, the needy, the outcast and the prisoner.

5

Abortion: Its Legal and Moral Aspects in Catholic Theology

Within the past few years the question of abortion has been raised with greater frequency in Roman Catholic journals and discussions. These considerations reflect the growing debate within society itself about abortion and abortion laws. Most Americans are familiar with the abortion debate in this country culminating with the decision of the Supreme Court. However, these discussions have been world-wide, and recently there has been a growing body of Catholic writing on abortion especially in France, Belgium, Italy and Germany.[1]

This chapter will not attempt a detailed exposition of all that has been written on this subject, but rather will try to present the state of the question in Roman Catholic the-

---

[1] E.g., *Avortement et respect de la vie humaine*, Colloque du Centre Catholique des Médecins Français (Paris: Éditions du Seuil, 1972) ; *Abtreibung—Pro und Contra*, ed. J. Gründel (Würzburg: Echter, 1971) ; D. Mongillo, F. D'Agostine, F. Compagnoni, "L'Aborto," *Rivista di Teologia Morale*, IV (1972) , 355-392.

ology, indicating the ways in which Catholics can and should approach both the legal and the moral aspects of abortion. Thus the essay is limited to Roman Catholic theology with the realization that such theology must be in dialogue with all the discussions on the question.

LEGAL ASPECTS

The relationship between law and morality has often been a matter of debate both within Roman Catholicism and within the broader human community. In the broader perspective the issuance of the Wolfenden Report in England calling for the removal of laws penalizing homosexual acts between consenting adults in private sparked an interesting controversy about the relationship between law and morality.[2] In the Roman Catholic context the question arose in the United States in the 1960's in the debate about artificial contraception.[3] Also the discussions about religious liberty touched on this question. Today the question has come to the fore both in the United States and in Europe in the light of lively debates about abortion laws.

In the contemporary Catholic literature I find two opposed solutions to the theoretical question of the relationship between law and morality with which I cannot agree. The one solution is closely associated with an older Roman Catholic approach about the function of law in society. In such a perspective all of reality is governed by the eternal law which is the plan for the world existing in the mind of God. The eternal law is the source of all other laws. As the basic foundation of all moral authority the eternal law gives binding force to every other law, which in some way is a partici-

---

2 Sir Patrick Devlin, *The Enforcement of Morals* (Oxford: Oxford University Press, 1959) ; H. L. A. Hart, *Law, Liberty and Morality* (New York: Vintage Books, 1963) .

3 Norman St. John Stevas, *Life, Death and the Law* (Bloomington, Indiana: Indiana University Press, 1961) .

pation in the eternal law. The natural law is the participation of the eternal law in the rational creature. The divine or eternal law, as it appears in the revealed law of God or in the natural law, does not cover all the particular questions and individual circumstances existing in different cultures and places. It is the function of the state to apply the natural laws which are basic and unchanging to concrete sociological and historical conditions.[4]

The primary function of civil law is to apply the natural law to these particular circumstances, for human law is really only an extension of natural law in the changing circumstances of different cultural and historical situations. However, such an approach realizes that at times it might not be possible to apply the natural law, and the lawgiver might even have to tolerate those things which are opposed to natural law. Sometimes it is more harmful to society to insist that the natural law be followed perfectly. In the past there were debates about the legalization of prostitution. In such cases the wrong action is accepted or tolerated as a lesser of two evils.

In summarizing the present debate about abortion laws among Catholics in Italy, Dionigi Tettamanzi claims that the arguments pro or con in proposing a middle position allowing abortion in some indicated conditions but not abortion on demand are based on the juridical principle of the possible toleration of the lesser evil just as in the case of the acceptance of prostitution. Within such a framework, G. Davanzo argues in favor of a relaxed law which will allow abortion in some circumstances, but other authors deny that such a practice can be tolerated as a lesser evil.[5]

---

[4] Franz Böckle, *Fundamental Concepts of Moral Theology* (New York: Paulist Press, 1968). It should be pointed out that this opinion was expressed by Böckle a few years ago, and it was then the more common teaching among Catholic theologians.

[5] Dionigi Tettamanzi, "L'attuale problematica morale-giuridica sull'aborto," *La Scuola Cattolica*, C (1972), 185-187.

Such a theoretical understanding of the statement of the question, which could admit of either a positive or a negative response, coheres with a previously accepted Catholic understanding of the function of law, but it is not in agreement with the tradition of common law and the reality of pluralistic democratic societies. Recall the similarities with the older Catholic approach to religious liberty, which would in some circumstances tolerate the fact that the state did not recognize the true Church of Jesus Christ. Objective truth is the primary norm, and error has no rights according to such an approach. However, in some circumstances the separation of Church and state can be tolerated.[6]

An opposite approach sees the function of law almost totally in very pragmatic terms as merely reflecting the mores of a particular society at any given time. Robert Boyer, S.J., in arguing for an abortion law that permits abortion in certain indicated circumstances emphasizes that the law does not represent any juridical ideal. Law comes into existence through the struggles of different people with different ideas living in society.[7] One must recall that there is a compromise aspect about law. The function of law is not to determine what actions of men are good and which are bad but, in considering what is lived and accepted in the community, to bring about a social equilibrium which permits each one to live according to his convictions and ethic while safeguarding as well as possible the general interest. Although Boyer does occasionally admit a teaching function of law,[8] he emphasizes the pragmatic aspect of law in society, which follows the accepted convictions and life styles of the community.

---

6 John Courtney Murray, *The Problem of Religious Freedom* (Westminster, Md.: Newman Press, 1965), pp. 7-17; Pius Augustin, *Religious Freedom in Church and State* (Baltimore: Helicon, 1966).

7 Robert Boyer, S.J., "Légalité et moralité face à l'avortement," *Lumière et Vie*, XXI, n. 109 (Aout-Octobre 1972), 48-49.

8 *Ibid.*, pp. 53-54.

My objection to such an approach is its one-sided over-emphasis on the pragmatic in reaction to the idealism of the first approach. There will always be a pragmatic aspect to law in a pluralistic society, but at times law must also have a prophetic and teaching role so that society itself is changed. One only has to recall the efforts in the United States on behalf of racial equality to show that law does have a moral or ideal aspect as well as a pragmatic aspect. This ideal aspect is even more apparent in questions of social matters such as minimum wage laws or guaranteed annual wage.

My approach to the question is analogous to the position developed in the Declaration on Religious Freedom of the Second Vatican Council. Religious freedom implies that the individual is free from external coercion to act in a manner contrary to his beliefs and is not restrained from acting in accord with his beliefs (n. 2). However, the document recognizes that there are limitations on the exercise of the right of religious liberty, since it is exercised in human society.

In the use of all freedom the moral principle of personal and social responsibility is to be observed. But the Declaration on Religious Freedom goes on to indicate the need for some juridical limitations because society has the need to protect itself against possible abuses. Society must safeguard a genuine public peace, a public morality and the rights of all citizens.

A footnote by John Courtney Murray in a popular American edition of The *Documents of Vatican II* explains that the Declaration on Religious Freedom employs the concept of public order as the juridical norm controlling the action of government in limiting or inhibiting the exercise of the right to religious freedom. Public order includes a threefold content. It is an order of justice by which the rights of all citizens are effectively safeguarded and provision is made for the peaceful settlement of conflicts of rights. Secondly, it is an order of peace; but public peace, especially in the light of a Catholic theological understanding of the state, is classically the work of justice and not the result of oppression by the police. Thirdly, public order involves an order of morality, but this does not necessarily imply that society must live a shared morality on all points.[9] In my judgment it refers to that fundamental public morality which is necessary for men to live together in society with the realization that there may be great differences of opinion and of action existing within society on specific moral questions.

In applying such a standard to questions of morality in a pluralistic society one must begin with an acknowledgement of the rights of the individual to act in accord with the dictates of his own conscience. The limiting principle justifying the intervention of government is based on the need to protect other innocent persons and the public order. I make the protection of other innocent persons a separate category so as to highlight its importance. Thus there is established a juridical principle which can be followed in determining the relationship between law and morality.

However, there are other factors coming from the meaning of law itself which must also be considered. The general principle holds that law must be good law. Under this heading it is necessary that a particular law must be enforceable. Likewise, law must be equitable. If a law against abortion, for example, discriminates against a particular class in society then it is not good law. In addition an individual law must contribute to the overall good of society and the function of law in preserving and promoting that good. If a law is frequently being disobeyed and not observed, one can wonder if it contributes to the overall purpose of law in society. The aspects mentioned in this paragraph under the general functions of law point out that there are some im-

---

9 *The Documents of Vatican II*, ed. Walter M. Abbott, S.J. (New York: Guild Press, 1966) , p. 686.

portant pragmatic aspects to the question of the relationship between law and morality.

A second important consideration is the nature of law in a pluralistic society. Paul Ramsey has described democracy as a form of just war in which opposite opinions are reconciled through the ballot box which then prevents violence and bloodshed.[10] Within a pluralistic society one must recognize the rights of others and the resulting differences in thoughts and actions. In the light of this, one might very well conclude that in striving for a particular law even in the question of abortion, such an attempt might be both futile and divisive. Likewise, lawmakers or legislators are conscious of the compromises that must be made in the enactment of laws. Thus, for example, in the matter of abortion, a legislator who would prefer a very strict law against abortion might support a more moderate abortion law to prevent the acceptance of abortion on demand. Citizens must keep this aspect in mind in their own discussions and actions in favor of particular pieces of legislation.

In the light of this understanding of the relationship between law and morality a Roman Catholic could for various reasons arrive at any one of the three generic types of abortion laws: almost absolute condemnation, regulated abortion allowed on the basis of certain indications, no law whatsoever or the possibility of the decision being made in accord with the conscience of the mother. The proper understanding of the relationship between law and morality indicates there is great room for different prudential decisions to be made in this area. Thus there can be no such thing as *the* Catholic opinion on the question of abortion laws. Even among those who believe that we must act as if human life is present from the very beginning, there is the possibility of

---

10 Paul Ramsey, *Christian Ethics and the Sit-In* (New York: Association Press, 1961) , p. 104.

divergent opinions about what the law should be in our society.

As a matter of fact Roman Catholics have opted for all three different approaches to abortion laws. Roman Catholics have been generally associated with the position in favor of strict abortion laws which usually allow an exception only in a conflict with the life of the mother. Robert Drinan, S.J., however, has developed a case proposing that there be no criminal sanctions on abortion.[11]

My own opinion based on a consideration of the factors mentioned above argues in theory for a modified abortion law that restricts abortion to certain indicated reasons such as those mentioned in the Model Penal Code ratified by the American Law Institute in 1961. Such an approach is consonant with any willingness from the viewpoint of morality to allow a greater number of conflict situations in which abortion is acceptable even though I would not accept the A.L.I. criteria as moral criteria. Likewise, the more pragmatic aspect of law and legislation in a pluralistic society makes such an approach seem more feasible. I willingly acknowledge some drawbacks with such an approach, but they seem to be outweighed by the advantages. The criterion of grave psychological harm to the mother could be stretched to include just about anything. From a more theoretical viewpoint such a law would set the precedent that fetal life could be taken for a sufficient reason. However, there is no practical feasibility that such a moderate law could now come into being in the United States after the Supreme Court decision.

---

11 Robert F. Drinan, S.J., "Catholic Moral Teaching and Abortion Laws in America," *Proceedings of the Catholic Theological Society of America*, XXIII (1968), 118-130; Drinan, "Abortion and the Law" in *Who Shall Live?*, ed. Kenneth Vaux (Philadelphia: Fortress Press, 1970), pp. 51-68; Drinan, "The Jurisprudential Options on Abortion," *Theological Studies*, XXXI (1970), 149-169.

Such an understanding of the relationship between law and morality and its interpretation in the question of abortion help clarify other aspects of the discussion. Very often one hears the charge that Roman Catholics should not impose their morality on others. In passing it should be pointed out that opposition to abortion is not only a Catholic position but is shared by others in our society. There is an aspect in which that axiom about not imposing one's morality on others is true, but from another perspective it definitely calls for nuancing. If such an axiom were accepted in too simplistic a way, it would totally separate morality from the political life of society. It was precisely the moral conviction of many people that moved them to oppose the action of their country in Vietnam. Moral reasons have been proposed as the reason for changing laws against discrimination and for changing our current welfare laws. Thus there cannot be a strict dichotomy between law and morality.

In the older Catholic approach, however, as mentioned above, there was a tendency of too easily identifying law and morality. In the particular question of abortion laws if someone thinks that human life is present in the fetus, one can work for a law that condemns or radically restricts abortion. One's moral position on abortion will have some effect on his position on abortion law. Within our pluralistic society such people have a right to work for their convictions and safeguard the fetus. Likewise someone with the same moral convictions might find other reasons for not backing such a law. Law and morality are different but not totally dichotomous.

MORAL ASPECTS

A position paper on the morality of abortion from the Roman Catholic perspective must of necessity be somewhat selective. The following pages will center on three specific facets—the correct statement of the official teaching of the hierarchical magisterium, the possibility of dissent and the present state of debate within Roman Catholicism.

Proper Statement of the Teaching

The most succinct and correct statement of the official teaching of the hierarchical magisterium is: direct abortion is always wrong. Pope Paul's encyclical *Humanae Vitae* condemns "directly willed and procured abortion, even if for therapeutic reasons."[12]

A very accurate summary of the reasoning and statement of the Catholic position was given by Pope Pius XII in a 1951 address to an Italian family group.

> Innocent human life, in whatsoever condition it is found, is withdrawn, from the very first moment of its existence, from any direct deliberate attack. This is a fundamental right of the human person, which is of general value in the Christian conception of life; hence as valid for the life still hidden within the womb of the mother, as for the life already born and developing outside of her; as much opposed to direct abortion as to the direct killing of the child before, during or after its birth. Whatever foundation there may be for the distinction between these various phases of the development of life that is born or still unborn, in profane and ecclesiastical law, and as regards certain civil and penal consequences, all these cases involve a grave and unlawful attack upon the inviolability of human life.[13]

The ultimate basis of the teaching on abortion comes from the sanctity or dignity of human life. However, the precise teaching on abortion requires two more specific judgments

---

12 *A.A.S.*, LX (1968) , 490.
13 *A.A.S.*, XLIII (1951) , 857.

before it can be accurately articulated and formulated. The first judgment concerns the question of when human life begins. The second judgment involves the solution of conflict situations.

On this question of the beginning of human life there has been and still is a difference of opinion among Catholic theologians. Catholic Canon Law in its history often acknowledged a theory of delayed animation and did not propose the same penalties for abortion before animation and abortion after animation although both abortions were considered wrong. St. Thomas Aquinas and a majority of the medieval theologians held such a view of delayed animation.[14] Even in the twentieth century there were still many Catholic theologians maintaining the theory of delayed animation.[15] Pope Pius XII implicitly acknowledges this difference in the long citation given above. Although Catholic teaching allows diversity on the theoretical question of when human life begins, in practice the question was solved by saying that one must act as if life is present from the beginning. If there is doubt whether or not life is present, the benefit of the doubt must be given to the fact that there is human life present.[16]

Such an understanding should guide Catholic statements on abortion especially when voices become raised and shrill with the attendant problems of oversimplification and sloganeering. Abortion from the viewpoint of Catholic teaching thus should not be called murder or infanticide because even Church teaching acknowledges that human life might not be present there. One must strive to be as accurate as possible in these matters.

[14] John T. Noonan, Jr., "Abortion and the Catholic Church: A Summary History," *Natural Law Forum*, XII (1967), 85-131.

[15] H. M. Hering, O.P., "De tempore animationis foetus humani," *Angelicum*, XXVIII (1951), p. 19.

[16] John Canon McCarthy, *Problems in Theology*, Vol. I: *The Sacraments* (Westminster, Md.: Newman Press, 1956), pp. 15-21.

Likewise, one distorts the true Catholic teaching by claiming that Catholic teaching forbids all abortion. In reality Catholic teaching does acknowledge the existence of some conflict situations which are solved by the application of the principle of the double effect. Direct abortion is always wrong, but indirect abortion can be permitted when there is a proportionate reason. The two most famous examples of indirect abortion are the cancerous uterus and the ectopic pregnancy. Pope Pius XII emphasized that he purposely used the term direct abortion or direct killing because indirect abortion could be permitted.[17] He defined direct killing as a deliberate disposition concerning innocent human life which aims at its destruction either as an end in itself or as the means of attaining another end that is perhaps in no way illicit in itself.[18]

Unfortunately statements in the past about the Catholic position have not always been as accurate and precise as they should have been.

Possibility of Dissent

Recently Roman Catholic theology has publicly recognized that a good Roman Catholic can dissent from the authoritative or authentic, noninfallible papal teaching on artificial contraception. The question also arises: is dissent possible on the question of the condemnation of direct abortion? Chapter One has already indicated the existence of a more broad and general right to dissent in specific moral questions.

The teaching on direct abortion does belong to the category of authentic or authoritative, noninfallible hierarchical teaching. This teaching has been proposed in various responses of different Roman congregations and especially in

---

17 *A.A.S.*, XLIII (1951) , 859.
18 *Ibid.*, 838.

the encyclical *Casti Connubii* of Pope Pius XI. Pius XII frequently reiterated and explained in his allocutions the condemnation of direct abortion. The Pastoral Constitution on the Church in the Modern World of the Second Vatican Council spoke of abortion as an infamy and an unspeakable crime, but unfortunately did not make explicit the necessary distinction between direct and indirect abortion.[19] However, this question was really not a central consideration in this document. Obviously the comments made in this document are to be interpreted in the light of the general Catholic teaching on the subject. *Humanae Vitae,* the encyclical of Pope Paul VI, carefully restated the condemnation of direct abortion even if done for therapeutic reasons.[20]

The historical tradition indicates there was a solid historical basis for the teaching that has been expressed with greater precision from the time of St. Alphonsus as the condemnation of directly willed and procured abortion.[21] Perhaps the greatest deviation in the historical tradition concerns the expulsion of an inanimate fetus to save the life of the mother and even the reputation of the mother. John of Naples, a somewhat obscure fourteenth century theologian whose work is known to us only through citations from oth-

---

[19] Richard A. McCormick, S.J., "Past Church Teaching on Abortion," *Proceedings of the Catholic Theological Society of America*, XXIII (1968), 133-37.

[20] *A.A.S.,* LX (1968), 490.

[21] Noonan, *op. cit.* Note that in my judgment Noonan misinterprets the position of Thomas Sanchez and of Arthur Vermeersch. Germain G. Grisez, *Abortion: The Myths, The Realities and the Arguments* (New York and Cleveland: Corpus Books, 1970), pp. 117-184. Grisez also misinterprets Sanchez, for he holds like Noonan that Sanchez would allow the abortion of an inanimate fetus to save the life of the mother which might be threatened if it were known that she had conceived through sinful intercourse. On p. 168 Grisez maintains about Sanchez that apparently he alone in the Catholic tradition holds such an opinion. Although Sanchez did not hold such a position, in the next paragraph in the text I mention some Catholic theologians who did hold such a position.

ers, apparently allows the abortion of an inanimate fetus to save the life of the mother. The animated fetus cannot be aborted.[22] This opinion was also maintained by Antoninus of Florence. However Antoninus expressly denied the liceity of abortion to save the life of the mother if the fetus is already animated. He also expressly condemned the abortion of an inanimate fetus if the purpose was merely to hide the sin of the mother.[23] Later Sylvester da Prieras presented his opinion in the same manner.[24] The same opinion was maintained by the influential Martin Azpilcueta, better known as Doctor Navarrus.[25]

A theologian named Torreblanca exerted a great influence on some seventeenth century theologians. Torreblanca taught that before animation a woman may procure an abortion if because of the birth she is in danger of death or even of losing her reputation. In this case the fetus is not yet animated and her action is not homicide. Torreblanca cites seven authors in favor of his opinion, but he mistakenly cites Antoninus, Sylvester, Navarrus and Sanchez as favoring his position which they did not do in the case of abortion to protect the reputation of the woman.[26]

Leo Zambellus explicitly following Torreblanca held that if it is licit to procure an abortion before animation to save the life of the mother it is also licit in order to save her reputation.[27] John the Baptist de Lezana allowed abortion before

---

22 John of Naples is cited by both Antoninus of Florence and Sylvester da Prieras in the places referred to in the next two footnotes.

23 S. Antoninus, *Summa Theologica* (Verona, 1760), Pars III, Tit. VII, Cap. III.

24 Sylvester Prierate, *Summa Sylvestrina* (Antwerp, 1569), Medicus n. 4.

25 Martinus Azpilcueta, *Enchiridion sive Manuale Confessariorum et Poenitentium* (Venice, 1593), c. XXV, n. 60-64.

26 Franciscus Torreblanca, *Epitome Delictorum sive De Magia* (Lyons, 1678), Lib. II, Cap. XLIII, n. 10.

27 Leo Zambellus, *Repertorium Morale Resolutorium Casuum Conscientiae* (Venice, 1640), Medicus, n. 11.

animation in the case of a noble woman or a nun who sinned
with a man and feared death or loss of reputation or scandal
if her sin were known, but he accepted the expulsion in these
cases only if it is the last available means.[28] John Trullenchus cited Torreblanca and Pontius (wrongly in this case) as
permitting the abortion of an inanimate fetus as the last
remedy in perserving a pregnant girl's life or reputation.
Trullenchus himself denied such an opinion, but he admitted
that the affirmative opinion is not improbable.[29] Gabriel of
St. Vincent also argued against the possibility of abortion of
the inanimate fetus, but he did admit some extrinsic probability as did Trullenchus.[30] The majority of theologians
did not accept such an opinion.[31] On March 2, 1679, among
sixty-five errors condemned by the Holy Office was the following :"It is licit to procure an abortion before the fetus is
animated lest the girl be killed or lose her reputation if the
pregnancy is detected."[32]

This historical section is included because other writers do
not mention Torreblanca and those depending on him. The
recognition of this fact indicates that even in the historical
development there was some vacillation among Roman Catholic theologians, but the opinion permitting abortion of the
inanimate fetus to save the reputation of the mother did not
really arise again after the condemnation of 1679. In the
question of therapeutic abortion even of an animated fetus

---

[28] Joannes Baptista de Lezana, *Summa Questionum Regularium seu de
Casibus Conscientiae* (Venice, 1646) , Tom. III, Abortus, n. 5.

[29] Joannes Aegidius Trullenchus, *Opus Morale* (Barcelona, 1701) , Tom.
II, Lib. V, Cap. I, Dub. 4.

[30] Gabriellus a S. Vincentio, *De Sacramentis,* Pars IV, De Matrimonio,
Disp. VII, Qu. V, n. 42.

[31] The following theologians cite the opinion proposed by Torreblanca,
but they do not follow it: Zanardus, Amicus, Franciscus Bonae Spei, Azor,
Diana, Sporer.

[32] *Enchiridion Symbolorum Definitionum et Declarationum de Rebus Fidei
et Morum,* ed. H. Denzinger, A. Schönmetzer, *et al.* (32nd ed.; Barcelona:
Herder, 1963) , n. 2134.

to save the life of the mother, John R. Connery claims there was no official condemnation by the Church until the nineteenth century.[33]

In comparing the teaching on abortion with the Church's teaching on contraception it should be noted that John T. Noonan, Jr., who has extensively studied the historical tradition on both questions, argues strenuously in favor of the Catholic teaching on abortion while he disagrees with the traditional condemnation of contraception.[34] There do exist some few vacillations in the historical development, but one could still find there the general basis for the present teaching of the Catholic Church. The crucial problem remains the fact that life itself changes and develops so that one cannot give absolute value to a tradition which merely repeats the past and does not enter into dialogue with present experience and with the discontinuities which can exist in the present even though one could also conclude that there are no such discontinuities.[35]

Thus from the fact that the condemnation of direct abortion belongs to the authoritative and authentic, noninfallible papal teaching and from the fact there is a long historical tradition which despite some vacillations serves as a basis for such a teaching, one cannot legitimately conclude that there cannot be dissent from, or possible change in, the Catholic Church's teaching on direct abortion. In fact I argue there can be both dissent from and change in the accepted Catholic teaching denying direct abortion.

---

33 John R. Connery, S.J., "Grisez on Abortion," *Theological Studies,* XXXI (1970) , 173.

34 John T. Noonan, Jr., *Contraception: A History of Its Treatment by the Catholic Theologians and Canonists* (Cambridge: Harvard University Press, 1965) .

35 The understanding of the value of the historical tradition as expressed in this sentence is similar to the opinion expressed in a roundtable discussion by René Simon, *Avortement et respect de la vie humaine,* p. 233.

The possibility of dissent from authoritative, noninfallible Church teaching has been demonstrated in Chapter One
on the basis of the Church's own self-understanding of the
assent due to such teaching.[36] The earlier chapter pointed
out that the possibility of dissent rests on the fact that in
specific moral judgments on complex matters one cannot
hope to attain a degree of certitude that excludes the possibility of error. In more complex matters one must consider
many different facets of the question and circumstances so
that one cannot expect to exclude all fear of error.

The present teaching of the Church on abortion depends
on two very important judgments—the judgment about
when human life begins and the judgment about the solution
of conflict situations involving the fetus and other values
such as the life of the mother. Even our brief historical summary indicates that in the past there has been some dispute
on both these issues. The following section will furnish additional proof of the possibility of dissent based on the fact
that some Roman Catholic theologians are now dissenting
from and disagreeing with the accepted teaching of the
Church on the condemnation of direct abortion. One can
rightly suppose that the dissent will become even more prev-
alent in the future. Thus even in the question of the morality
of abortion it is impossible to speak about *the* Roman Catholic position as if there cannot exist within Catholicism a
legitimate dissent from that teaching.

Present State of the Debate

Until a few years ago there was no debate within Catholicism on the question of abortion. Earlier there had been

---

[36] See also, Joseph A. Komonchak, "Ordinary Papal Magisterium and
Religious Assent," in *Contraception: Authority and Dissent*, ed. Charles E.
Curran, (New York: Herder and Herder, 1969) , pp. 101-126.

other discussions on the question of craniotomy and the possibility of killing the fetus to save the life of the mother, but there was no dissent from the authoritative teaching proposed in *Casti Connubii.* Today there is an incipient debate within Catholicism which deserves to be brought to public attention and discussed, but there is comparatively much less dissent on abortion than on artificial contraception.

Within the last few years most episcopal conferences have made statements defending the accepted Catholic teaching.[37] In the United States Germain Grisez has published a detailed study on abortion which, with one small exception (the possibility of killing the fetus to save the mother) , defends the traditional opinion. As mentioned, John Noonan and others have also defended the existing teaching. However, there are some theological voices both here and abroad which have begun to disagree with the official teaching.

The remainder of this paper will review the recent discussion within Roman Catholicism. The fact that his discussion is comparatively new in Roman Catholicism can be documented by comparing what is mentioned here with the discussion of Roman Catholic theologians as recorded by Callahan in his far reaching study on abortion published in 1970.[38] Our present discussion will neither repeat the work done by others such as Callahan nor will it attempt to be totally exhaustive. Rather representative opinions will be outlined and criticized.

The first crucial question in the moral judgment on abortion concerns the beginning of human life. Here there have been some recent divergences from the Catholic teaching

---

37 For a summary of these, see D. Mongillo *et al.,* pp. 374-377.

38 Daniel Callahan, *Abortion: Law, Choice and Morality* (New York: Macmillan, 1970) , pp. 409-447.

which insisted at least in practice on the fact that one had to act as if human life is present from the time of conception. Daniel Callahan in his study has described three generic theories about the beginning of human life—the genetic, the developmental and the social consequences approach.[39] In the recent Catholic discussions I see two different approaches proposed. The first approach can be called the individualistic approach with almost exclusive dependence on biological or physical criteria. The second type can be called a relational approach, which is unwilling to accept just physical criteria and argues for what it would call more personalistic criteria for the beginning of human life.

The first characteristic of the relational school is the unwillingness to accept a determination of when human life begins on the basis of biological criteria alone. The destination of the embryo to become a human being is not something which is inscribed in the flesh alone but depends not only on the finality inscribed in the biological aspects but even more so on the relation of acceptance and recognition by the parents who engage themselves in the act of procreation. Thus it is fruitless to look for a biological moment in which human life begins even if it would be possible to determine such a moment.[40]

Bernard Quelquejeu likewise denies that fecundation alone marks the beginning of human life, for the fruit of conception becomes human only through a procreative will expressed by the mother, the parents and in some way by society itself.[41] Jacques Marie Pohier explicitly mentions the fact that in other societies the decision about accepting one

39 *Ibid.*, pp. 378-401.
40 Bruno Ribes, S.J., "Recherche philosophique et théologique," *in Avortement et respect de la vie humaine,* p. 200.
41 Bernard Quelquejeu, O.P., "La volonté de procréer," *Lumière et Vie* XXI, n. 109 (Aout-Octobre 1972), p. 67.

into the life of the tribe or the society was made after birth. Although disagreeing with such an approach, he contends that the motivation behind it was an attempt to show respect for life and the obligation of the society to care for the life which is accepted into it. Such approaches do show the relational aspect of acceptance which is required for truly human life.[42]

If the biological criteria are not sufficient, then one must ask what are the criteria for determining the existence of human life. Based on the notion of procreation as a free act of the parents and on the importance of relationship these authors indicate the need for an acceptance by the parents and to some extent by society itself. Louis Beirnaert rejects an objectivist view which sees the fruit of conception as a being in itself when contemporary epistemology shows the participation of culture and of a knowing or recognizing element in the very constitution of the object of discourse. A human interrelation implies the recognition of the other as similar—the human face of the other. But this similarity is not present in the fetus or embryo. But even before this face is present the parents by their acceptance of the fetus especially through giving a name make the fetus a subject who has a place in the world of men. It is not a child until the decision of the parents anticipates the human form to come and names it as a subject.[43]

One can raise the question about when the relational recognition and acceptance take place. At least in some explanations it appears that this can take place any time before birth. For example, Jacques Marie Pohier, O.P., argues that

---

42 Jacques-Marie Pohier, O.P., "Réflexions théologiques sur la position de l'église catholique," *Lumière et Vie*, XXI, n. 109 (Aout-Octobre, 1972), p. 84.
43 Louis Beirnaert, S.J., "L'avortement est-il infanticide?," *Études* CCCXXXIII (1970), 522.

there are economic, psychological, cultural and even faith
aspects of human life in addition to the biological aspects.
What is the human life which God wants for man? In effect
all depends, even from the point of view of God on the possibility that men have to sustain a human life for that which
will be born from this embryo.[44] Bruno Ribes asserts that
in all the cases in which the relationship between the infant
and the parents does not exist now or will not exist at birth
one has the duty to ask about the legitimacy of allowing such
a child to be born.[45]

These authors generally take very seriously the fact that
many people in our contemporary society obviously do not
have difficulty in terminating a pregnancy under certain
somewhat broad criteria. Bernard Quelquejeu calls for an
entirely new theological methodology in the light of such
experience. One can no longer begin with established moral
principles and apply them to these different cases, but rather
one must begin with the moral experience as manifested in
these different decisions. The experience of women who
decide to have an abortion definitely constitutes a true
source of moral reflection—a *locus theologicus.*[46]

Although I admit to some uneasiness in making the judgment about the beginning of human life, I cannot accept the
relational approach described above. In reality it seems that
some of the authors themselves do still hold a biological and
individualistic criterion—birth. Apparently none of them is
willing to apply the relational criterion once the child is
born, but some would be willing to apply it before this time.
If one accepts only a relational approach in terms of recognition by parents and somewhat by society itself, there seems

---

[44] Pohier, *Avortement et respect de la vie humaine,* p. 179.
[45] Ribes, *Avortement et respect de la vie humaine,* p. 202.
[46] Quelquejeu, pp. 57-62.

to be no reason to draw the line at birth. After birth these relationships could so deteriorate that one could judge there was not enough of a relationship for truly human existence.

Likewise, it is necessary to realize the problems existing on the other end of life; namely, the time of death. All the standards acceptable today for determining death are based on the individualistic understanding of man as determined primarily by physical or biological criteria. Death is understood by some as the breakdown of the three basic human systems of circulation, respiration and brain. Some might want to define death only in terms of brain death, but all these understandings of death and tests for the presence of death follow an individualistic model. There would seem to be great problems in allowing a relational criterion which could then claim that death has occurred when human relationships are no longer present.

In addition, the relational criterion which is proposed does not itself accept a full mutuality of relationships. One could press on with this criterion to say that truly human relations must be mutual and thus the child needs to acknowledge and recognize the gift of the parents before there is a truly human relationship present.

I do not want to deny the importance of relationality in human life and existence, but at the very beginning of human life or at the end of human life we are obviously not dealing with human life in its fullest actuality. Here we are dealing with the bare minimum which is necessary for individual human existence. Men do exist in relationships, but more fundamental and basic is the fact that human beings are individuals called to enter into relationships with others in the growth and development of their own human lives.

Some proponents of this approach are not the only ones who mention the theoretical importance of the fact that many women see no moral problems in their decision to have an abortion. I agree that the experience of people is an important consideration in moral theology. Catholic moral theology itself must recognize this, for it has accepted a natural law on the basis of which all people can arrive at ethical wisdom and knowledge. Thus one cannot write off the experience of people who are not "good Catholics" or "good Christians." However, on the other hand, one must also recognize that the experience of people can be wrong. Human limitation and sinfulness affect all our judgments and decisions. In many aspects of life we realize that even conscientious people are not able to agree on what is right or wrong. We know from history that the human race has unfortunately accepted some human behavior such as slavery and torture which we are not willing to accept today. Yes, one cannot neglect the experience of people who have made their decision in a particular matter, but such experience must always be subject to critical reflection.

The second generic approach to the question of the beginning of human life sees the basis of human life in terms of the presence of a human individual and usually employs physical or biological criteria to establish this fact. Such an approach, like the previous one, could insist on a developmental or process understanding of the development of human life, but it will still be necessary to draw some lines about when individual human life is present.

One could, from this perspective, adopt the time of birth or even the time of viability. In my judgment birth and viability tell us where the individual is or can be and not necessarily what the individual is. It is important to acknowledge that at this time, to my knowledge, no Catholic theologians explicitly propose birth as the beginning of human life.

Joseph Donceel has written often on the subject and espouses a theory of delayed animation which in his judgment is the teaching which Thomas Aquinas proposed not on the basis of his admittedly inaccurate biological knowledge but on the basis of his philosophical theory of hylomorphism.[47] According to the Thomistic theory, the soul is the substantial form of the body, but a substantial form can be present only in matter capable of receiving it. Thus the fertilized ovum or early embryo cannot have a human soul. Man's spiritual faculties have no organs of their own, but the activity of "cogitative power" presupposes that the brain be fully developed, that the cortex be ready. Donceel admits that he is not certain when the human soul is infused into the matter, and he draws what appears to be a somewhat strict criterion in the light of his above understanding. The least we may ask before admitting the presence of a human soul is the availability of these organs: the senses, the nervous system, the brain, and especially the cortex. Since these organs are not ready during early pregnancy, he feels certain that there is no human person until several weeks have elapsed.[48]

John Dedek, after reviewing some of the theological literature on the question of the beginning of human life, admits there is doubt. He resolves the problem in practice by balancing off the probability of life and the reasons justifying abortion. He allows abortion up to the beginning of the third week for such circumstances as rape or even grave socioeconomic reasons. He even states there is a prudent doubt until the twelfth week and perhaps even until the fetus is technically viable, although he has really given no proof for the latter part of that statement. Only very serious reasons such as grave danger to the physical or mental health of the

---

[47] Joseph F. Donceel, S.J., "Abortion: Mediate or Immediate Animation," *Continuum*, V (1967), 167-171; Donceel, "A Liberal Catholic View," in *Abortion in a Changing World*, ed. Robert E. Hall, M.D. (New York: Columbia University Press, 1970), I, 39-45; Donceel, "Immediate Animation and Delayed Hominization," *Theological Studies*, XXXI (1970), 76-105.

[48] Donceel, *Theological Studies*, XXXI (1970), 83, 101.

mother or some very serious physical or mental deformity of the child could justify an abortion during that time.[49]

W. Ruff has proposed that individual life begins with the cortical function of the brain. Spiritual animation takes place at this time. Contemporary medicine also tests for death by the irreversible loss of the functioning of the cortex. The same test seems to be logical for the beginning of human life.[50]

In a matter as complex as this I have to admit there is some basis for these proposals, but I cannot accept them. Actual human and personal relations do not really take place until after birth. Truly spiritual activity does not take place until after birth. In my judgment the basis for these actions is not qualitatively that more present because there is now a cortex in the brain. There is still a great deal of potentiality and development which is required. I do not see the rudimentary emergence of these organs as a qualitatively different threshold which can determine the difference between human life and no human life.

The argument about the consistency of tests for the beginning of human life and the end of human life does have some attractiveness. Frankly, I see it as a good approach with those who do not believe that human life is present until much later. In this whole question of life it is important to respond with some logical consistency to the questions raised about the beginning of human life and about the end of human life. However, one must realize what the test is trying

---

[49] John F. Dedek, *Human Life: Some Moral Issues* (New York: Sheed and Ward, 1972), pp. 88-89.

[50] Wilfried Ruff, S.J., "Das embryonale Werden des Individuums," *Stimmen der Zeit*, CLXXXI (1968), 107-119; Ruff, "Das embryonale Werden des Menschen," *Stimmen der Zeit*, CLXXXI (1968), 327-337; Ruff, "Individualität und Personalität im embryonalen Werden," *Theologie und Philosophie*, XLV (1970), 24-59.

to measure. The irreversibility of the coma is the decisive factor in the test for death. The test tries to measure if there is present any immediate potentiality for spontaneous life functioning. At the beginning of life this can already be present before there is measurable electrical activity of the brain.

My own particular opinion is that human life is not present until individuality is established. In this context we are talking about individual human life, but irreversible and differentiated individuality is not present from the time of fecundation. The single fertilized cell undergoes cell division, but in the process twinning may occur until the fourteenth day. This indicates that individual human life is not definitely established before this time. Likewise in man there is also some evidence for recombination—one human being is formed from the product of more than one fertilization.[51] Thus I would argue that individuated human life is not present before this time. Corroborating evidence is the fact that a great number of fecundated ova are expelled from the uterus before they could ever reach this stage of the fourteenth day.

Notice that my argument is based on the concept of individuality which employs biological data to determine when individuality is present. The appearance of rudimentary organs in my judgment does not constitute a qualitative threshold marking the beginning of individual human life for there is still much development which is necessary. In my discussion I have purposely refrained from using the term person or personal life because as argued above the actual signs of such personal life do not seem to be present until well after birth. Obviously many Roman Catholic theolo-

---

51 André E. Hellegers, "Fetal Development," *Theological Studies*, XXXI (1970) , 4-6.

gians still argue that human life begins or probably begins at conception and confirm this argument from genetics which reminds us that there is present from the very beginning a unique genetic package. However, I do not believe there is yet present the individuality which is required.

An important study that needs to be done in this whole area is the question of probabilism and what to do when there is some doubt. My own tendency is to draw the line earlier so as to give the benefit of the doubt to individual existing human life. The older official Catholic teaching which is still maintained by many Catholics explicitly employs probabilism in this question. In one way or another this must enter into all the judgments which are made on this question. It would be an important contribution to indicate how various authors do deal with this concept.

The second crucial moral question concerns the solution of conflict situations in which the life of the fetus is in conflict with the life of the mother or with some other value. Catholic theology has traditionally solved such conflict situations in the question of abortion by the concept of direct and indirect abortion. Direct abortion is always wrong, but indirect abortion may be permitted for a sufficient reason. The basis of the distinction between direct and indirect as noted earlier is found in the nature and direction of the physical act and its effects.

In the question of abortion according to traditional Roman Catholic teaching the only possible conflict situation involves two innocent individuals and is solved by the application of the principle of direct and indirect abortion. In other cases outside the womb Catholic theology also admits the unjust aggressor situation in which the unjust aggressor, even if the aggressor is in no way subjectively guilty for what he is doing, can be repulsed by killing if necessary to protect life or other values proportionate to life. Thus anyone familiar with

Roman Catholic moral theology recognizes that more possible conflict situations have been admitted for life outside the womb than for life inside the womb.

There is comparatively widespread dissatisfaction among Roman Catholic theologians today about the resolution of conflict situations by the concept of direct and indirect effects. Even some who maintain most of the traditional Catholic teaching admit that in some cases the fetus may be killed to save the life of the mother even though the general and even official interpretation of the older teaching would not allow it.[52] Germain Grisez argues that the principle of double effect in its modern formulation is too restrictive insofar as it demands that even in the order of physical causality the evil aspect of the act not precede the good. Grisez then gives some illustrations in which he would admit abortion to save the life of the mother provided no other act must intervene to accomplish the good effect.[53]

Other Catholic theologians have given even more radical theoretical interpretations to the understanding of the principle of the double effect. Many Catholic theologians today would be willing to accept in principle my earlier stated solution to the problem of conflict situations in abortion.[54] "Conflict situations cannot be solved merely by the physical structure and causality of the act. The human values involved must be carefully considered and weighed. . . . As a Christian any taking of life must be seen as a reluctant necessity. However, in the case of abortion there can arise circumstances in which the abortion is justified for preserving

---

52 Edouard Pousset, "Etre humain déjà," *Études,* CCCXXXIII (1970), 512-513; Roger Troisfontaines, "Faut-il légaliser l'avortement?", *Nouvelle Revue Théologique,* CIII (1971), 491.
53 Grisez, pp. 333-346.
54 For a perceptive summary of some of the recent debate on this question, see Richard A. McCormick, S.J., "Notes on Moral Theology," *Theological Studies,* XXXII (1971), 80-97; XXXIII (1972), 68-86.

the life of the mother or for some other important value commensurate with life even though the action itself aims at abortion 'as a means to the end'."⁵⁵ Richard McCormick after studying six different modifications of the concept of the direct effect also concludes that one cannot decisively decide the morality of the conflict situation on the basis of the physical structure of the act but ultimately on the basis of proportionate reason.⁵⁶

In this light the question arises about what constitutes a proportionate reason. In other conflict situations in the past especially in the case of unjust aggression, Catholic theology has been willing to equate other values with physical human life itself. Manuals of moral theology justified the killing of an unjust aggressor as a last resort in defense of one's life, bodily integrity, spiritual goods "of greater value than life or integrity" such as the use of reason or conservation of reputation in very important matters; and material goods of great value.⁵⁷ In my opinion such a balancing of values could also be present in conflict situations involving abortion. Thus abortion could be justified to save the life of the mother or to avert very grave psychological or physical harm to the mother with the realization that this must truly be grave harm that will perdure over some time and not just a temporary depression.

From my theological perspective there is also another theoretical justification for abortion in some conflict situations based on a theological notion of compromise. The theory of compromise recognizes the existence of human

⁵⁵ *A New Look at Christian Morality* (Notre Dame, Indiana: Fides Publishers, 1968) , p. 243.

⁵⁶ Richard A. McCormick, S.J., *Ambiguity in Moral Choice* (Milwaukee: Marquette University, 1973) .

⁵⁷ Marcellinus Zalba, S.I., *Theologiae Moralis Summa*, Vol. II: *Theologia Moralis Specialis* (Madrid: Biblioteca de Autores Cristianos, 1953) , pp. 276-277.

sinfulness in our world because of which we occasionally might be in a position in which it seems necessary to do certain things which in normal circumstances we would not do. In the case of abortion, for example, the story as reported about women in Bangladesh who were raped and would no longer be accepted in their communities if they bore a child out of wedlock illustrates a concrete application of the theory of compromise.

A fair assessment of contemporary Catholic moral theology indicates a growing dissatisfaction with the concept of direct killing which in the case of abortion would call for a greater number of conflict situations, even though some might disagree with my understanding of proportionate values or with my other justification for abortion on the basis of compromise.

Although some Catholic theologians today are questioning and denying the traditional Catholic teaching in the area of abortion, it is necessary to realize precisely what they are saying. I have not read any Catholic theologian who holds that the fetus is just tissue in the womb of the mother or that the woman may abort for any reason whatsoever. No Catholic theologian to my knowledge accepts abortion of the fetus as just another form of contraception needing no more justification than any other use of contraception. At times I feel that some Catholic theologians are so involved in intramural discussions about abortion that they do not emphasize that their opinions also differ quite markedly from many others in our society who seem to see nothing at all wrong with abortion. My own position does differ somewhat from the accepted Catholic position both about the beginning of human life and the solution of conflict situations, but I am adamantly opposed to any position which does not recognize some independent life in the fetus and which justifies abortion as just another form of contraception.

In closing this summary of contemporary Catholic moral theology on the moral aspects of the question of abortion it is important to recall that this chapter has presented just the newer and different opinions which have appeared in the last few years. These positions are not held by the majority of Catholic theologians but there is sizable and growing number of Catholic theologians who do disagree with some aspects of the officially proposed Catholic teaching that direct abortion from the time of conception is always wrong.

6

Sterilization: Exposition, Critique and Refutation of Past Teaching

The question of the morality of sterilization in the teaching of the Roman Catholic Church has recently been raised in a number of different contexts. Vasectomy, since it is very efficient and a comparatively simple procedure, has become very popular with many people in our society.[1] In a specifically Catholic context a recent court decision in Billings, Montana, ordered a Catholic hospital to perform a sterilization in the specific case of a woman who was going to deliver a baby by caesarean section.[2]

There is a third context within which questions of sterilizations arise—problems connected with the retarded.[3] Sterilization is often recommended as a form of protection for a retarded girl who through force or her own ignorance may

---

[1] G. Parker, "Voluntary Male Sterilization," *Lancet* (January 1967), I, 219-220.

[2] L. Cary, "Court Ordered Sterilization Performed at St. Vincent Hospital Billings," *Hospital Progress*, LIII (December 1972), 22.

[3] M. S. Bass, "Pastoral Counselling on Voluntary Sterilization for Retarded Individuals," *Pastoral Psychology*, XX (December 1969), 33-40.

be induced into having sexual intercourse. Also it often happens that a retarded girl is not able to care for her own feminine hygiene, thus placing a very great burden on her family and those caring for her. Sterilization is recommended as a means of preventing the menstrual bleeding which becomes so burdensome in this case.

In 1971 the American bishops promulgated a new set of "Ethical and Religious Directives for Catholic Health Facilities," which include the following directives concerning sterilization:

18. Sterilization, whether permanent or temporary, for men or women, may not be used as a means of contraception.

20. Procedures that induce sterility, whether permanent or temporary, are permitted when: (a) they are immediately directed to the cure, dimunition or prevention of a serious pathological condition and are not directly contraceptive (that is, contraception is not the purpose), and (b) a simpler treatment is not reasonably available. Hence, for example, oophorectomy or irradiation of the ovaries may be allowed in treating carcinoma of the breast and metastasis therefrom; and orchidectomy is permitted in the treatment of carcinoma of the prostate.

22. Hysterectomy is permitted when it is sincerely judged to be a necessary means of removing some serious uterine pathological condition. In these cases, the pathological condition of each patient must be considered individually and care must be taken that a hysterectomy is not performed merely as a contraceptive measure, or as a routine procedure after any definite number of caesarean sections.[4]

---

[4] These directives are available from Department of Health Affairs-USCC, 1312 Massachusetts Ave., N.W., Washington, D.C. 20005. For a critical evaluation of these directives including a negative reaction to the section on

EXPLANATION OF THESE DIRECTIVES

These specific directives are substantially the same as the previous guidelines and are in keeping with the generally accepted teaching on sterilization proposed by the papal teachings and explained by Catholic theologians before 1963.[5] Pius XI in his encyclical *Casti Connubii* in 1930 was mainly concerned with eugenic sterilization as imposed by state laws.[6] The Holy Office responded on February 24, 1940, that the direct sterilization of a man or woman whether perpetual or temporary is forbidden by the law of nature.[7]

The textbooks of Catholic moral theology generally discussed sterilization under the heading of mutilation, although it constitutes a distinctive type of mutilation.[8] Mutilation is governed by the principle of totality. According to Pope Pius XII the principle of totality affirms that the part exists for the whole, and that, consequently, the good of the part remains subordinate to the good of the whole; that the good of the whole is the determining factor in regard to the part, and can dispose of the part in its own interest.[9] Man can thus legitimately sacrifice a part of his organism for the

---

sterilization, see "Catholic Hospital Ethics: The Report of the Commission on Ethical and Religious Directives for Catholic Hospitals Commissioned by the Board of Directors of the Catholic Theological Society of America," *Proceedings of the Catholic Theological Society of America*, XXVII (1972), 241-269. Further debate about these directives can be found in *The Linacre Quarterly*, XXXIX (1972) and *Chicago Studies*, XI (1972), 279-318.

5 The date 1963 is employed because it was only in this year that Roman Catholic theologians began to publicly question the hierarchical teaching on artificial contraception. Today it is safe to say that the majority of Catholic theologians who are currently involved in research and writing disagree with this hierarchical teaching.

6 *Acta Apostolicae Sedis*, XXII (1930), 565.

7 *A.A.S.*, XXXII (1940), 73.

8 E.g., Marcellinus Zalba, S.I., *Theologiae Moralis Summa*, Vol. II Cristianos, 1953), pp. 263-270.

9 *A.A.S.*, XLIV (1952), 787.

good of the whole. In this case good medicine is good morality because sound and conscientious medical practice permits a mutilation only when this is for the genuine good of
the patient and when that same good cannot be obtained by
some simpler and more reasonably available means.

Sterilization, however, constitutes a special type of mutilation because it concerns the generative faculties of man. The
individual does not have the same stewardship and dominion
over his generative faculties which he has over the other
parts of his body. The generative faculties of man do not
exist only or even primarily for the good of the individual but
for the good of the species. The whole being and finality of
the other parts of man are totally subordinate to the good of
the individual, but the generative faculties cannot be totally
subordinated to the good of the individual. The generative
functions and organs have a twofold aspect and meaning.
Man does not have the right to subordinate the generative
aspect of these functions to the good of the individual. Only
when these generative organs and functions in themselves
and apart from their generative function cause harm to the
whole person, may they be suppressed or sacrificed for the
good of the whole.[10]

Pope Pius XII addressed this particular aspect of the question in his talk to the Italian Society of Urologists on October 8, 1953. If the generative organ (e.g., fallopian tube,
testicle) is itself diseased or can truly be called pathological
or if the organ itself is not diseased but its preservation or

---

[10] Denis O'Callaghan, "Fertility Control by Hormonal Regulation," *Irish
Theological Quarterly*, XXVII (1960), 1-4. This summarizes the generally
accepted reasoning proposed by the hierarchical teaching and in the theological explanations. Note that some authors such as O'Callaghan have
later changed their views on this question. O'Callaghan's explanation here
is a good example of Catholic moral theology's attempt to base morality on
the physical teleology of the organs themselves. He speaks of the innate
teleology of the generative organs.

functioning directly or indirectly entails a serious threat to the whole body, then the organ can be removed.[11] The specific cases mentioned in Directive 20 of the Catholic Hospital Code exemplify this type of situation.

The principle is thus established that direct sterilization is morally wrong, for man is not able to sacrifice the generative functions *qua* generative for the good of the individual. Indirect sterilization of the generative functions not *qua* generative but *qua* relating to the individual is permitted for a proportionate reason when there is no simpler treatment readily available. In indirect sterilization the action has multiple effects one of which is sterilizing, but the sterilization is neither directly done nor directly intended. The generative function is only indirectly sacrificed or suppressed.

Pope Pius XII described direct sterilization as that which aims at making procreation impossible as both means and end.[12] The Pope later applied this principle to the case of the anovulant pills. In common parlance these pills are often referred to as contraceptive pills, but strict theological terminology classifies them as a form of sterilization. Contraception interferes with the sexual act as such, whereas sterilization interferes with the sexual faculty; as in this case, by preventing ovulation. The anovulant pills constitute a temporary sterilization. Such medication, according to the Pope, may be used to treat a malady of the uterus or of the organism. "But one causes a direct sterilization, and therefore an illicit one, whenever one stops ovulation in order to preserve the uterus and the organism from the consequences of a pregnancy which they are not able to stand."[13]

Examples given by Pope Pius XII well illustrate the difference between direct and indirect sterilizations. Sterilization

---

11 *A.A.S.*, XLV (1953) , 673-674.
12 *A.A.S.*, XLIII (1951) , 843, 844.
13 *A.A.S.*, L (1958) , 735.

is often recommended to prevent a new pregnancy because of the danger to the life and health of the mother. However, it is a direct sterilization and consequently immoral if the danger arises from other diseased organs such as the heart, the kidneys or the lungs. The sterilization is direct because the danger arises only if voluntary sexual activity brirgs about a pregnancy. The danger does not arise from the presence or normal functioning of the generative organs or from their influence on other diseased organs.[14]

In the light of this official papal teaching, theologians discussed other possible cases which came to their attention.[15] The first question to arise chronologically concerned punitive sterilization. Punitive sterilization was mentioned by Pope Pius XI in his encyclical *Casti Connubii*. The original version of the official text seemed to condemn it, but later the Pope corrected the text in such a way that the question of punitive sterilization was left open for debate among theologians.[16] Although the majority of theologians condemned punitive sterilization, those who defended it had to reconcile it with the later condemnation of direct sterilization. The influential Francis Hurth, for example, argued that such a sterilization was not direct. One could also argue to the liceity of punitive sterilization on the basis of analogy

---

[14] *A.A.S.*, XLV (1953) , 675.

[15] Gerald Kelly, S.J. summarizes well and accurately the magisterial teaching and the theological discussions on sterilization. For a good summary bringing together much of what he wrote on the subject see, John C. Ford, S.J. and Gerald Kelly, S.J., *Contemporary Moral Theology*, Vol. II *Marriage Questions*, pp. 315-377. In addition one can find helpful discussions of the Catholic teaching on sterilization in the standard works on medical ethics which include the following: Edwin F. Healy, S.J., *Medical Ethics* (Chicago: Loyola University Press, 1956) ; Gerald Kelly, S.J., *Medico-Moral Problems* (St. Louis: The Catholic Hospital Association, 1958) ; Charles J. McFadden, O.S.A., *Medical Ethics*, 4th ed. (Philadelphia: F. A. Davis, 1958) ; Thomas J. O'Donnell, S.J., *Morals in Medicine* (Westminster, Md.: Newman Press, 1956) .

[16] *A.A.S.*, XXI (1930) , 564, 565; 604.

with the right of the state to take the life of the criminal which right has generally been admitted in theory by Catholic theologians although today many would (rightly I believe) argue against capital punishment. In some theories punitive sterilization would be a direct sterilization, but the principle would be nuanced to read that the direct sterilization of the innocent on one's own authority is wrong.[17]

Another case involved the weakened and scarred uterus which was frequently discussed by Catholic moralists. Is it permissible to remove a uterus which in the opinion of competent physicians has been so badly damaged by previous caesarean sections that it would likely create a serious danger for the mother in a future pregnancy because of rupturing? Theologians differed in their responses. Some argued that such a procedure would be a direct sterilization, for the danger is not now present and arises only when and if there is a new pregnancy.[18]

Others argue that the sterilization was only indirect. The root cause is the organ itself which can be regarded as pathological because it is not able to carry out its proper functioning without danger to the mother. There are two effects of such an action, one of which is sterilization, but the effect which is directly done and directly intended is the removal of the "pathological organ" to prevent a future hemorrhage.[19] E. Tesson added a further refinement. In such a case it cannot be *a priori* excluded that the doctor is permitted to tie the tubes rather than remove the uterus. By this

---

17 For a summary of opinions on this matter, see John Canon McCarthy, *Problems in Theology*, Vol. II, *The Commandments* (Westminster, Md.: Newman Press, 1960) , pp. 124-129.

18 Francis J. Connell, C.SS.R., *Father Connell Answers Moral Questions* ed. Eugene J. Weitzel (Washington: Catholic University of America Press, 1959) , pp. 174, 175.

19 For an exposition of this opinion and a summary of the whole debate, see Kelly, *Medico-Moral Problems*, pp. 215-217.

process one isolates the uterus which is a less radical procedure than the removal of the uterus.[20]

In the 1960's another question came to the fore in the light of the predicament of the sisters in the Congo in danger of rape who took the pill to prevent the possibility of conception. Most Catholic theologians allowed the use of the pill or any other contraceptive in those circumstances on the basis of legitimate defense against the possible consequences of unjust aggression.[21]

Punitive sterilization and sterilization in the form of defense against the possible consequences of unjust aggression in rape modified somewhat the teaching condemning direct sterilization. However, in both these cases there are parallels with the question of the direct taking of life. Some Catholic theologians in the middle 1960's argued that the exceptions in the cases just mentioned tended to indicate the arbitrariness of the whole Catholic teaching on sterilization.[22] Although I too am opposed to such a teaching, I believe there is a logical consistency to it even with the exceptions mentioned above provided that one grants the basis on which the whole teaching is based.

The application of this accepted teaching to the questions raised at the beginning of this chapter have all been answered except for those arising in the case of retardation. There does seem to be a true parallel between the sterilization of the retarded girl to prevent the possible conception which might follow from the fact that through fear or igno-

---

[20] E. Tesson, "Discussion Morale," *Cahiers Laennec*, XXIV (Juin 1964), pp. 69-70. This entire issue is devoted to the question of sterilization.

[21] This question was first discussed and adjudged affirmatively by P. Palazzini, F. Hürth and F. Lambruschini in *Studi Cattolici*, V (1961), 64-72. These were three very influential Roman theologians.

[22] For a development of this approach and with reference to other authors, see Thomas A. Wassmer, S.J., *Christian Ethics for Today* (Milwaukee: Bruce Publishing Co., 1969), pp. 177-182.

202 New Perspectives in Moral Theology

rance someone takes advantage of her and has sexual intercourse with her, and the sterilization of those who are in
danger of rape. The condition of the retarded girl is more
permanent and could call for the more permanent form of
sterilization. I would, however, add the important caution
that society must respect the rights of the retarded which all
too often are not safeguarded.

In the case of sterilization to prevent the menstrual bleeding of a girl who is not able to provide for her own hygiene,
there seems to be a true case of indirect sterilization. The
menstrual bleeding for this particular girl causes her hygenic
problems and difficulties and may even necessitate that she
be removed from her family environment because her family
cannot care for her. The sterilization is indirect because there
are two effects, the suppression of the menstrual bleeding
and the sterilization, but what is directly intended and directly done is the suppression of the menstrual bleeding.

One might retort that the menstrual bleeding is normal
and does not constitute a pathological condition. However,
the sterilization can still be indirect if the normal functioning of the generative organs is detrimental to the health of
the whole person as in the case of cancer of the prostate or
cancer of the breast. Even though the physical health of the
girl might not be injured in this case, the bleeding is detrimental to the total well-being of the person. John Connery,
S.J., in 1954 perceptively pointed out that the good of the
whole which could justify a mutilation and even an indirect
sterilization is not just the good of the body or the good of
the physical organism but the total good of the person.[23]
Thus I argue that even in the context of the accepted Catholic teaching until the 1960's, sterilization in the two cases
concerning the retarded is a morally acceptable procedure.

---

23 John R. Connery, S.J., "Notes on Moral Theology," *Theological Studies,*
XV (1954) , 602.

COUNTER CATHOLIC POSITIONS

I disagree with the past Catholic teaching on sterilization and maintain that in practice Catholics can dissent from the authoritative Church teaching condemning direct sterilization.

The condemnation of direct sterilization as proposed by Catholic moral theologians before 1963 involves three related but different moral principles—the principle of stewardship which determines the power that man has over his body and its organs, especially in this case his sexual organs; the principle of totality; and the principle of the double effect by which indirect sterilization is distinguished from direct sterilization. Many theologians in the last few years have disagreed with the teaching which was generally accepted before 1963, but they have proposed different reasons for their disagreement. My disagreement with the accepted teaching goes to the most basic and fundamental level—the stewardship which man has over his sexuality and generative functions. Those who disagree primarily by questioning the concept of direct and indirect or the principle of totality without going to the ultimate level do not, in my judgment, adequately come to grips with the question of sterilization.

In the question of sterilization a non-Roman Catholic such as Joseph Fletcher and a Catholic writer such as Thomas Wassmer have insisted on their disagreement with the concept of direct and indirect sterilization.[24] Wassmer sees inconsistencies in the condemnation of direct sterilization when sterilization is allowed as punishment or as defense. Although he does consider the other questions of the principle of totality and the stewardship which man exercises over

---

[24] Joseph Fletcher, *Morals and Medicine* (Boston: Beacon Press, 1960), pp. 141-171. Fletcher does mention the other aspects of sterilization, but uses this discussion primarily to question the concept of direct and indirect effects.

his generative organs or his sexuality, Wassmer devotes the greater part of his article to the distinction between direct and indirect sterilization.[25]

Perhaps this emphasis is explained by the fact that Wassmer was writing somewhat early in the controversy about sterilization. In addition Wassmer was obviously using this occasion to express his disagreement with the notions of direct and indirect effects and also with the concept of intrinsically evil. I too have difficulties with the accepted explanation of the principle of the double effect with its understanding of what is direct, but the question of sterilization must be ultimately resolved on a deeper level. Why did the accepted teaching say that direct sterilization is wrong and why do many contemporary theologians argue that direct sterilization is morally acceptable?

Others approach the question of sterilization in terms of revising the principle of totality. The principle of totality also exercised an important influence on the questions of transplantation and experimentation, for these were forms of medical operations which were generically treated as mutilations and considered in the light of the principle of totality.

On the basis of the principle of totality it seemed impossible to justify either transplantation or experimentation. Catholic teaching enunciated by the Popes and explained by the theologians insisted that the part could be sacrificed only if its meaning and finality were totally seen in terms of the whole for which it was sacrificed. Thus the state cannot sacrifice an individual for the good of the state because the individual has a meaning and finality apart from the state. In reaction to the pretensions of totalitarian states, Pope Pius XII stressed the fact that the physical organism of human beings, unlike the moral unity of the state or of the com-

---

25 Wassmer, pp. 174-192.

munity, has a unity of its own in which each of the members; e.g., hand, foot, heart, eye, is an integral part destined in its whole being to be inserted into the totality of the organism itself. Such a rationale appears to limit the application of the principle of totality just to physical organisms. Some few theologians thus denied the morality of transplantation and experimentation, but the majority found other justifying reasons, especially charity.[26] Later, however, Pope Pius XII himself maintained that to the subordination of particular organs to the organism one must add the subordination of the organism to the spiritual finality of the person himself.[27] Martin Nolan has interpreted this papal teaching to indicate that the total good of the person is achieved in activating oneself in one's innermost reality which is relationship to God and to others. The human person and his good are seen in terms of relationship to God and to others. On the basis of this understanding, Nolan now employs the principle of totality to justify both transplantation and experimentation and thus reconciles charity and the principle of totality.[28]

Such a revised understanding of the principle of totality could also be applied to sterilization. Perhaps even in sterilization, according to Nolan, the discussion should not be confined to the organs in question and their relationship to the organism, but rather the good of the whole man and his relationship to his family, community and the larger society must be taken into account.[29] Such an approach echoes the often heard complaint that an older Catholic theology emphasized too much the finality of particular organs and did

26 Gerald Kelly, S.J., "Pope Pius XII and the Principle of Totality," *Theological Studies*, XVI (1955) , 373-396.

27 *A.A.S.*, L (1958) , 593, 594.

28 Martin Nolan, "The Principle of Totality in Moral Theology," in *Absolutes in Moral Theology*, ed. Charles E. Curran (Washington: Corpus Books, 1968) , pp. 237-248.

29 *Ibid.*, p. 244.

not give enough attention to the person and to his relationships with others.

Totality has been expanded to justify sterilization in two
different ways. Warren Reich succinctly pointed out both
possibilities and described the first as an attitude among
some Catholic theologians to extend the principle of totality
to apply to all those pathological cases in which the life of
the mother is imperiled by a new pregnancy.[30] One recently
approved and promulgated Policy Manual for a Catholic
hospital does accept such an approach. "In our view, this
'isolation procedure' describes quite well how a tubal ligation
may be a good and necessary procedure in applying the
principle of totality to a woman who, because of a serious
pathological condition other than a damaged uterus, may not
be able to support a future pregnancy without grave danger
to her life and health."[31] Somewhat similar proposals are
now under discussion in some dioceses in the United States.

In evaluating such an approach one must honestly recognize that such a proposal runs counter to the explicit teaching of Pius XII. Also, in my judgment the approaches as
stated here are too limited. The Policy Manual limits the
justification of tubal ligation to cases in which there is a
pathological condition of the mother and a permanent major
threat to her life and health.[32] Such a requirement calls for
a much more serious reason than is required in other mutilations. Economic, sociological or demographic reasons are
apparently judged not sufficient. Also the policy does not
explicitly allow for the sterilization of the male in such cases

30 Warren Reich, "Medico-Moral Problems and the Principle of Totality:
A Catholic Viewpoint," in *Medico-Moral Ethics for a Hospital Ministry* (VA
Pamphlet 10-95), p. 40.

31 *Policy Manual for Committee to Advise on Requests on Obstetrical/
Gynaecological Sterilization Procedures* (London, Ontario, Canada: St. Joseph's Hospital, 1973), p. 11.

32 *Ibid.*

even though this is a much simpler medical procedure. While I applaud such attempts to break away from the teaching of the past, this particular reasoning does not go to the ultimate level on which the question must be settled.

Another approach invoking the principle of totality to justify sterilization argues that the marriage or the family itself constitutes a totality and a part may be sacrificed for the good of the marriage or the totality of the family.[33] A number of Catholic theologians have advocated this line of reasoning which overcomes many of the objections to the first extension of the principle of totality. However, such reasoning logically involves a discussion of the stewardship over sexuality and generative functions.

In my judgment the proper level for the discussion of sterilization is the stewardship which man exercises over his sexuality and his generative functions. Since sterilization was first categorized by theologians as a surgical operation, it was treated in the manuals of moral theology under the heading of mutilation and brought into the area primarily governed by the principle of totality. A somewhat similar problem arose in the questions of experimentation and transplantation which were placed in this same category.

There are many convincing reasons to justify the contention that sterilization must ultimately be considered in terms not of the difference between direct and indirect, not primarily on the basis of the principle of totality, but in the light of the stewardship that man has over his sexuality and his generative faculties. From the ethical perspective this means that sterilization must be seen in the same basic terms as contraception.

Even before the overt controversy in Roman Catholicism about contraception, Gerald Kelly pointed out the need to

[33] Quentin de la Bedoyere, "Sterilization and Human Reason," *New Blackfriars*, XLVIII (1966/67), 153-156; Wassmer, pp. 185-192.

distinguish between noncontraceptive mutilation and contraceptive mutilation which is defined as "any procedure which is either explicitly or implicitly directed to the permanent or temporary suppression of the power of procreation."[34] Thomas J. O'Donnell, who strongly upholds the condemnation of direct sterilization, recognizes where the issue ultimately lies, for he defines direct sterilization as directly contraceptive sterilization and distinguishes it from indirect sterilization.[35] Kelly argues that, except for the cases of punitive sterilization and consent to compulsory sterilization, the discussions of contraceptive sterilization belong more properly not to the treatise on mutilation but to the treatise on the abuse of sexual faculties.[36]

The widespread discussions about the anovulant pill in Roman Catholic theology in the 1960's indicate again that sterilization must be considered under the rubric of man's stewardship over his sexuality and his generative faculties. The anovulant pill was popularly called the contraceptive pill, and the debate was characterized as a debate over contraception. However, in accord with strict ethical terminology the anovulant pill involved sterilization and not contraception. Contraception interferes with the act of sexual intercourse, whereas sterilization interferes with the generative faculty. The pill interferes with the generative faculty by preventing ovulation. In technical terminology the pill brings about a temporary sterilization. Pope Pius XII in his condemnation of the pill as direct sterilization and Catholic theologians debating the pros and cons of the issue realized

---

[34] Gerald Kelly, S.J., "The Morality of Mutilation: Towards a Revision of the Treatise," *Theological Studies*, XVII (1956), 328.

[35] Thomas J. O'Donnell, S.J., "Sterilization," *New Catholic Encyclopedia* XIII, pp. 704, 705. For O'Donnell's continued opposition to direct sterilization, see Thomas J. O'Donnell, S.J., "Hospital Directives: A crisis in Faith," *Linacre Quarterly*, XXXIX (1972), 143.

[36] *Theological Studies*, XVII (1956), 331.

that they were talking about sterilization and not contraception.

Dialogue with Protestant and Jewish ethicians also indicates that the question is basically the same as the question of contraception. Sterilization is not discussed primarily in terms of the principle of totality. Those non-Catholic authors who frequently agree with many Catholic positions in the question of medical ethics disagree on contraception and sterilization. Their argumentation points out that both these questions must be considered in terms of man's stewardship over his sexuality and generative functions.[37]

It lies beyond the scope of this paper to marshall the theological and ethical arguments in favor of the morality of artificial contraception, since these arguments have been formulated so often in the last few years. In general those who accept artificial contraception understand human sexuality in terms of its relationship to the individual person, to his spouse or family and to all of society. In the light of these multiple relationships the individual has stewardship over his sexuality and his reproductive functions. He has the right to intervene in these functions in the light of the multiple relationships, but this does not per se give anyone else, e.g., the state, the right to intervene or coerce the individual in the control of his reproductive functions.

A Roman Catholic advocating the moral liceity of direct sterilization must also respond to the fact that such a pro-

---

[37] E.g., Immanuel Jakobovits, *Jewish Medical Ethics* (New York: Bloch Publishing Co., 1959), pp. 159-169; Paul Ramsey, "Freedom and Responsibility in Medical and Sexual Ethics: A Protestant View," *New York University Law Review* XXXI (1956), 1189-1204. One might expect that Anglican theologians who are closer to the Roman tradition in moral theology might discuss the question primarily in terms of the principle of totality. This is exemplified in Robert M. Cooper, "Vasectomy and the Good of the Whole," *Anglican Theological Review* LIV (1972), 94-106. Unfortunately, Cooper does not acknowledge the theoretical and practical possibilities of dissent within Roman Catholicism on the question of sterilization.

posal is against the authoritative teaching of the Church. The right to dissent from the authoritative teaching on contraception has been sufficiently demonstrated in many places. Interestingly, even proponents of the official teaching on sterilization before *Humanae Vitae* admitted that the magisterial commitment to the condemnation of direct sterilization was not as strong as in the case of contraception.[38] *Humanae Vitae*, citing both *Casti Connubii* and the 1940 response of the Holy Office, puts the condemnation of direct sterilization in the same paragraph as the condemnation of contraception.[39] Thus in proving the possibility of dissent from contraception, one also proves the possibility of loyal Catholics dissenting from the condemnation of direct sterilization.

Despite the basic similarity between sterilization and contraception there are some morally significant differences. Sterilization especially in terms of vasectomy and tubal ligation tends to be permanent, so there should be a reason commensurate with the fact that the individual may lose his or her reproductive potential to justify such actions. Sterilization also does involve a greater interference in the human system, and there may be some side complications which arise. This ultimately rests on medical facts, but it is a factor that must be taken into account in any prudent decision regarding sterilization.

This position is very similar to that briefly proposed by Richard A. McCormick, S.J.. McCormick rightly indicates that sterilization and contraception must be considered together, but points out that the possible permanent nature of surgical sterilization constitutes a profound human caution, but does not lead to an absolute exclusion of surgical steril-

---

38 Ford and Kelly, pp. 315-318.
39 *A.A.S.*, LX (1968) , 490.

ization.[40] My difference with McCormick, if there is any difference, is one of emphasis. I think there are many occasions when other reasons can justify the permanent destruction of the reproductive capacity although it is important to realize the far-reaching consequences of surgical sterilization.

The thrust of this article has been to situate and evaluate properly the Catholic teaching on sterilization. Proper ethical discourse must place sterilization in the same generic category as contraception, governed by the stewardship which man has over his sexuality and generative functions. Those who like myself argue in favor of contraception must logically also accept so-called direct sterilization with the realization that the more permanent nature of some sterilization and its more radical interference in bodily functions must enter into the decision about the proportionate reason justifying sterilization.

[40] "Medico-Moral Opinions: Vasectomy and Sterilization," *Linacre Quarterly*, **XXXVIII** (1971), 9, 10.

7

Divorce: Catholic Theory and Practice in the United States

This chapter is an interpretive and critical analysis of the recent developments, both in theory and in practice, on the question of divorce among Catholics in the United States.[1] There are two important limitations on this study. First, the study will consider explicitly only the American theory and practice, but with the realization that this has obviously been influenced by what is being said and done elsewhere in the world. Second, only the question of divorce and remarriage will be considered although it is necessary to point out that even more pressing is the need to develop a better theology and spirituality of Christian marriage itself. The discussion

---

1 For helpful surveys dealing with some aspects of the question to be treated here, see William W. Bassett, "Divorce and Remarriage—The Catholic Search for a Pastoral Reconciliation," *The American Ecclesiastical Review*, CLXII (1970), 20-36; 92-105: Richard A. McCormick, S.J., "Notes on Moral Theology" *Theological Studies*, XXXII (1971), 107-122; XXXIII (1972), 91-100; Seamus Ryan, "Survey of Periodicals: Indissolubility of Marriage," *The Furrow*, XXIV (1973), 150-159; 214-224; 272-284.

will center on three different aspects of the question—the legal provisions with special emphasis on marriage tribunals or Church courts; extralegal approaches often referred to as internal forum or pastoral solutions; and the more theoretical aspect of a change or revision in the teaching of the Church on the indissolubility of a consummated marriage between two baptized persons.

There is one methodological difficulty that must be pointed out. If one argues that the Roman Catholic Church should change its teaching on indissolubility, this change greatly affects the approach taken to the question of legal provisions or marriage tribunals and pastoral solutions. For the sake of discussion in this study the consideration of the first two questions of the legal provisions and pastoral solutions for those who are divorced and remarried will generally accept the present teaching of the Church. The third section will develop my reasons for changing the teaching and practice of the Church on indissolubility; but by prescinding from this position in the first two questions the conclusions reached about legal provisions and pastoral solutions will be able to stand, even if one does not accept the more radical conclusion proposed in the third section.

PART I: LEGAL PROVISIONS AND MARRIAGE TRIBUNALS

According to Catholic teaching and practice, a consummated sacramental marriage (*ratum et consummatum*), that is, a consummated marriage between two baptized persons, is indissoluble. A sacramental marriage which is not consummated may be dissolved by the Pope or by solemn religious profession of one of the parties. If one or both of the parties in a marriage is not baptized, then there are two possible ways of dissolving the marriage. The Pauline privilege asserts that when there is a valid marriage between two unbaptized persons and one becomes baptized, the converted party obtains the right to remarry if the unbaptized party refuses to peacefully live with the newly baptized. According to the so-called Petrine privilege or privilege of the Faith, any marriage in which at least one party is unbaptized may be dissolved by the Pope. At the present time this dissolution of the marriage is not granted unless there is a conversion to Roman Catholicism, but in the past such dissolutions have been granted even when there has been no conversion.

There are three generic reasons for annulments of marriages in Church law. The first exists when there has been an invalidating impediment such as impotence, a previously existing marriage bond, etc. The second generic reason is the lack of due canonical form which in general calls for a Catholic to be married before a priest and two witnesses. The third generic type concerns cases of defective consent which can be based on such realities as ignorance, lack of the ability to carry out the essential reality of marriage, force and fear, or other factors that might prevent the persons involved from giving a true matrimonial consent. In cases of this third type there is involved the formal court trial, whereas in other cases such as the dissolution of the bond, lack of canonical form, or the invalidating impediment of a previous bond, the procedure is more administrative or a summary judicial procedure and not a formal trial as such.[2]

The procedures and substantive rules followed in all Church marriage cases are those set down in the Code of

---

2 Church law is found in the *Codex Juris Canonici.* The substantive aspects of the law about marriage are found in Book Three, Canons 1012-1143. The procedural norms for courts are found in Book Four. The better-known English commentaries on marriage used often in the United States include: T. Lincoln Bouscaren and Adam C. Ellis, *Canon Law: A Text and Commentary* (2nd rev. ed. Milwaukee: Bruce Publishing Co., 1955), pp. 453-644; Marcian J. Mathis and Nicholas W. Meyer, *The Pastoral Companion: A Handbook of Canon Law,* (12th ed., Chicago: Franciscan Herald Press, 1961), pp. 167-305; John A. Abbo and Jerome D. Hannan, *The Sacred*

Canon Law. Since the cases of all formal trials are subject to appeal to the Roman Rota, one would not expect great originality in the jurisprudence followed by diocesan marriage tribunals. However, there have been some significant developments on the American scene that have brought about changes in the procedures employed and in the number of affirmative sentences that have been reached by Church courts.

Procedural Norms

Significant changes have been brought about in the procedural norms for formal courts largely through the efforts of the Canon Law Society of America which deserves commendation for many efforts made to revise Church law and structure in all areas of Church life. A survey sponsored by the Canon Law Society of America covering the year 1968 reveals the inadequacy of the tribunal system at that time. 134 out of 146 American dioceses responded. 58 reported that no decision was rendered in a formal trial during 1968; 18 tribunals published one decision in a formal trial in first instance in the same year; 19 tribunals published two decisions in formal trials in the first instance in 1968. In fact only 442 formal decisions were made in the whole United States in that year although 1,554 cases were pending in Rome. In addition there were 3,277 privilege of the faith cases sent to Rome and 325 *ratum et non consummatum* cases for all the American tribunals.[3]

Canons: A Concise Presentation of the Disciplinary Norms of the Church, 2 vols. (2nd rev. ed.,; St. Louis: B. Herder Book Co., 1960), pp. 160-412. For more specific and contemporary information, see *The Tribunal Reporter*, ed. Adam J. Maida (Huntington, Indiana: Our Sunday Visitor, Inc., 1970); Lawrence G. Wrenn, *Annulments* (Hartford, Conn.: Canon Law Society of America, 1970); *Matrimonial Jurisprudence, United States, 1968-1971* (Hartford, Conn.: Canon Law Society of America, 1973).

[3] "Committee Report on Regional Tribunals," *Proceedings of the Thirty-First Annual Convention of the Canon Law Society of America*, (1969), pp. 143-155.

In addition, the survey of the Canon Law Society revealed an inordinate delay in the major areas of tribunal work. The process in privilege of the faith cases averaged 2 years and 5 months; the process in nonconsummation cases averaged 2 years and 8 months. In both these cases the final decision can only be made in Rome. In the formal trials the average time was 3½ years in the local tribunal of first instance with more time required for appeals to other courts. An appeal was always required if the first decision was against the existence of a marriage bond.[4]

These statistics are jarring. Obviously a great injustice was being done to many Catholics who were not able to have their cases adjudicated. Even the few who had their case processed were forced to wait an inordinate length of time for any decision. In the light of this situation the Canon Law Society has called for a number of reforms. In September of 1968 the Society endorsed the work of a subcommittee chaired by Msgr. Stephen J. Kelleher, Chief Judge of the Archdiocese of New York, and recommended to the American bishops a series of procedural changes. After approval by the American bishops, these proposals were revised somewhat in dialogue with Rome and finally approved for a three year experimental period beginning July 1, 1970.[5]

The major provisions of these twenty-three procedural norms are the following: Additional tribunals are declared competent to hear cases; permission to have just one judge and not three; no mandatory appeal required after a decision affirming the marriage was null and void from the beginning; the recognition that the moral certitude required of a decision is generated by the prevailing weight of that evidence

---

4 *Ibid.,* pp. 144-145.
5 Lawrence G. Wrenn, "The American Procedural Norms," *The American Ecclesiastical Review,* CLXV (1971), 175-186; Thomas J. Lynch, "Streamlining Marriage Courts," *The Homilectic and Pastoral Review,* LXIX (1968-9), 833-838.

which has a recognized value in law and jurisprudence. The new norms also provide that the whole process should not take more than eight months.[6] In the *Motu Proprio, Causas Matrimoniales,* Pope Paul VI determined new norms for the universal Church in expediting marriage procedures, but these are used in the United States only when they expand what is contained in the twenty-three procedural norms. In general these norms for the universal Church are still more restrictive than the experimental norms for the United States. One less restrictive provision is that a layman may be one of the judges in a tribunal with three judges.[7]

Lawrence G. Wrenn, Chief Judge of the Archdiocese of Hartford, sees a most important theoretical difference between the new procedural norms and the 642 canons of Book Four of the Code of Canon Law. Although the letter from Cardinal Villot granting the original three year experimental use of the new norms insisted that the canons of Book Four of the Code of Canon Law are not abrogated, Wrenn maintains that twenty or thirty procedural norms are all that should ever be needed. The Canons of Book Four not only fail to work in practice, but they mirror a type of law proposed for a society based on fear and distrust rather than the law that should characterize the community of the Church. Church law must reflect what the Church is—a community of love and not just an ordinary political society.[8]

---

6 "Commentary on the Procedural Norms," *The Jurist,* XXXI (1971), 406-422.

7 "Causas Matrimoniales," *Acta Apostolicae Sedis,* LXIII (1971), 441-446. An English translation may be found in *The Jurist,* XXXI (1971), 668-672.

8 Wrenn, *The American Ecclesiastical Review,* CLXV (1971), 175-186. It should also be remembered that the provisions of Book Four were envisioned to resolve all types of controversies in the Church community, redress of wrongs, adjudication of rights and facts, etc. Thus these procedures were not designed specifically for marriage cases which for all practical purposes are the only cases now handled.

When the experimental period of three years elapsed, there appeared to be great reluctance in extending these norms. Rome finally approved their continued use for one more year but with the understanding that after one year these procedures will no longer be allowed.[9] The latest available statistics in comparison with the 1968 statistics indicate some improvements have been made through these new norms and other procedures. During 1971 the United States' tribunals annulled or prepared for annulment something less than 3,000 apparently valid marriages. Lawrence Wrenn estimates that perhaps twice that many people received a preliminary hearing as to the merits of their case.[10]

Other procedural improvements have been made by individual diocesan tribunals. Interrogation by telephone is much quicker and less cumbersome than appointing a priest interrogator who really knows nothing about the case to obtain the testimony of witnesses. By telephone the people directly involved in the case can acquire the testimony of needed witnesses. Tape recorders can also be used efficiently in transcribing testimony rather than the more time consuming typing of all the testimony. The Diocese of Brooklyn has developed a one-day oral trial which is a vast improvement over past procedures.[11] Circuit courts, regional courts and frontier courts have all been used in various dioceses of the United States.[12]

---

9 The August 1973 *Newsletter* of the Canon Law Society of America cites the rescript dated June 20, 1973, from Cardinal Villot containing this information.

10 Lawrence G. Wrenn, "Marriage—Indissoluble or Fragile?" in *Divorce and Remarriage in the Catholic Church,* ed. Lawrence G. Wrenn (New York: Newman Press, 1973), p. 144.

11 Gerald J. Arella, "Approaches to Tribunal Practice—A Resumé of Ten Years Experience," *The Jurist,* XXXI (1971), 489-505.

12 Dennis J. Burns and Bertram Griffin, "Tribunal Procedure," *Proceedings of the Thirty-Fourth Annual Convention of the Canon Law Society of America* (1972), pp. 76-82.

Important Substantive Developments

Although one should not expect many substantive innovations in the jurisprudence of local tribunals, there have been some trends and developments of great import in American jurisprudence. American canonical practice has spurred the development and extension of the papal power to dissolve nonsacramental marriages which was championed in theory by Pietro Gasparri, the architect of the present Code of Canon Law. In 1924 a series of decisions affirmed the papal power to dissolve a marriage between a baptized person and a nonbaptized person who then converted to the Catholic faith and entered marriage as a Catholic. The so-called Helena case was the first of these cases to be published and had a great influence in the United States because of the frequency with which such cases occur in this country. This was a case of dissolution of a marriage where the Church had not given a dispensation. The Monterey-Fresno case of 1947 was the first reported instance in which a marriage between a Catholic and an unbeliever entered with a dispensation from the Church was dissolved. The Monterey-Fresno case of 1955 marked another step forward because here the marriage between a Catholic and an unbeliever was dissolved on the petition of the Catholic party who had obtained a dispensation to marry the unbeliever in the first place. In the late 1950's the papal power was extended even further. Marriages were dissolved between two unbelievers so that one of the parties remaining an unbeliever could be married to a Catholic.[13] Note the late and rapid development of this most significant theory and practice.

---

13 Rene Leguerrier, "Recent Practice of the Holy See in Regard to the Dissolution of Marriages Between Non-Baptized Persons Without Conversion," *The Jurist* XXV (1965), 453-465; John T. Noonan, Jr., "Papal Dissolution of Marriage: Fiction and Function," *Proceedings of the Thirty First Annual Convention of the C.L.S.A.* (1969), pp. 89-95.

This so-called privilege of the faith was used more extensively in the United States than elsewhere, for here there was the combination of a large number of people who were both divorced and not baptized. Some dioceses did not accept such cases because of the danger of scandal, but gradually more and more dioceses took advantage of this solution. However, the privilege or favor of the faith raises not only practical problems of scandal but also theoretical problems. The Catholic Church often talked about the natural law indissolubility of marriage, but now it recognized that most of the marriages in the world (only a minority would be between two baptized persons) could be dissolved by the Pope.[14]

In late August of 1970, the American bishops were informed that at an earlier date and without previous notice the practice in privilege of the faith cases had been changed. Dissolutions would be granted only if there was a conversion. There would be no dissolutions without conversion. This sudden change caught American dioceses with over five thousand petitions in process. Both the American bishops and the Canon Law Society have asked for the older practice to be restored, but to date the restrictive practice of requiring a conversion is still in effect.[15]

Perhaps the most innovative substantive contribution of American tribunal practice involves the good faith solution adopted by the Archdiocese of Chicago in the late 1940's. The good faith solution arose in the context of prospective converts, especially blacks, who wanted to become Catholics but had a previous marriage bond. Often it was impossible to assemble the necessary data and testimony for a formal

---

14 John T. Noonan, Jr., *Power to Dissolve: Lawyers and Marriages in the Courts of the Roman Curia* (Cambridge, Mass.: Belknap Press of Harvard University Press, 1972) , pp. 368-392.

15 *Proceedings of the Thirty-Second Annual Convention of the Canon Law Society of America* (1970) , p. 108.

trial. A list of procedures was drawn up to handle such cases in the 1950's. If there is an insoluble doubt about the validity of the first marriage, the promoter of justice determines the present marriage is not to be attacked and gives a document to this effect to the party involved. The parties are left in good faith about their present marriage. If the first marriage is certainly valid, then the parties should separate or a brother-sister arrangement can be proposed, but only in the rarest of cases may the good faith solution be applied here. Good faith is ordinarily had if both parties were not Catholic at the time they entered a second marriage and thought in the eyes of God that this was a good marriage. Insoluble doubt is often present because of the defective intention against the permanency of marriage based on the fact that most of these people believed they could divorce and re-marry if their first marriage did not work out.[16]

This interesting pastoral solution also raised some questions. Some argue that the solution was primarily a moral solution and did not need to be handled juridically by the tribunal but could be employed by the individual priest. Could this good faith solution be applied to Catholics? Could these procedures be a paradigm for handling all marriage cases and abolish more formal tribunal procedures?[17] In many ways the Chicago good faith solution was a pioneering approach which helped set the stage for many other possibilities.

Most of the formal tribunal cases in many dioceses today involve the lack of psychic maturity on the part of the couple so that they are unable to posit the necessary consent required for marriage or unable at the time of the marriage to fulfill the essential obligations of marriage. This question was

[16] Raymond G. Carey, "The Good Faith Solution," *The Jurist*, XXIX (1969) 428-435.
[17] *Ibid.*, pp. 436-438.

first discussed in the American literature by John R. Keating in various articles on the psychopathic and sociopathic personalities.[8] It has been developed in the literature and in the courts so that it now appears to be the approach taken in the majority of formal cases in the jurisprudence of American tribunals. This approach has been described in different ways (the incapacity to marry, the sociopathic personality, essential incompatibility, lack of due discretion), but the basic reality is the same.[19]

Recent tribunal jurisprudence develops the argument along the lines that there is a relative incapacity to fulfill one or more of the essential elements of marriage. Note well that the incapacity is relative so that the individuals involved might well be able to enter a valid marriage with a different person. The essential elements in marriage in the present canonical understanding are permanency, fidelity, and the object of the contract—the *ius in corpus alterius*. Even in this admittedly narrow view of the object of the marriage contract (the common life is restricted to the ability to engage in marital intercourse in a human fashion), one can

---

18 John R. Keating, "The Caput Nullitatis in Marriage Cases," *The Jurist*, XXII (1962), 391-411; Keating, "Marriage of the Psychopathic Personality," *Chicago Studies*, III (1964), 19-38; Keating, "Sociopathic Personality," *The Jurist*, XXV (1965), 429-438; Keating, "The Legal Test of Marital Insanity," *Studia Canonica*, I (1967), 21-36. These articles grew out of his doctoral dissertation—John R. Keating, *The Bearing of Mental Impairment on the Validity of Marriage—An Analysis of Rotal Jurisprudence* (Rome: Gregorian University Press, 1964).

19 Representative articles include the following: John T. Finnegan, "Current Jurisprudence Concerning the Psychopathic Personality," *The Jurist*, XXVII (1967), 440-453; Finnegan, "The Capacity to Marry," *The Jurist*, XXIX (1969), 141-156; Stephen J. Kelleher, "Relative and Absolute Incapacity to Marry," *The Jurist*, XXIX (1969), 326-331; Stanley J. Ogorzaly, "The Law in Psychological Inability Cases," *The Jurist*, XXX (1970), 103-106; Marion Justin Reinhardt and Gerard J. Arella, "Essential Incompatibility as Grounds for Nullity of Marriage," *The Catholic Lawyer*, XVI (1970), 173-187. For the actual practice in some courts, see *Matrimonial Jurisprudence, United States*, 1968-1971, pp. 16-26; 110-180.

have canonically acceptable proof that the partners were not able to oblige themselves to what they verbally promised to do. In many cases of marital breakdown, this relative incapacity is present. Psychiatric and psychological proof can readily be obtained. It is even easier to prove if one wants to broaden the essentials of the marital contract so that the object is no longer limited to the right to marital intercourse in a human way but now includes what an older theology called the secondary ends of marriage—marital affection, the love union of husband and wife and mutual help. Recent Rotal decisions indicate that this is now an acceptable approach but even sticking with the older jurisprudence the essential incompatibility existing between these two persons can be commonly accepted as causing a marriage to be null and void.[20]

History

In 1972 John T. Noonan, Jr., published his *Power to Dissolve: Lawyers and Marriages in the Courts of the Roman Curia*.[21] William W. Bassett of the School of Canon Law of Catholic University of America who has written extensively on questions of marriage has lavishly praised Noonan's work as the finest study of the Canon Law on marriage since Es-

---

[20] The description in the text follows closely that provided by Reinhardt and Arella, *The Catholic Lawyer*, XVI (1970), 173-187. Reinhardt, Arella, and their associates have established in the tribunal of Brooklyn what is generally regarded as the most efficient and effective tribunal in the United States. Reinhardt, however, in a later article indicates that often in practice the incapacity was found to be absolute and not just relative. See Marion J. Reinhardt, "The Incidence of Mental Disorder," *Studia Canonica*, VI (1972), 209-225. For a discussion of recent Rota jurisprudence maintaining the need of the capacity for an interpersonal relationship of love between the spouses, see Cyril Murtagh, "The Judicial Importance of *Amor Conjugalis*," to be published in *The Jurist* XXXIII (1973).

[21] John T. Noonan, Jr., *Power to Dissolve: Lawyers and Marriages in the Courts of the Roman Curia* (Cambridge: Belknap Press of Harvard University Press, 1972).

mein and Joyce.[22] John J. Reed, S.J. of Woodstock College in a very negative review claims that Noonan's study is neither serious, objective nor competent.[23]

Noonan's long, well documented volume unfolds in seven chapters. Each of the first six chapters takes one particular case heard by the Roman Tribunals from the seventeenth to the twentieth century that illustrates a particular question or questions—coercion and free consent, virginal marriage, conditional contract, relationship of consummation to indissolubility, mental incapacity, intention to exclude children, intention against indissolubility, invalid dispensation of a diriment impediment. Noonan traces each particular case in its historical setting, cites the pertinent legislative enactments, theological and canonical opinions, jurisprudential precedents and unfolds not only the complete legal aspects of the case but also describes all the parties involved and enters into the various personal aspects of the case. A scholarly approach, exact historical research and pleasing literary style contribute to give engrossing illustrations of the way in which the Church court system functions and at the same time to indicate the historical development of important theological and canonical teachings and practices.

In my judgment Noonan's work is most praiseworthy and a very valuable contribution to our knowledge and appreciation of the workings of Church courts in the area of marriage. I do have some comparatively minor criticisms. His scope encompasses so much that one occasionally wonders, especially in his treatment of the persons involved in the system, if he too neatly explains some things just in reference to this one particular case when there had to be so many more complex influences present in their lives and in their decision-making. The title is misleading, since only one section deals

---

22 William W. Bassett, book review in *The Jurist,* XXXII (1972) , 420.

23 John J. Reed, book review in *Theological Studies,* XXXIV (1973) , 173.

with the papal power to dissolve marriages. If he insisted on keeping the present title, Noonan should have developed a comment briefly made in the book and asserted by him elsewhere; namely, ". . . the capital point that psychologically and sociologically the nullification of a marriage and its dispensation are the same; hence the history of indissolubility is tied to the history of the process of nullity."[24]

The book closes with eleven pages that serve as a summary but also can be read as Noonan's own judgment (negative) on the adequacy of the court system to serve the intended purpose of strengthening the indissolubility of Christian marriage and giving justice to the parties involved. Perhaps it would have been better to eliminate this section and to publish his own personal conclusions at much greater length in a separate article. The section as it stands is too brief to be adequate and can readily detract from the objective tone of the entire work. Occasionally Noonan employs terminology in this conclusion which is somewhat inaccurate or perjorative in its implications; for example, he uses "policy" to denote the fact that indissolubility has to be weighed with other values or he speaks about a marriage being invalid at the "option" of the courts.[25] One cannot criticize Noonan for any omissions, but it would be helpful if someone of Noonan's superior ability could indicate how the court system grew up in terms of the relationship of the Church to the social and civic life of various countries especially Italy.

Historical scholarship serves a great purpose in showing the temporal, historical and cultural influences in the development of any teaching. Especially in some Catholic circles there is always the tendency to view the teaching and practice of the Church on matters of marriage as coming

---

[24] John T. Noonan, Jr., book review of *Le Lien Matrimonial* in *The Jurist*, XXXII (1972) , 426.
[25] Noonan, *Power to Dissolve*, pp. 393, 403.

from the hand of God and failing to see the truly human side. As Noonan notes there was great flexibility and room for many different interpretations in determining the teaching and practice on Christian marriage. Many of the decisions that were made were the result of various types of balancing values or even of compromise. Noonan's masterful analysis shows why some interpretations were made instead of others. Some of the cases decided one way at a particular time in history would have been decided exactly the opposite at a different time. A juridical system seems unable to preserve and protect the values of Christian marriage.[26]

One of the most pervasive features of the court system was the length of time required for decisions to be finally rendered. These long delays certainly involved an injustice for the parties concerned, although Noonan might have phrased his perception of this fact a little more judiciously than when he states: "Accepting delays as a method, the managers of the system passively acknowledged that the indissolubility of marriage could be subordinated to other values. Papal practice itself impaired the symbol of indissolubility."[27] In my judgment Noonan's book furnishes strong evidence that the legal provisions and court system enshrined in the practice of the Church really failed to achieve its twofold purpose of safeguarding the values of Christian marriage and at the same time giving justice to Christian people.

---

[26] Noonan himself makes this point on the basis of the fact that the system did nothing to preserve the marriages of the litigants as effective symbols of the love union of Christ and his Church (pp. 398-399). In a sense this is unfair because one cannot expect the court system to do this when it is dealing with breakdowns in marriages. Also there is the theoretical problem of the exact meaning of that marital love union which could be interpreted in terms of fidelity even if there is no return or mutuality. Noonan's book does show clearly, in my judgment, that the juridical process reduced the reality of marriage to a juridically manageable concept and thus distorted the true meaning of Christian marriage.

[27] Noonan, *Power to Dissolve*, p. 396.

Criticism of Present Legal Provisions and Tribunals

The first type of criticism concerns changes in the existing Church teaching and law on marriage which could be brought about without modifying the basic presupposition that consummated sacramental marriage is always indissoluble. One suggested change involves the teaching of canon 1014 that the existence of the bond enjoys the favor of the law so that the petitioner must prove his freedom to marry since the benefit of the doubt goes to the existence of the bond.[28] However, the newly adopted procedural norms in the United States by allowing for a moral certitude based on a preponderance of evidence seem to have already changed somewhat the original presupposition of canon 1014.

Many commentators today admit the inadequacy of the canonical understanding of marriage as a contract. William Bassett in an excellent review article calls the canonical definition of marriage radically imperfect, for it is not a definition of marriage at all but rather the agreement of two persons to enter the state of life or the lived relationship of marriage. Marriage cannot be reduced merely to a contract but must be seen as a living relationship of love in the service of life.[29]

---

[28] James R. Hertel, "Save the Bond? or Save the Person?" *America*, CXVIII (Feb. 17, 1968), 217-220. Hertel has also published for a more general audience a small, helpful book which also incorporates this and other suggestions for change in the Church's practice in marriage courts while still retaining courts and the present teaching of the Church. James R. Hertel, *When Marriage Fails* (New York: Paulist Press, 1969). For another discussion of needed reforms, see Bernard Häring, "A Theological Appraisal of Marriage Tribunals," in *Divorce and Remarriage in the Catholic Church*, pp. 18-26.

[29] Bassett, *The American Ecclesiastical Review*, CLXII (1970), 92-94. Bassett also mentions other needed revisions. Also William W. Bassett, "The Marriage of Christians—Valid Contract, Valid Sacrament?" in *The Bond of Marriage*, ed. William W. Bassett (Notre Dame, Indiana: University of Notre

Restricting marriage just to a contract distorts its true meaning, but such a distortion is even more objectionable when the essential object of the contract is merely the right to marital sexual intercourse. The essential object of marriage must include much more than just this, for it involves the personal union of husband and wife—a relationship which some canonists in the past have referred to as the *affectio maritalis.* If Christian marriage is seen as a covenant rather than a contract and if the object of the covenant is more than just the right to sexual intercourse, there could be drastic changes in our understanding of the validity of some marriages. It could very well be that the couple was unable to oblige themselves to such a loving permanent union because of some type of psychic inability to take upon themselves this relationship. As noted earlier, this approach is being employed in some Church courts to declare the invalidity of such marriages.[30]

Another criticism rejects the identification of sacramentality with the contract. The sacrament of marriage can never be reduced merely to a contract. In addition many object to identifying the existence of sacramentality with the fact that both parties are baptized. True Christian sacramentality demands more than just the baptism of the partners, for there is required some understanding of Christian marriage as symbolizing the total commitment of Jesus to the Church. At the very minimum the mere fact of baptism cannot be identified with sacramentality.[31] From such a perspective

Dame Press, 1968) , pp. 117-179. This book deserves special mention because it contains the papers presented at a symposium on the bond of marriage sponsored by the Canon Law Society of America in October 1967. Various articles from this symposium will be frequently cited in the course of this study.

[30] Murtagh, *The Jurist,* XXXIII (Summer, 1973) . See also Paul F. Palmer, "Christian Marriage: Contract or Covenant?" *Theological Studies,* XXXIII (1972) , 617-665.

[31] Leo M. Croghan, "Is Baptism the Decisive Factor?" *America,* CXVIII (1968) , 222-223; Edward J. Kilmartin, "When Is Marriage a Sacrament?" *Theological Studies,* XXXIV (1973) , 275-286.

it is evident that many marriages do not attain that level which is necessary for sacramentality so that such marriages could then be dissolved.

A final criticism concerns the concept of consummation. The present canonical discipline understands consummation only in terms of physical consummation brought about by an act of sexual intercourse. The aspect of marriage as a love union, however, also calls for some type of consummation.[32] Thus in the context of a broader notion of consummation it should be obvious that there are a good number of marriages which are never truly consummated. Here too there would be the possibility of dissolving these marriages.

All of these suggested modifications would have, from one perspective, three distinct advantages. First, they would not call for a radical change in the present teaching of the Catholic Church on the indissolubility of consummated sacramental marriages. Second, they would be much more in keeping with a more contemporary theological understanding of the reality of marriage. Third, they would provide a much greater flexibility so that a greater number of marriages could be annulled on the basis of such understandings. However, one must also realize that many of these suggested changes would be much more difficult to determine in a juridical way. The present definitions of consummation or sacramentality, for example, are quite readily discernible and verifiable, but the newer understandings do not have the exactitude which is based solely on the objective evidence of either the baptism of the partners or an act of sexual intercourse.

There is also a call for continuing procedural changes. Our Church courts could very well incorporate many of the protections and due process regulations found in the common

---

[32] Dennis Doherty, "Consummation and the Indissolubility of Marriage," in *Absolutes in Moral Theology?* ed. Charles E. Curran (Washington: Corpus Books, 1968), pp. 211-231; Theodore Mackin, "Consummation: Of Contract or of Covenant?" *The Jurist*, XXXII (1972), 213-223; 330-354.

law tradition. A trust system should be much more willing to accept the testimony of the person without requiring that much more additional proof. Also many procedures such as the privilege of the faith cases and the dissolution of a non-consummated marriage are now solved ultimately in Rome, but these cases should be handled on a local level. Such changes would certainly make the operation of tribunals much more effective.

For some the above-mentioned criticisms do not go far enough. A more radical solution is required. The tribunal or court system is no longer adequate for handling marriage cases and should be abolished.

A call for the abolition of the marriage tribunal was first made publicly by Msgr. Stephen J. Kelleher, the Officialis or Presiding Judge of the Marriage Court of the Archdiocese of New York, who had spent most of his priestly ministry in tribunal work. His article, "The Problem of the Intolerable Marriage," published in the September 14, 1968, issue of *America* is an eloquent and moving appeal made by a man whose pastoral experience has brought him to see that the marriage tribunal no longer serves its purpose. Stopgap measures such as more tribunal personnel, more impediments, or a covenant understanding of marriage rather than a contract approach are not sufficient. Marriage courts themselves must go. The personal responsibility of the couple themselves becomes the ultimate factor in determining the freedom to marry, although he also sees the need for some type of local Church commission at times to make a community judgment about a particular case.[33]

This short, courageous article has exerted great influence, but from a theological perspective there are a number of shortcomings. The article does not distinguish adequately

---

[33] Stephen J. Kelleher, "The Problem of the Intolerable Marriage," *America*, CXIX (September 14, 1968) , 178-182.

the three separate but interrelated questions which are in-volved—the Catholic Church's teaching on the indissolubil-ity of consummated sacramental marriages, the pastoral practice of not allowing divorced and remarried Catholics to participate in the Eucharist and the sacramental life of the Church, and the use of marriage courts and tribunals as the vehicle of carrying out the marriage practice of the Church. Kelleher himself in his article does not explicitly call for a change in the Church's teaching on indissolubility, although at times his insistence on personal responsibility in making the decision to remarry seems to imply it.[34] Likewise, the au-thor himself recognizes that he does not solve the tension between insisting on personal responsibility and acknowl-edging the need for some ecclesial overseeing.

In the fall of 1973, Kelleher published a book which de-velops his original thesis in greater detail. Now he readily acknowledges that the Church must change its teaching on indissolubility. The book does not pretend to be primarily a scholarly treatise, but the author competently uses most of the accessible scholarly data to support his thesis.[35]

In my judgment Kelleher presents a convincing argument in general, but I do have some critical observations. From a theoretical viewpoint the most important point made by Kelleher revolves around the need to change the teaching of the Church on the indissolubility of marriage. However, his own personal experience has been in the area of the marriage courts themselves so that he spends much time talking about the inadequacies of these procedures. If one accepted his basic thesis about the need to change the teaching of the Church on the indissolubility of marriage, then there would

[34] The editors of *America* in a later editorial interpret Kelleher as not denying the teaching of the Church against divorce, *America*, CXIX (1968), 428.

[35] Stephen J. Kelleher, *Divorce and Remarriage for Catholics?* (Garden City, N.Y.: Doubleday & Co., 1973).

really be no need to develop at great detail many of the inadequacies of the tribunal system. Again he does not completely solve the tension between the individual responsibility in making such a judgment about remarriage and some overseeing role by the local Church community. It seems that the thrust of his book prevents him from giving enough importance to some of the ecclesial aspects of the question and also from stressing the notion of indissolubility as the radical demand of Jesus and the goal and ideal of every Christian marriage.

Others have also joined in the call to abolish the tribunal. Leo Croghan who also was involved for some time in tribunal work maintains that the tribunal should be abolished because its procedures really do not correspond to the actual demands of the present time. But at this time he upheld the indissolubility of marriage based on the Scriptures.[36] Croghan went on to explain in a short autobiographical article his own sense of continuing disillusion with tribunal work. Like Kelleher, he later argues for the fact that the Church should now change its teaching on indissolubility.[37]

In its 1970 meeting the Canon Law Society of America appointed a subcommittee "to study whether the canonical institution of ecclesiastical tribunals is the proper institution for the determination of the validity of marriages and to propose those changes necessary to ensure an effective pastoral concern of the Church for the sacredness of the institution of marriage, and the rights and obligations of the parties to Christian marriages."[38]

---

36 Leo M. Croghan, "Marriage Law and Real Life," *America*, CXXI (1969) , 352-355.

37 Leo M. Croghan, "Farewell to the Tribunal," *America*, CXXIII (1970) , 227-229.

38 *Proceedings of the Thirty-Second Annual Convention of the C.L.S.A.* (1970) , pp. 111, 112.

Lawrence Wrenn was appointed chairman of the committee and his committee published a book containing articles by the various members.[39] Unfortunately the studies do not all focus on the specific question under discussion. Most illuminating is the concluding essay written by Wrenn himself, who is the Officialis of the Archdiocese of Hartford and has written frequently on the subject of matrimonial jurisprudence. Wrenn urges that the tribunal system is both meaningless and disfunctional in the American church. He also argues that the Church should change its teaching on indissolubility so that marriage is no longer seen as indissoluble but as fragile. Wrenn maintains that the judgment about remarriage and participation in the Eucharist and the sacramental life of the Church should be made on the local parish level. The judgment should take account of the fact that the first marriage has irremediably broken down and there are signs of repentance insofar as possible in the life of the individual concerned.[40]

Others continue to urge that the Church must always use marriage courts because only in this way can the rights of individuals be adequately safeguarded. Naturally there are many changes that should be brought about in the court system, but it would be somewhat anomalous in this day when reform in the Church centers on protecting the rights of individuals that some people want to do away with the court system in marriages.[41]

I agree with the judgment that matrimonial tribunals are not an adequate institution to achieve the purpose of the

---

[39] *Divorce and Remarriage in the Catholic Church*, ed. Lawrence G. Wrenn (New York: Newman Press, 1973) .

[40] Lawrence G. Wrenn, "Marriage—Indissoluble or Fragile?" in *Divorce and Remarriage in the Catholic Church*, pp. 134-149.

[41] Gerald J. Arella, "Case for the Marriage Court," *America*, CXXVII (1972) 316-320; Marion J. Reinhardt, "Updating the Marriage Tribunal," *America*, CXIX (1968) , 429-433.

Church in safeguarding Christian marriage and even in upholding the indissolubility of marriage as well as in providing a means of justice for Catholics. My personal conviction that the Church should change its teaching and practice on the indissolubility of Christian marriage obviously influences such a negative judgment on the tribunal system, but the arguments against the existence of the tribunal system still have validity apart from the contention that the Church should change its basic teaching.

The Catholic Church has not always had a tribunal or court system to deal with marriage cases. Such a system has been an historical development and must be judged by its effectiveness in pursuing the goal of upholding the sacredness and meaning of Christian marriage, even indissolubility, and for providing justice for the Catholic faithful. The judgment on the performance of the marriage tribunals in the past must be negative. Noonan's historical study shows the injustices involved both because of the fact that many people could not take advantage of the tribunal system and the long delays for those who did become involved in the system. The statistics for the United States in 1968 show only too well the grave injustice that was being done to many Catholic people because there was no possibility for them to go to the Church courts for justice.

Despite the improvements that have been made in the procedural norms, and even if these new procedures were to be continued, the tribunal system will still become even more inadequate in terms of the amount of work which is to be done. Lawrence Wrenn estimates there were 120,000 civil divorces granted in 1971 from presumably valid marriages of Catholics. If there is truly a lack of due discretion or essential incompatibility in many of these cases which would have rendered such marriages invalid to begin with, then there should be a huge number of Catholics who would be

able to present their cases before the tribunals. Even the best
marriage tribunals today are handling a comparatively insignificant number of cases in terms of the many cases that
can be presented by Catholics seeking justice.[42] Ironically,
as tribunal officials realize the need to provide for many more
cases, the inadequacy of the system becomes more apparent.

The present procedures do not even seem to safeguard the
indissolubility of marriage which they were intended to safeguard. In Pauline privilege cases and in privilege of the faith
cases natural bonds of marriage are dissolved with little or
no consideration given to the whole question of the indissolubility that to some extent is present in such bonds. If the
Catholic party in a marriage did not marry in the acceptable
canonical form, then the marriage is declared null even
though there might be true moral obligations which arose
from such a promise having been given. In reality the sincere
canonist tries to find some point of law which would help
to prove the invalidity of a previously existing bond or give
some grounds for the dissolution of such a bond without any
real consideration of the indissolubility which might be inherent in that particular bond.

The existential reality is that some marriages break down
and then the individuals involved try to see if in the eyes of
the Church they can enter a second marriage. The present
process really has nothing to do with the reality of the breakdown of the first marriage, but is rather concerned with possible grounds on which the first marriage can be annulled or

---

[42] Wrenn gives the generous estimate only 10% of those who have a
right to a Church judgment about the validity of their marriage would have
received such a hearing. Each year the backlog will only grow. *Divorce and
Remarriage in the Catholic Church*, pp. 144, 145. Statistics to be presented
to the 1973 meeting of the Canon Law Society of America by a committee
headed by Father Dennis Burns of Boston point out the continuing inadequacies of the tribunal system in the United States.

can be dissolved. The tribunal official with a sincere desire to help people will try to find some legal reason to buttress his case, but in reality this often appears even to the people themselves to be a loophole which has no relationship to the existential reality. Such a process then cannot and does not engender a feeling of confidence or respect for the sacredness of marriage or even the indissolubility of marriage on the part of those it is designed to serve.

Certain historical circumstances which are definitely not present today influenced the creation of the tribunal system as we know it. In those different historical circumstances the Church took upon itself many of the social and civic responsibilities for the regulation of marriage. Society no longer looks to the Church for doing this so that many reasons explaining the growth and development of the present system are no longer existing today. The Church does not need a tribunal or court system to regulate the teaching and practice of marriage even if it continues to maintain the indissolubility of consummated sacramental marriages.

There are also two very significant practical reasons for asserting that the tribunal system will cease to function in the future. First, many of those who are calling for the abolition of the tribunal are often people who have been deeply involved in tribunal work and dedicated their lives to make the system work. Through their own personal experience they have come to the conclusion of the ineffectiveness of this approach. In the future it appears that many priests will not want to dedicate themselves to this work so that it will be very difficult to find people willing to man the staffs of tribunals.

There is even a more cogent indication signaling the future demise of the tribunal system. Now many in practice are already circumventing the tribunal through internal forum or pastoral solutions which will be described below. These internal forum solutions are multiplying with great rapidity and take advantage of the theological thinking on marriage as covenant as well a better understanding of consummation and sacramentality. Tribunal reform, even if it were a good thing, will not take place soon enough to stem the growth of internal forum solutions. More and more in the immediate future the tribunal will be bypassed since its procedures are inadequate even given the fact of the Church's teaching on the indissolubility of marriage.

As historical institutions marriage tribunals must be judged by their practical effectiveness in safeguarding the values of Christian marriage including indissolubility and by providing justice for those who have recourse to them. For all the above reasons a negative judgment has been formulated about the tribunal today. However, there is a deeper and less historically conditioned aspect to this question. Can the marriage tribunal set up on the model of justice courts in political society ever adequately serve the needs of the Church? Even accepting the identification or great similarity between the Church and other civil societies there is difficulty with obtaining justice in marriage cases within the framework of the tribunal system. Legal justice, even in the Thomistic understanding, remains inherently imperfect. *Epikeia* or equity is the crown of justice. The equity or *epikeia* aspect of justice cannot be codified because by its very nature it depends upon the unique circumstances of the case. Thus only a rough and imperfect justice, not true justice, can be achieved through these means.[43]

There are not only similarities between the Church and a human political society, but there are also some differences. The external forum of the Church is not just the same as the juridical forum of any other society but rather must manifest and be a sign of the reality of the Church as the community

---

[43] Vernon J. Bourke, "Marital Fidelity and Philosophy," in *Divorce and Remarriage in the Catholic Church*, pp. 59-61.

of those gathered together in the bonds of love around the risen Lord.[44] The teaching and practice of the Church on marriage must manifest both in its procedural and substantive aspects the reality of the Church and of Christian marriage. Procedurally the current tribunal system really mirrors a society based more on fear and distrust than a society based on trust and love. Our matrimonial tribunals are not truly sacramental signs of what should be the real life of the Church. Substantively in the light of a juridical approach the reality of Christian marriage has been reduced to a permanent and indissoluble contract giving rights to sexual intercourse. The true significance and meaning of Christian marriage have been greatly distorted by the necessity of trying to understand the sacrament of marriage primarily in juridical terms.

The juridical system and the procedures used by the Catholic Church for the processing of marriage cases in history, in actual practice in the United States and in theory are inadequate for achieving their stated purposes even granting the present teaching of the Church on the indissolubility of consummated sacramental marriages. There is an ecclesial aspect to the questions involving marriage and marital breakdowns, but I believe that a pastoral approach rather than a strictly juridical approach is a better instrumentality. A pastoral approach could more speedily and efficaciously consider the number of cases which must be handled, and at the same time pastoral procedures seem to reflect better the reality of the Church as well as its concern in the question of marriage. A pastoral approach would also avoid some of the distortions of Christian marriage which have obviously arisen because of the overriding juridical concerns. However, this chapter will not now develop in great detail what such procedures should be. This entire first part has been proposed

---

44 Peter Huizing, "Law, Conscience and Marriage," *The Jurist*, XXX (1970), especially, 17-20.

on the presupposition that sacramental consummated marriages are indissoluble. Part Three will develop my reasons advocating a change in the Church's teaching on indissolubility. The conclusion will then briefly sketch the appropriate pastoral role of the Church in the light of the presupposition that indissolubility is a goal but not an absolute norm for Christian marriage.

PART II: INTERNAL FORUM OR PASTORAL SOLUTIONS

In the last few years a new phenomenon has appeared—a pastoral solution to marriage cases in which people involved in what is canonically an invalid marriage have been reconciled with the Church in the form of full participation in the Eucharist and in the sacramental life of the Church. These are sometimes referred to as good faith solutions or internal forum solutions, but there are important nuances and differences in the terms employed.

The good faith solution first appeared in the United States through the practice of the Archdiocese of Chicago. Converts to the Catholic faith who were in good faith about their present marriage were allowed to remain in their present marriage even though there had been a previous marriage. In April 1966, *The Homiletic and Pastoral Review* published an influential and pioneering article by B. Peters, T. Beemer and C. van der Poel—"Cohabitation in 'Marital State of Mind'." The main concern was participation in the sacrament of the Eucharist for Catholics involved in an invalid second marriage. The authors first showed that such a union was not the reality called concubinage because the relationship was stable, permanent and based on true marital affection.[45]

---

[45] B. Peters, T. Beemer and C. van der Poel, "Co-Habitation in 'Marital State of Mind'," *The Homiletic and Pastoral Review*, LXVI (1965-66), 566-568.

Unfortunately the article does not clearly differentiate two different types of cases—those whose first marriage is really not valid and those who did have a true or valid first marriage. Also the realities of good faith and God's forgiveness are more important for the discussion than the marital state of mind.

The various reasons proposed for excluding such people from receiving the sacraments are reviewed by these authors and judged not to be pertinent in every case. First, a personal sinful condition is not always present. Even if there were guilt in the beginning, this particular couple often cannot and should not separate because they have contracted obligations to one another and to their families. Their good faith must be shown in terms of their willingness to fulfill all their obligations and also to live in general a good Christian life. Second, an invalid marriage has affected the ecclesial standing of the partners. The article does not discuss this question under the aspect of canonical excommunication but rather insists that in all our lives there will always be some scars of sin and no one is without wrinkle or spot. Thus the fact of some sinfulness should not necessarily exclude a person from ecclesial communion. Third, scandal would be taken if such people received the sacraments. The authors argue that scandal should not be a great obstacle if the whole matter is properly explained to the Christian people.[46]

Despite some vagueness and lack of distinctions, the article has rightly had a great effect on theory and practice in the United States. The fact that *The Homiletic and Pastoral Review* later notified its readers that the Congregation for the Doctrine of the Faith disapproved of these opinions and issued a formal *monitum* does not seem to have had much practical effect.[47] Some theologians reacted negatively,[48]

---

46 *Ibid.*, pp. 570-577.
47 *The Homiletic and Pastoral Review*, LXVIII (1966-67), 390.
48 E.g., Richard A. McCormick, "Notes on Moral Theology," *Theological*

but others basically accepted the approach proposed here. In the process of discussion the two different categories were clearly distinguished: 1) those whose first marriage was invalid from the beginning but the invalidity could not be proved canonically; 2) those whose first marriage was true and valid but it is now irremediably broken.

John T. Catoir in 1967 expressly considered the first case and argued that it was a matter of equity although at times there might be a problem with scandal. Thus if the marriage could not be canonically proven invalid, still the reality of invalidity was present and such persons should be allowed access to the sacramental life of the Church.[49]

In the same vein I argued that in the light of the inherent inadequacy of law in general and of the particular inadequacies of present Church discipline (e.g. the presumption in favor of the bond, impoverished notion of consummation, overemphasis on the physical aspects of marriage and consummation) in many cases of marital breakdown there would be no true marriage from the beginning even though this could not be proven in the external forum. In these cases the couple could in good conscience enter into the Eucharistic life of the Church. Even in cases where there was a true marriage at the beginning my reasoning briefly pointed out that such persons did not always have the sinful condition or ecclesial unworthiness that would exclude them from the Eucharist.[50]

In October 1968, the Canon Law Society set up a committee to investigate the internal forum solutions for deserving persons involved in canonically insoluble marriage cases. The report of the committee made by Ladislas Örsy as well

Studies, XXVII (1966), 622-624. Note that McCormick has since changed his opinion as will be pointed out later in the text.

[49] John T. Catoir, "The Church and Second Marriage," *Commonweal*, LXXXVI (1967), 113-117.

[50] Charles E. Curran, *A New Look at Christian Morality* (Notre Dame: Fides Publishers, 1968), pp. 226-231.

as articles on the subject commissioned by the committee appeared in *The Jurist,* XXX (1970), 1-74.[51]

Anthony Kosnik in his article treats just the case in which there is sufficient evidence to provide moral certitude that from the beginning something essential was lacking for a true Christian marriage. In such cases he argues that pastorally such people can fully participate in the sacramental life of the Church although consideration must be given to the possible fact of scandal.[52] Bernard Häring, who had been advocating his approach in lectures throughout the United States in the late 1960's, urges internal forum solutions in both cases, but perhaps he does not distinguish carefully enough three different arguments proposed in the course of his paper—the fact that some marriages may existentially die so that marriage is not indissoluble; the good faith of the spouses about their present marriage; and the mercy and the forgiveness of God which will always be present for the sinner.[53]

Leo Farley and Warren Reich in their combined article consider both types of cases, but rightly give more attention to the harder case; that is, where there was a true marriage from the beginning, but it has now broken down. These authors view a second marriage under the sign of forgiveness. God's mercy and forgiveness are always offered to the sinner. If the second marriage is stable and the partners are showing signs of the Christian life in their marriage and in their daily life, then such persons should not necessarily be excluded from the Eucharist for reasons of personal sinful-

---

51 Ladislas Örsy, "Intolerable Marriage Situations: Conflict Between External and Internal Forum," *The Jurist,* XXX (1970), 1-14.

52 Anthony Kosnik, "The Pastoral Care of Those Involved in Canonically Invalid Marriages," *The Jurist,* XXX (1970), 31-44.

53 Bernard Häring, "Internal Forum Solutions to Insoluble Marriage Cases," *The Jurist,* XXX (1970), 21-30.

ness and unworthiness. Likewise there often is no ecclesiastical unworthiness present. The appendix to their article rightly indicates that very often there is no excommunication contracted by the parties. The Church as a sign of forgiveness should also manifest mercy and forgiveness to truly repentant spouses in a second marriage.[54]

Although I disagree with some more peripheral aspects of their article (e.g. the unnecessarily long discussion of the marital disposition of the couple), I believe Farley and Reich have made a real advance by concentrating on the harder case of a previously existing true marriage. Likewise they have advanced the argumentation by prescinding from their own opinion that the Church should change its teaching on indissolubility. They appeal to the mercy and forgiveness of God to allow full participation in the Eucharistic life of the Church to those involved in a second marriage even if the previous marriage was true and valid.

Richard A. McCormick, in one of his admirable yearly summaries of periodical literature in moral theology which have exerted such great influence in the United States over the past few years, summarizes these and other approaches to the pastoral solution of canonically insoluble marriage cases. McCormick distinguishes the good faith solution from what one author calls the human frailty solution. He has difficulties with the solution proposed by Farley-Reich and others. McCormick prefers to use the good faith solution but realizes that this solution does not apply to cases in which the couple acknowledges there was a previously true marriage. He thus limits the pastoral solution just to those cases in which there was no true marriage from the beginning, al-

---

[54] Leo C. Farley and Warren T. Reich, "Toward 'An Immediate Internal Forum Solution' for Deserving Couples in Canonically Insoluble Marriage Cases," *The Jurist*, XXX (1970), 45-74.

though rightly commenting that many cases would be included under this category.[55]

McCormick fears that the second solution as proposed by Farley-Reich and others would have to confront the traditional teaching on the indissolubility of consummated, sacramental marriages which apparently he is unwilling to do at this time.[56] I disagree. A pastoral solution to the case of a second marriage where there was a previously valid first marriage based on the sign of God's forgiveness does not necessarily entail a denial of the teaching of the Church on the indissolubility of consummated, sacramental marriages. It is based on God's forgiveness and can presuppose the wrong in the breakdown of the first marriage and even in entering a second marriage. Likewise, it recognizes that the argument cannot be based only on the good faith of the parties because such good faith about no previous marriage bond might not always be present. For the sake of discussion I am prescinding from my conviction that a Catholic can act on the presupposition that indissolubility is not an absolute norm.

The committee of the Canon Law Society of America considering the internal forum question recognized the need to distinguish carefully both cases. In the case of those who believe in good faith their first marriage was invalid, the following solutions are offered: within the existing legislation perhaps the courts could accept as evidence the oath of the parties about the status of their first marriage, thus providing a way to bridge the gap between the internal and external forums; outside the present legal format, there could be a committee in every diocese operating in a pastoral and not a juridical way helping the parties form their conscience; on

---

55 Richard A. McCormick, "Notes on Moral Theology," *Theological Studies*, XXXII (1971) , 113-122.

56 *Ibid.*, pp. 120-121.

a sacramental level the priest should advise the parties to follow their well formed consciences and participate in the sacraments. In the case of those who did have a previous, true marriage, the committee recognized the matter was not mature for any legal conclusion, but they agreed on one recommendation: if a priest by way of counsel in the forum of conscience permits a person living in such a union to have access to the Eucharist, no legal action should be taken against such a priest.[57]

In June 1971, the Catholic Theological Society of America appointed a committee to study the question of the pastoral ministry to divorced and remarried Catholics. This report was published as the work of the committee (no action was taken by the Society as a whole on the report) in the *Proceedings* of the 1972 Convention. If a couple judges in their conscience on the basis of objective criteria that the previous marriage was not a true marriage, the community, although it will not officially celebrate the second marriage, should respect the conscience of those who have entered such marriages. Note that the committee does not touch the case in which there was a true marriage existing from the beginning. On the question of those already involved in a second marriage the committee report tends to put together both the cases in which there was not a true marriage from the beginning and those in which there was. The reason justifying the possibility of sacramental reception in the second case stems from the obligation which the parties have contracted with one another and with their family.[58]

This document and other articles raise the question not only about the reception of the sacraments for those already

---

[57] Örsy, *The Jurist*, XXX (1970), 12-13.
[58] "The Problem of Second Marriages: An Interim Pastoral Statement by the Study Committee Commissioned by the Board of Directors of the Catholic Theological Society of America," *Proceedings of the Catholic Theological Society of America*, XXVII (1972), 233-240.

involved in second marriages but also the question of the conscience formation of those who now wish to enter a second marriage. In this context there also arises a question about the role of the priest in the second marriage that Catholics want to celebrate. Again I believe it is necessary to distinguish the two types of cases. When there was no true marriage to begin with, there is certainly no difficulty with a couple deciding to marry and with a priest advising a couple to marry and fully participate in the sacramental life of the Church.

What about the priest celebrating such a marriage? John Catoir reasons that in this situation it lies beyond his competency and jurisdiction both in the ecclesial forum and in the civil forum for the priest to celebrate an official Catholic marriage. He advises that there be a civil marriage but that the priest can later give a private blessing.[59] Coyle and Bonner even speak of a private ceremony with a Eucharist and exchange of vows but caution that the couple should usually have a civil marriage.[60] In practice I follow the approach described by Coyle and Bonner. I do not think that now I can officially witness such a marriage in the eyes of the Church, for such a witness would say in the external forum that the Church recognizes such a marriage as valid, but in reality this is not the position of the Church at the present time. After explaining this to the couple I propose a somewhat small but not totally private celebration involving a Eucharist and an exchange of vows which in conscience we are convinced is a true marriage in the eyes of God.

---

[59] John T. Catoir, "When the Courts Don't Work," *America*, CXXV (1971), 254-257. Catoir, who was the presiding judge of the tribunal of the diocese of Paterson, New Jersey, sees the advantages of such an approach existing side by side with the tribunal system.

[60] Alcuin Coyle and Dismas Bonner, *The Church Under Tension: Practical Life and Law in the Changing Church* (New York: Catholic Book Publishing Co., 1972), p. 91.

In the second case in which there was a true previous marriage, there is no difficulty in proving that Catholics can at times enter new marriages and that priests can so advise if one accepts, as I do, that the Church should change its teaching on indissolubility and see it as a goal or ideal which is not always able to be attained. In practice I also have a small Eucharistic celebration and an exchange of vows after a civil ceremony in this case.

Even prescinding from that more radical position, it still might be possible to prove that Catholics can in good conscience enter such a second marriage. Here by presupposition the couple cannot be in good faith about the marriage they are contemplating because they acknowledge there exists a true previous marriage. Those who justify sacramental participation for a couple already involved in such a second marriage base their approach on the sign of forgiveness. Such a position often admits the fact that the second marriage was wrong but now the couple have assumed new obligations towards one another and perhaps to a family which they should not break. True acceptance of God's forgiveness means only they do what it is possible for them to do at this time, but they should not now separate. However, one could try to construct an argument for entering such a marriage based on the forgiveness of God. There seems to be some lack of consistency at least in the existential order, although not a total inconsistency, in permitting people already involved in such second marriages to be reconciled with the sacramental life of the Church, but in denying that they can in good conscience enter such a marriage. The forgiveness of God is offered for whatever failures brought about the breakdown and separation of the first marriage. This forgiveness is extended to the recognition that the forgiven but frail person needs a new marriage.

I grant that this argument has its weaknesses, but it appears to be the best argument that can be made for justifying such a second marriage without disagreeing with the Catholic teaching on the indissolubility of consummated sacramental marriages. Coyle and Bonner justify the entrance into such a second marriage on the basis that good faith might be there from the beginning,[61] but by definition in this case there cannot be good faith because the couple honestly recognizes a true previous marriage. It is on this level (i.e., in considering entering into a second marriage and not in considering Eucharistic reconciliation for those already involved) that McCormick could best try to make his point that it cannot be accepted without denying the present teaching of the Church.

In this connection a brief word is necessary on scandal. Scandal can obviously be avoided if the practice of internal forum cases is properly explained to all the Christian people. Yet there remains a very important aspect of pastoral care in this matter which is too often neglected. The Church as such must show a real concern for those people who in the past have lived according to the teaching and external forum practice of the Church. In their own conscience they thought they were being most loyal to the teaching of the Church and generously sacrificed in order to remain faithful. To them we owe great respect and pastoral help so that they can now accept the decision of others when they themselves felt they could not make the same decision and still be loyal Catholics.

The practice of internal forum solutions is now quite well known and frequently employed in the United States. Secular newspapers and Catholic publications have called it to the attention of the general public for the last few years.[62]

---

61 *Ibid.*

62 On December 22, 1970, *The New York Times* devoted a front page story to recent developments in the Catholic Church on divorce and remarriage. One salient paragraph states: "Another extra-judicial development resulting from the apparent inadequacy of the formal system is the growing willingness of priests to marry persons for the second time even though

In fact, as mentioned before, in my estimation this practice is now so well entrenched that it not only exists side by side with the tribunal system but is becoming the primary way in which marriage cases are handled in practice because of the inherent weaknesses and cumbersome procedures of the existing legal system.

While the theory and practice of internal forum or pastoral solutions has been growing, another practice, the expansion of the good faith approach first proposed by the Chicago Archdiocese, has also been creatively employed in some dioceses. The Catholic press referred to the fact that a number of dioceses including Portland, Oregon; Pueblo, Colorado; Mobile, Alabama; Boise, Idaho have used this approach.[63]

In June 1972, Bishop Robert E. Tracy of Baton Rouge, Louisiana, in a pastoral letter indicated the procedures to be employed in good conscience solutions. A good conscience decree is issued by the Chancery Office to the couple involved. The good conscience applies in the following cases: a) where there is every indication a substantative law has been transgressed which would make the first marriage invalid, but this is not provable in a court of law; b) where both parties in a previous marriage were non-Catholics and now one of the parties in a second marriage wishes to be converted and has a good conscience about the present marriage; c) when a Catholic, who may have a transgression of

they have not received an annulment or dissolution of their first marriage. These are normally done rather quietly" (p.42). Also Edward Wakin, "They Remarried in Good Conscience," *U.S. Catholic*, XXXVIII (June 1973), 19-22. I have found in the recent literature about divorce and Catholics two articles which do not accept or do not mention the internal forum solution as a possibility—David T. McAndrew, "Pastoral Ministry to the Invalidly Married," *The Homiletic and Pastoral Review*, LXXIII (1973), 26-30; William J. Nessel, "The Catholic Divorcee—A Pastoral Approach," *The Homiletic and Pastoral Review*, LXXIII (1973), 10-16.

[63] *National Catholic News Service (Domestic)*, Aug. 17, 1972; pp. 17-19.

existing canonical legislation with regard to the first marriage, nevertheless truly believes in his own conscience and seems to be sincere in his judgment that his first marriage was not a true marriage but that his present marriage is.[64] It should be noted that such an approach is truly an external forum approach even though it is not provided for in the existing universal law of the Church.

I applaud the creative pastoral action taken by Bishop Tracy and others, but I have a reservation about this approach. Neither at the present time nor as an ideal solution in the future do I think that this should be a process handled by the Chancery Office or by the tribunal. The ultimate decision is made by the couple themselves with this decision then accepted or ratified by the local ecclesial community in a pastoral way and not by the Chancery Office.

On August 17, 1972, John Cardinal Krol of Philadelphia as President of the National Conference of Catholic Bishops issued an official statement noting that the matter of pastoral care of divorced people is under study by the Holy See which does not want any individual diocese to introduce procedures contrary to the current discipline until the matter has finally been decided for the universal Church. Krol cautioned that the mere fact that the matter is under study does not in any way prove that a change will take place.[65]

On April 11, 1973, the Congregation of the Doctrine of the Faith sent a letter to Bishops in which the Congregation urged all concerned to be diligent in remaining faithful to the teaching of the Church regarding the indissolubility of marriage and to put such teaching into practical effect through the tribunal system. "In regard to admission to the sacraments, the Ordinaries are asked on the one hand to stress observance of current discipline, and on the other

---

64 *Catholic Mind,* LXX (1972) , 5-7.
65 *Ibid.,* pp. 7-8.

hand, to take care that the pastors of souls exercise special care to seek out those who are living in an irregular union by applying to the solution of such cases, in addition to other right means, the Church's approved practice in the internal forum."[66]

Some news accounts from Rome said the proper understanding of approved internal forum solutions applied only to the brother-sister relationship.[67] This interpretation will be very hard to maintain in practice in the light of the conclusions reached by the special committees of both the Canon Law Society of America and the Catholic Theological Society of America. In my judgment the internal forum solutions of both types will continue to grow even though dioceses do not reinstate their good conscience approach with its official decrees given by the Chancery Office.

PART III: THE CATHOLIC CHURCH'S TEACHING ON THE INDISSOLUBILITY OF MARRIAGE

According to Catholic teaching every marriage is intrinsically indissoluble while consummated sacramental marriages are both intrinsically and extrinsically indissoluble. As noted earlier, the marriages which are intrinsically indissoluble may be dissolved by the power which is claimed for the Church and the Pope. In the popular mind the Catholic Church has always been associated with the teaching on the indissolubility of marriage. There has been no recent disagreement within Roman Catholicism on this teaching until the past few years.

The first important development was the publication of Victor J. Pospishil's *Divorce and Remarriage: Toward a New Catholic Teaching* in 1967. Pospishil's work has rightly been

---

[66] *Clergy Newsletter,* Archdiocese of Washington, May 1973.
[67] *National Catholic News Service,* June 19, 1973, pp. 24-25.

criticized, but its publication stands as a landmark—the first serious call for change in the Catholic Church's teaching on divorce. There are many inadequacies in his argument which later commentators have criticized and corrected. The book also illustrates the difficulty of a comprehensive scholarly discussion of the question of divorce because of all the different competencies involved—scriptural, historical, theological and legal. Although a somewhat serious book, it cannot be described as scholarly or as developing original research.[68]

Pospishil's thesis maintains that "the Catholic Church recognizes that she possesses from her divine Founder the unlimited power of the keys, the authority to grant total divorce and to permit the remarriage of divorced Christians."[69] His solution rests on the distinction between intrinsic indissolubility (the parties themselves cannot dissolve the marriage) and extrinsic dissolubility (the Church with the power of the keys can dissolve truly Christian marriages). Pospishil proves his assertion by developing three major aspects of the question—the biblical evidence, the historical evidence and contemporary evidence. An appendix of more than sixty pages gives the important historical references.

I disagree with Pospishil's explanation of his basic thesis. Divorce in his view is primarily a juridical and ecclesial question which can be solved by appealing to the power of the Church. I see divorce as primarily a moral and personal question with ecclesial overtones. Pospishil's solution appears too extrinsic, reflects an ecclesiology that defines the Church

---

68 Victor J. Pospishil, *Divorce and Remarriage: Towards a New Catholic Teaching* (New York: Herder and Herder, 1967). Also see José Montserrat-Torrents, *The Abandoned Spouse,* tr. Garry MacEoin (Milwaukee: Bruce Publishing Co., 1969). This translated book is quite similar to Pospishil's, but it appeared later on the American scene and has not been as influential.
69 *Ibid.,* p. 17.

merely in terms of its powers given by Christ and does not seem consonant with the data. Pospishil's biblical section remains very inadequate for he employs a quite fundamentalistic approach to the Scripture and makes no references whatsoever to contemporary biblical literature. In this biblical section he cites no contemporary biblical exegetes and is content to follow the approach taken by William O'Connor, but O'Connor's article was published in 1936.[70] The historical section is overtly apologetic for his position and often seems to skip over possibly different interpretations. The section on the Council of Trent goes into the historical background of Trent, but fails to build on the work done by Lang and Fransen. However, these and other major criticisms cannot detract from the significance of the publication of Pospishil's book, since he first raised the question in public consciousness and in many ways set the parameters for future discussion. This section will now briefly examine the development of the various aspects of the question.

Sacred Scripture

Before 1967 American Scripture scholars generally understood the New Testament as furnishing the basis for, or being in general agreement with, the Roman Catholic teaching on the indissolubility of marriage. This indissolubility of marriage was quite clearly taught in Mark 10:2-12 and Luke 16:18 as well as in the teaching of Paul (1 Cor. 7). However, there was the problem created by the famous exception clauses in Matthew 19:9 (*me epi porneia*), Matthew 5:32 (*parektos logoy porneias*) and the so-called Pauline privilege of 1 Corinthians 7.

---

[70] The first citation to O'Connor's article on p. 24 fails to mention the volume number or the year of the *Ephemerides Theologicae Lovanienses* in which it appeared. The bibliography on p. 209 refers to Vol. XIII, 1963. This represents a rather significant typographical error, for the actual year of publication is 1936.

Although Catholic Scripture scholars very often no longer accepted the traditional Catholic explanation of the Matthean exceptions as referring to the possibility of separation but not remarriage after adultery, nonetheless they proposed solutions which would still be compatible with the Catholic teaching on the indissolubility of marriage. Bruce Vawter in an often cited survey of the literature mentioned various approaches that have been taken. He rejects the so-called traditional Protestant opinion allowing divorce after adultery as well as the popularly held Catholic teaching admitting separation but not remarriage after adultery. He likewise criticizes the theory proposed by Bonsirven that *porneia* translates the technical rabbinical term *zenut* which denotes illegitimate marriages. Vawter himself proposed a variation of the preterition theory. According to this theory in general Jesus merely bypasses the whole problem of *porneia* while excluding all ,other alleged reasons. Vawter's approach understands *porneia* as referring to the *erwat dābār* of Deuteronomy 24:1. Thus Jesus states his absolute refusal of divorce and remarriage, "Deuteronomy 24:1 notwithstanding."[71]

In 1967 Vawter changed his opinion. The teaching of Jesus is a command about the absolute indissolubility of marriage directed to the conscience of Christians. It is not merely an unrealizable ideal nor only a counsel as contrasted with a precept, but at the same time it cannot be considered as a divine law binding in all and every circumstance. Exceptions can and have been made even in the early Church (the Matthean exceptions and 1 Corinthians 7) and also by the Roman Catholic Church which today admits dissolubility in some cases. Vawter in this article interprets the Matthean exceptions to be redactional adaptations presumably reflect-

---

[71] Bruce Vawter, "The Divorce Clauses in Mt. 5:32 and 19:9," *The Catholic Biblical Quarterly*, XVI (1954), 155-167. A preterition theory was also championed by Thomas V. Fleming, "Christ and Divorce," *Theological Studies*, XXIV (1963), 106-120.

ing an interpretation of Jesus' words current in the Church of the first gospel. Vawter now understands *porneia* in the exception clauses to be the *zenut* which denotes illegitimate marriages, thereby adopting the position proposed by Bonsirven.[72]

A quite similar position was proposed independently at about the same time by Dominic Crossan at the symposium on the bond of marriage sponsored by the Canon Law Society in October 1967. Crossan also sees the exception clauses in Matthew as a later redaction and understands *porneia* according to the rabbinic interpretation proposed by Bonsirven.[73]

Scripture scholars in the United States thus began to question the scriptural basis for the present Catholic teaching and practice on divorce. Why the change? First, Scripture scholars obviously felt the greater freedom which was now present in Catholic theology so they could question the scriptural basis of the Catholic teaching on divorce. It was now possible to propose theories at variance with the Church's teaching in this area.[74] Second, through an acceptance of modern scriptural approaches the exception clauses, whatever their meaning, were now interpreted as later redactions and not as the word of Jesus. It would seem that Jesus did speak in an absolute way about the indissolubility of marriage, but that some accommodations were made in the early Church as is evident not only in the teaching of Paul in 1 Corin-

---

[72] Bruce Vawter, "The Biblical Theology of Divorce," *Proceedings of The Catholic Theological Society of America,* XXII (1967), 223-243.

[73] Dominic Crossan, "Divorce and Remarriage in the New Testament," in *The Bond of Marriage,* pp. 1-33.

[74] Obviously some exegetes still accepted the teaching proposed by the hierarchical magisterium. Aidan Mahoney, for example, admitted that the Matthean clauses allow an exception but this exception does not depart from the traditional teaching of the Church. See Aidan Mahoney, "A New Look at the Divorce Clauses in Mt. 5:32 and 19:9," *The Catholic Biblical Quarterly,* XXX (1968), 30.

thians 7 but also in the newer interpretations of Matthew's exception clauses. It seems to me that this realization is a very important difference between the first and the second article written by Vawter who in his earlier article accepted the whole Matthean passage as the words of Jesus, but then came to see the exception clauses as a later redaction.

Third, the Sermon on the Mount context of the exception clause in Matthew added a very significant context for the interpretation of the divorce saying. Both Crossan and Vawter refer explicitly to this context and realize that Jesus' teaching on divorce must be understood in the light of the radical teachings of Jesus proposed in the Sermon on the Mount.[75] Catholic moral theologians led by Bernard Häring started to give greater attention to the ethical teaching of the Sermon on the Mount as proposing radical ethical demands with the realization that at times some accommodation is necessary.[76] I pointed out that the teaching on divorce participated in the eschatological tension created by all the radical demands of Jesus, but the Catholic Church in the instance of divorce has not taken this into account. In this world where the fullness of the eschaton is not yet present there will always be some need to make accommodations with the ethical ideal proposed by Jesus and to realize that some people will not be able to accomplish these radical demands.[77]

A fourth reason contributing to the new interpretation of the Scriptures was based on the recognition that the Catholic Church itself and its present practice and teaching do make

---

[75] Crossan, *The Bond of Marriage*, pp. 29-33; Vawter, *Proceedings of the Catholic Theological Society of America*, XXII (1967), 241-243.

[76] Bernard Häring, "The Normative Value of the Sermon on the Mount," *The Catholic Biblical Quarterly*, XXIX (1967), 375-385. Both Vawter and Crossan refer to this article.

[77] *A New Look at Christian Morality*, pp. 16-21.

some exceptions in the absolute teaching of Jesus on divorce. The extensive expansion of the privilege of the faith cases in the last few decades was bound to raise questions. Especially, if one realizes that from the beginning of creation there was to be no divorce, then it is hard to justify some aspects of the present teaching of the Church.

There is continuing debate about the exact meaning of the exception clauses.[78] Thomas L. Thompson maintains that the more correct meaning of Matthew 19 does not allow exceptions, but on the basis of Paul's teaching divorce can be allowed even in sacramental marriages when other important spiritual values such as peace are at stake.[79] Myles Bourke in an admittedly cursory study examines the different interpretations given to the exception clauses in Matthew and concludes that the teaching of the Scriptures is not clear. Bourke himself contends that the Christian is bound to the eschatological demand of absolute indissolubility, but in this fallen aeon such an eschatological demand is not always attainable.[80] The debate about the exact meaning of the exception clauses will obviously continue to take place, but nonetheless there is a growing number of Catholic scholars who understand the entire New Testament evidence as calling for a change in the present teaching and practice of the Church on the indissolubility of marriage.

---

[78] Two items of interest outside the American literature as such deserve mention. For a summary of some recent opinions on the Scriptural teaching on divorce, see S. Ryan, *The Furrow*, XXIV (1973), 150-159. The complexity of the problem is illustrated by the fact that Wilfred Harrington published an article in 1972 changing the position he proposed in an article in 1970. Wilfred Harrington, "Jesus' Attitude Towards Divorce," *Irish Theological Quarterly*, XXXVII (1970), 199-209; Harrington, "The New Testament and Divorce," *Irish Theological Quarterly*, XXXIX (1972), 178-187.

[79] Thomas L. Thompson, "A Catholic View on Divorce," *Journal of Ecumenical Studies*, VI (1969), 53-67.

[80] Myles M. Bourke, "An Exegesis of the Divorce Texts in the New Testament," *Diakonia*, IV (1969), 39-43.

The Historical Evidence

Victor Pospishil concludes on the basis of his interpretation of the historical data that in the East there has been an uninterrupted evolvement of the idea that marriages ought to be permitted to be dissolved and that at least innocent partners be allowed to remarry, while in the West only after the reform of Cluny in the tenth century and the foundation of the first universities can it be said that the Western Church established a clear policy and teaching prohibiting divorce.[81] Anthony Bevilacqua summarizes a long historical study with the firm conviction that the weight of evidence from the Fathers, Roman Pontiffs, and the Councils of the first millenium of Christianity strongly supports the indissolubility of marriage.[82] These two contrasting opinions illustrate the problem connected with a proper interpretation of the history of the Church's teaching on divorce. Bevilacqua, like Pospishil, appears to be more of an apologist than a detached scholar, for he somewhat regularly comments on disputed passages (e.g. Lactantius,[83] Basil,[84] Asterius[85]) that it cannot be established with certitude that the authors allowed remarriage after divorce.

John T. Noonan, Jr., has added to our historical knowledge of the early period of the Church by seeking to discover what we can know of the Christian teaching on divorce from the laws of Christian emperors which did allow divorce. Noonan concludes that the historical evidence establishes that for a substantial period of time marriages were viewed

---

81 Pospishil, pp. 49 and 44.

82 Anthony J. Bevilacqua, "The History of the Indissolubility of Marriage," *Proceedings of the Catholic Theological Society of America*, XXII (1967), 253-308.

83 *Ibid.*, p. 261.

84 *Ibid.*, p. 275.

85 *Ibid.*, pp. 279-280.

by many Christians as dissoluble, but that in itself does not prove that the later development toward indissolubility was wrong.[86]

A sharply critical reply to Pospishil was published in three languages by Henri Crouzel who maintains that in the primitive Church only Ambrosiaster and the Irish Canon of Patrick allowed for divorce and remarriage.[87] Pospishil's response to Crouzel appears somewhat weak and defensive relying mostly on citing other secondary sources who agree with some of Pospishil's interpretations of the Fathers and disagree with the rather minimalistic interpretation of Crouzel.[88]

The difficult problem of the proper interpretation especially of the teaching of the Fathers in the first six centuries will remain. In my judgment the following questions summarize many of the disputed points of interpretation. How accurately do the Fathers reflect the whole life of the early Church since they would have a special interest in exhorting people to a high moral life? Does explicit acceptance of divorce for the husband after adultery by the wife include the right to remarry? Does the prohibition of divorce for women mean that men were allowed to divorce? Does acceptance of civil law allowing divorce show an acceptance of the morality of divorce? Do the Fathers sometimes just point to an ideal and tolerate or accept the possibility that divorce and remarriage will be necessary for some people?

On the basis of the data available, I would make the following conclusions. It does seem that the Christian society

---

[86] John T. Noonan, Jr., "Novel 22," *The Bond of Marriage*, pp. 41-90.

[87] Henri Crouzel, "Remarriage after Divorce in the Primitive Church: A propos of a Recent Book," *Irish Theological Quarterly*, XXXVIII (1971), 21-41. See also Crouzel, *L'Eglise primitive face au divorce: Du premier au cinquième siècle* (Paris: Ed. Beauchesne, 1971).

[88] Victor J. Pospishil, "Divorce and Remarriage in the Early Church," *Irish Theological Quarterly*, XXXVIII (1971), 338-347.

as a whole did accept or at least tolerate the possibility of divorce and remarriage for some period of time. Some Fathers did speak only about the indissolubility of marriage and forbid divorce and remarriage—e.g. Hermes, Athenagoras, Ambrose and Augustine. It is obvious that Augustine then had a great influence on later developments in the Latin Church. Some few Fathers expressly accepted the possibility of divorce and remarriage while others tolerated the practice of remarriage after divorce. A good number of Fathers of the Church spoke about the possibility of divorce after the adultery of the wife or only forbade divorce by the wife, and it seems to me that this must have included at least for some of them the possibility of remarriage for the husband.

There seems to be greater agreement about the fact that some provincial councils as well as some penitential books indicate the acceptance of divorce and remarriage in some parts of the Church. Likewise it is clear that from the beginning of the second millenium the western Church insisted on the indissolubility of Christian marriage.

The facts about the exact teaching of the Fathers in the first six centuries of the Church are somewhat in dispute, but in addition there is also a problem of interpretation involving the reality that at least at some time and some places in the first thousand years of the Western Church divorce and remarriage were permitted. Those favoring the present Catholic teaching maintain there was development in the Church's understanding of the indissolubility of marriage much as there has been development in the attitude toward slavery. Some concessions were made in the past in certain circumstances, but the teaching has more clearly developed so that the Church came to see the indissolubility of Christian marriage as a demand of Christ. The other interpretation points out that divorce and remarriage were sanctioned in the past and can also be allowed today in various circumstances. Such an approach, which I accept, fits in well with the concept of indissolubility as a radical demand or true ideal but with the realization that all Christians cannot live up to this ideal.

The American scene has not produced any original research on the question of the teaching of the Council of Trent, but American authors are aware of the historical condition in which it was decided not to condemn the teaching and practice of the Eastern Church. The Tridentine teaching anathematizes anyone who asserts that marriage can be dissolved by reason of heresy, domestic incompatibility or willful desertion by one of the parties. A second canon anathematizes anyone who says the Church has erred in teaching that the marriage bond cannot be broken because of adultery.[89] Paul Palmer, Dupré and Bassett all point out that the teaching of Trent is not a solemn declaration of Faith, but Palmer sees in the teaching of Trent a strong commitment on the part of the Church to the indissolubility of marriage which cannot admit of change.[90] In the light of recent discussions about change and dissent in the Church I maintain that the teaching of Trent is not a definitive obstacle preventing a change of the present teaching.

Contemporary Life

Divorce is a fact of life for many Americans and also for many Roman Catholic Americans. There do not seem to be any exact statistics on the number of Catholics who are divorced in the United States. Pospishil in 1967 estimated that every year 70,000 Catholic couples terminate their marriage

---

[89] *Enchiridion Symbolorum Definitionum et Declarationum De Rebus Fidei et Morum*, ed. H. Denzinger and A. Schönmetzer, (32nd ed.; Herder: Barcelona, 1963), n. 1805, 1807.

[90] Paul Palmer, *Theological Studies*, XXXIII (1972), 649-650. Louis and Constance Dupré, "The Indissolubility of Christian Marriage and the Common Good," *The Bond of Marriage*, pp. 182-184; Bassett, *The American Ecclesiastical Review*, CLXII (1970), 36.

by divorce. He then estimated there were approximately 2,100,000 Catholic couples or 4,200,000 individual Catholics living either in invalid marriages or in obligatory isolation.[91] Wrenn estimates that in 1971 something like 120,000 civil divorces were granted for presumably valid marriages of Catholics.[92]

Early in the discussion Rosemary Ruether pointed out the changed understanding of the reality of marriage and Christian marriage in the contemporary world. Now, more so than ever before, marriage is truly a personal commitment of the individuals involved and thus can mirror much better the covenant relationship of Jesus with his Church. In the past there were many other considerations of a societal and even economic nature that prevented marriage from truly being the personal commitment of the spouses. However, this very fact also has the consequence that marriage as a loving union of the partners will more easily break up than a marriage which was based on other considerations. In addition, the sociological factor of the presence of the nuclear family now makes it much more difficult for a person who is divorced to find a place in society.[93]

Again there are two possible interpretations of the contemporary scene. Some would argue that the proposed changes really show how far we have come from the true Christian life and the Church should in no way give in to these modern tendencies but rather must continue to proclaim the fullness of its teaching. I accept a different understanding which sees these changes as signs of the times and argues for a more historically conscious approach. The gospel itself and Christian marriage will be better preserved in our

91 Pospishil, p. 85.
92 Wrenn, *Divorce and Remarriage in the Catholic Church*, pp. 144-145.
93 Rosemary Ruether, "Divorce: No Longer Unthinkable," *Commonweal* LXXXVI (1967), 117-122. See also Richard de Ranitz, "Should the Roman Church Recognize Divorce?" *Listening*, VI (1971), 60-70.

time by allowing for divorce and remarriage. In addition, unmarried adults over 25 years old have difficulty meeting a prospective spouse who was not married before.

Rational Arguments for Indissolubility

Both Pope Leo XIII and Pope Pius XI in encyclical letters appealed to natural law reasoning to prove the indissolubility of marriage.[94] In the more recent American literature Germain Grisez argues on the basis of rational ethics that divorce is a metaphysical evil and therefore metaphysically impossible. The commitment of the marriage partners is not only to one another but to a good beyond themselves—the hope of a child. Hence the partners themselves cannot dissolve this metaphysical bond of marriage. Grisez is forced to admit that the Church can dissolve some natural marriages and also that his own argument for indissolubility presupposes that contraception is always wrong.[95]

Louis and Constance Dupré argue that reason cannot prove the indissolubility of marriage. At most the arguments proposed by some Catholics in the past prove only a relative indissolubility or stability. Three essential values are at stake —the interpersonal relationship between the spouses, the well-being of children, and the good of society as a whole. But none of these requires absolute indissolubility; in fact, they at times favor the dissolution of marriage when there is no longer a loving and fruitful relationship present.[96]

---

[94] Pope Leo XIII "Arcanum divinae sapientiae," *Acta Sanctae Sedis,* XII (1889), 387; Pope Pius XI, "Casti connubii," *Acta Apostolicae Sedis,* XXII (1930), 572, 573.

[95] Germain G. Grisez, "Rational Ethics Says No," *Commonweal,* LXXXVI (1967), 122-125.

[96] Dupré, *The Bond of Marriage,* pp. 181-199. Substantially the same article by the Duprés appeared in a special issue of *America,* CXVIII (1968), 217-231, which was devoted to the questions of divorce and remarriage and has been cited previously. Also see Louis Dupré, "How Indissoluble is a Catholic Marriage?" *The National Catholic Reporter,* March 8, 1967.

I agree that none of the values involved argues for the absolute indissolubility of marriage. Likewise a rational perspective which tries to defend the present Catholic teaching and practice does not want to prove absolute indissolubility, for the Church admits that a natural bond can be dissolved by the power of the Church. There has been in the past and is now a great tension between the contention on the part of some Catholics that natural law proves the indissolubility of marriage and the practice that the Church itself claims power to dissolve the natural bond of marriage.

John T. Noonan, Jr., has again clarified our understanding by showing the role of natural law reasoning in the historical attempt to prove the indissolubility of marriage. The early canonists did not appeal to natural law. The classical university theologians of the middle ages, especially Thomas Aquinas, made some appeal to the fact that indissolubility responded to natural law instincts although these theologians did not claim that natural law universally forbade divorce. Thomas Sanchez, who died in the seventeenth century and is perhaps the most important and significant writer on marriage in Church history, declared that most probably the indissolubility of marriage is not based on natural law. St. Alphonsus Liguori, the eighteenth century moral theologian who has been named a doctor of the Church, maintained that indissolubility does arise from the law of nature itself.[97]

Insistence on the natural law origin of the indissolubility of marriage was a hallmark of the nineteenth and twentieth century papal teaching in the battle against civil divorce, but the twentieth century papal practice in dissolving natural unions seems to argue against such a position. Noonan concludes his study by observing, perhaps without sufficient

---

[97] John T. Noonan, Jr., "Indissolubility of Marriage and Natural Law," *The American Journal of Jurisprudence*, XIV (1969), 79-88.

nuance, that the natural indissolubility of marriage so inadequately demonstrated in nineteen centuries of debate, so little regarded by the classic canon law and some of its greatest commentators, and so recently asserted in polemic is no longer the basis of papal action.[98] In my mind there is no doubt that reason cannot prove the absolute indissolubility of all marriages and that there is some inconsistency in trying to assert both the present Catholic teaching and practice and a natural indissolubility of marriage.

Theological Reasoning

In my judgment the two most significant theological reasons adduced in the recent literature for the absolute indissolubility of Christian marriage stem from the notion of covenant love and from the fact that Christian marriage is a symbol of the union of Christ with his Church. Paul Palmer explicitly invokes the argument that covenant fidelity is the law of the gospel and more than just an ideal for Christian marriage, and he implicitly develops this approach throughout his article.[99] The covenant love by which Yahweh bound himself to his people and Jesus bound Himself to his Church must be the exemplar of the marital love of Christian husband and wife. However, God's covenant is a manifestation of his perfect fidelity to the promise that he had made. Covenant love emphasizes fidelity which commits self to another no matter what might happen in the future. Covenant love is not open to future revision and in no way depends upon changing circumstances or even on mutuality and reciprocity. Covenant love is truly the *agape* which God has first shown to us in his faithful love which in no way depends on any response.

---

[98] *Ibid.*, p. 94.
[99] Paul Palmer, *Theological Studies,* XXXIII (1972) , 649.

In responding to such an objection two observations suffice. First, the covenant fidelity of two Christians will to some extent always fall short of the eschatological perfection of the covenant fidelity of Yahweh for his people and of Jesus for his Church. Thus, because of the fact that we do live in the two aeons one cannot call for such fidelity on the part of Christian marriage. Second, the very nature of Christian love and of marital love does not necessarily include only that notion of a total willingness to give with a love that is self-sacrificing, spontaneous, unmotivated and in no way including mutuality, reciprocity or a response of any kind. Interestingly, Catholic theology in its long history has never accepted such a radical notion of Christian love based totally on self-giving and having no place for legitimate self-love and even for some mutuality and reciprocity. Marital love must also have those other elements and aspects which Catholic theology, as opposed to some forms of Lutheranism, has seen as a legitimate part of Christian love.[100] Permanency and fidelity remain radical demands of Jesus, but there are other aspects involved in the marital love of Christians because of which at times it is necessary to accept the reality of a breakdown in marriage.

Richard A. McCormick raises, at least for the sake of discussion, the objection that a second, third or even fourth marriage cannot be an effective symbol of Christ's faithful union with his Church, for such a reality would seem to dissolve the very notion of Christ's union with the Church.[101] The argumentation from signification or symbol tends to be somewhat broad and general especially when the earthly human reality symbolizes a divine mystery. In such a case the symbolism can never be perfect. No Christian marriage

---

[100] Compare the different approaches to *agape* in the Lutheran and Catholic traditions in the following: Anders Nygren, *Agape and Eros* (New York: Harper Torchbook, 1969) and M. C. D'Arcy, *The Mind and Heart of Love* (New York: Meridian Books, 1956) .

[101] Richard A. McCormick, *Theological Studies*, XXXII (1971) , 120.

is ever an adequate sign of the union of Christ with his Church, for every Christian marriage of necessity falls short. Marriage relationships in which love no longer exists even though there is no remarriage cannot be true signs of the loving union of God with his people. The union of Jesus with his Church certainly calls for fidelity, but it also includes other aspects which should be mirrored in Christian marriage. Human imperfection shows that marriage as a symbol will always be an imperfect sign of the union of Jesus with his Church.

A second marriage can still be a sign even though an imperfect sign of the total relationship of Jesus with his Church. A second marriage could also signify in its own way God's mercy and forgiveness and the fact that the people trying to express symbolically the union of God with his people do not yet live in the fullness of the eschaton. The imperfect aspect of this symbolism has been admitted in other areas. Second and third marriages have been permitted after the death of a spouse even though such marriages as signs mar the symbolism of the unique union of Jesus with his Church and were forbidden by some in the early Church. Likewise, the Christian tradition saw the union of the bishop with his diocese as a sign of the union of Jesus with his Church, but it now admits the fact that bishops can be transferred from one diocese to another.

Although the concept of covenant love and the symbolism of Christian marriage do not prove the absolute indissolubility of Christian marriage, they nonetheless are important aspects on which one must build a positive theology of marriage and the commitment of husband and wife to one another. Christian marriage is primarily a commitment of one spouse to the other as other, and not just a response to changing physical or psychic qualities or characteristics of the other. Likewise it does not depend primarily and in the first place on the reciprocity and mutuality of friendship but always tends to go beyond this toward the fullness of the commitment of Jesus to his Church. Precisely such a transcendent element present in Christian marriage is what gives permanency and fidelity to such marriages when one of the partners for one reason or other now has lost some of the qualities that might have made him or her attractive in the past or perhaps now is laboring under some difficulty or illness.

From the philosophical perspective I would argue that the possibility of making such a commitment to another person which in the last analysis transcends the changing circumstances of time and space in no way is a limitation on the freedom of man. But rather the fact that human beings are able to commit themselves to other human beings in a union which tends towards permanence is a sign of man's transcendence in overcoming his own creaturely distention in time and space. Such aspects of Christian marriage and spirituality must constantly be emphasized both in theory and in actuality, but at times it will happen that such a relationship is no longer possible.

It is beyond the limits of this essay to attempt a development of a theological understanding of Christian marriage. However, from indications already mentioned Christian marriage must be viewed in a more covenantal, relational and developmental way, breaking away from the contractual, substantialist and static approach of the past. In the light of such an approach the growth potential of Christian marriage for the individual couple is emphasized but at the same time the possibility of divorce and breakdown becomes greater.

Ecumenical Perspectives

Divorce in the past has been considered one of the fundamental practical differences between Catholics and Protestants. In the light of the recent ecumenical developments, it is only natural that Catholics, besides looking into their own tradition on this subject, should also study the approach to divorce existing within various Protestant communities.[102] From a theoretical perspective most of the interest has been in the teaching and practice of the Orthodox Church.

The interest in Orthodoxy's teaching and practice stems from many reasons.[103] The Orthodox do permit remarriage after divorce. They claim, and rightly so, that their practice has support from the very earliest days of the Church. There has been a long uninterrupted historical development to which they can point. The Council of Trent purposely did not condemn their particular approach although it did specifically condemn the teaching of Luther. There was no condemnation of the Oriental tradition by the Popes of the West in the first millenium. At some of the councils trying to bring about reunion there was no demand for a change in the Oriental practice, however, at other times both in reunion councils and in later statements by Popes after Trent there was a call for the Orthodox Catholics to profess the Latin tradition on the indissolubility of marriage. More recently the Decree on Ecumenism of Vatican II has been understood to accept the sacramental practice of the Eastern Church including the practice about marriage.[104] Archbishop Zoghby and Patriarch Maximos IV both appealed to this tradition in their speeches at Vatican Council II calling for a change in the Church's practice.[105]

---

102 John Charles Wynn, "Prevailing and Countervailing Trends in the Non-Catholic Churches," *Divorce and Remarriage in the Catholic Church*, pp. 65-88.

103 Bassett, *The American Ecclesiastical Review*, CLXII (1970), 34-36; Bernard Häring, *Divorce and Remarriage in the Catholic Church*, pp. 26-28; George A. Maloney, "Catholicism, Orthodoxy and Divorce," *Diakonia*, VII (1972), 297-300.

104 J. M. Kuntz, "Is Marriage Indissoluble?" *Journal of Ecumenical Studies*, VII (1970), 333-337.

105 These speeches are conveniently published together in *Diakonia*, IV (1969), 156-164.

What precisely is the teaching of the Orthodox Church on divorce and remarriage? In a paradoxical way Eastern Orthodoxy affirms the indissolubility of marriage and yet in her canonical regulations accepts divorce and remarriage. Marriage exists in an eschatological tension, for on the one hand, belonging to Christ and His Kingdom, it is indissoluble. On the other hand, subject to frailty and human weakness, marriages are constantly being dissolved in daily life. The Church itself acknowledges the fact that some marriages become spiritually dead, and divorce and remarriage are acceptable, but the Church as such does not divorce. Eastern Orthodoxy admits various reasons indicating when the marriage has truly become spiritually dead. Archbishop Iakavos in 1966 in an encyclical letter listed ten cases in which the Church accepts divorce and remarriage. Orthodoxy uses the term *economia* to refer to its compassionate acceptance of divorce and remarriage while still upholding the indissolubility of marriage.[106]

Some Roman Catholics may see in the Orthodox approach a way to maintain the traditional Catholic teaching on indissolubility while at the same time allowing reconciliation with the Church for those involved in or contemplating marriage after divorce. They seem to interpret *economia* as a pastoral solution which does not affect the objective teaching on indissolubility.[107] I do not believe this is either an

---

106 Alexander Schmemann, "The Indissolubility of Marriage: The Theological Tradition of the East," *The Bond of Marriage*, pp. 97-105; "Professor P. N. Trembelas on Divorce in the Orthodox Church," tr. George A. Maloney, *Diakonia*, IV (1969), 44-46; Lewis J. Patsavos, "The Orthodox Position on Divorce," *Diakonia*, V (1970), 4-15.

107 There is some doubt in my mind about the correct interpretation of the proposals of Archbishop Zoghby. He acknowledges his belief in the indissolubility of marriage but speaks of *economia* as a pastoral solution which is then compared to a dispensation (*Diakonia*, IV [1969] 156-161). William Bassett frequently refers to *economia* as a pastoral approach allow-

accurate interpretation of Orthodox teaching or an adequate solution for Roman Catholicism today. The objective order in which we live is a mixture of the two cities or the two aeons so that *economia* or compassion is more than just a pastoral approach. It qualifies the attitude of the Church to the reality of marriage and divorce in human existence this side of the fullness of the eschaton. In this world, indissolubility remains as a radical demand of Jesus and a goal but with the realization that sometimes divorce and remarriage will be a reluctant necessity. The canonical practice of the Orthodox Church seems to indicate that *economia* is more than just a pastoral solution but in its own way is an acceptance of divorce and remarriage. But in this case the Church itself does not divorce but merely acknowledges and accepts the possibility of divorce and remarriage.[108]

CONCLUSION

On the basis of all the foregoing evidence I conclude that the Roman Catholic Church should change its teaching and practice on divorce. Divorce and remarriage must be accepted as a reality in our world that at times can take place even without personal guilt on the part of the individuals involved. Indissolubility or permanency is a radical demand

---

ing a second marriage while a former spouse is living, but he distinguishes this from the question of the possibility of the Church's dissolving consummated sacramental marriages, which possibility he does not believe has been proved by the recent literature (*American Ecclesiastical Review*, CLXII [1970], 20-36). If Bassett is saying that the question is not about the power of the Church to dissolve marriages, I agree with him. However, I believe that he is saying more than this because he still affirms both extrinsic and intrinsic indissolubility while trying to make room for the pastoral approach of *economia* (pp. 29-30).

[108] Trembelas, *Diakonia*, IV (1969), 44-46; Patsavos, *Diakonia*, V (1970) 4-15.

of the gospel that is seen as a goal but not an absolute norm.[109]

Even those who do not agree with such an approach make some practical dispositions which in my judgment must ultimately lead to a change in theory. Although upholding the teaching of the Church on indissolubility, many still find different ways in practice to allow sacramental reconciliation and remarriage for many divorced Catholics. Such pastoral solutions which have been mentioned above furnish immediate pastoral help for many people, but in a theoretical order it appears incongruous to hold onto such approaches and also to the indissolubility of Christian marriage. The most frequently proposed pastoral approach maintains that many of these marriages were not valid or true Christian sacramental marriages from the beginning. To say after the fact that many marriages were not truly Christian marriages seems to be somewhat of a subterfuge, especially when the question is raised only after marriages have as a matter of fact broken down. If one were to carry out in practice such an understanding of Christian marriage, then one would have to say that very many Christian marriages really are never truly such. To accept such a conclusion would mean that the Church is adopting a somewhat sectarian approach with regard to the reality of Christian marriage as something which only the few or the perfect can ever achieve.

In the whole history of the discussion it seems to me that many problems and difficulties have arisen because of the

---

109 My position differs in some details from that proposed by Wrenn who contrasts the indissolubility-invalidity tradition with what he calls the fragility-illiceity tradition. This second tradition, which he now urges that the Church accept, sees the first marriage as a fragile union which needs special care; to break it and enter a second marriage is against the will of God and is gravely illicit (Wrenn, *Divorce and Remarriage in the Catholic Church,* p. 140). Wrenn still seems to see indissolubility in terms of an absolute norm rather than as a radical demand of the gospel and a goal for every Christian marriage.

juridical and ecclesiological perspective in which divorce and remarriage have been discussed in Roman Catholic thought. Marriage and divorce should be seen primarily in a moral or personal perspective with ecclesial overtones. In a juridical context great emphasis was placed on the power of the Church to determine all the legalities connected with marriage. In addition such an approach fostered the concept of marriage as a contract by which the bond of marriage was brought into existence as a juridical entity. The Church was thought to have power over the bond of marriage and the question was raised in terms of the power of the Church to dissolve marriages.

If divorce is seen in moral terms with ecclesial overtones, important ramifications follow. In this context one should not speak of the bond of marriage because such a concept is much more congenial to a juridical understanding of marriage. There is the marital commitment and relationship which may existentially break down even through no personal fault of the parties involved. The Church itself should recognize and at times accept this reality, but it does not really dissolve the bond of marriage for the marriage bond is not a juridical entity existing apart from the marital relationship.

The present practice and teaching of the Church assert the power of the Pope to dissolve certain marriages. John T. Noonan, Jr., on the basis of the historical evolution of the question points out that it is merely a legal fiction (legal statements used not fraudently but as techniques by which the law is often expanded and by which legal development is facilitated) to say that the Pope by virtue of his power of jurisdiction over the whole world dissolves marriages not as a man but in place of God.[110] The whole question of dis-

---

[110] John T. Noonan, Jr., *Proceedings of the Thirty-First Convention of the C.L.S.A.* (1969), 89-95.

solving marriages arises within a juridical context especially when the Church was fulfilling important civil and social functions in the area of marriage. I believe today it is also a legal fiction to speak of the Church or the Pope dissolving Christian marriages or any marriages. In these cases the Church just recognizes and acknowledges that the marital relationship has broken down and that a remarriage is possible.

What are the moral values that must be considered in the question of divorce and remarriage? I would emphasize the following moral values or concerns: the radical gospel demand of indissolubility as the ideal of Christian marriage, the realization that in this world not all are able to live up to the fullness of that ideal at times even without personal guilt, the gift of the forgiveness of God and the call to repent insofar as this is possible, the need to protect innocent persons, the provision for the children involved in a broken marriage. The couple or individuals involved in the light of these criteria make the judgment that their marriage has irremediably broken down or that it is spiritually dead and they can now remarry.

Although the decision on divorce and remarriage is a moral decision made by the parties themselves, there are ecclesial overtones because marriage involves more than just the parties themselves. A centralized court system does not furnish the best way to care for these ecclesial aspects of the question. The ecclesial acceptance of the reality of divorce and remarriage should be handled on a local level in a pastoral way by a small group representing the local community and mediating the community's willingness to celebrate a new marriage on the basis of the criteria mentioned above. It seems to me that only rarely would the community decide that on the basis of these criteria (e.g. refusal to provide for the children from a previous marriage or no signs of penance where this is called for and possible) they cannot celebrate a second marriage for a particular person. Perhaps there could be some slight differences in the rite for second marriages so that in this way one can indicate the ideal of indissolubility. In addition, the Church and the local community must do everything possible to foster the permanency and stability of all Christian marriages through education and training made available to people both before and during their marriages.

It is one thing to talk in a theoretical manner about what should be the teaching and practice of the Church in the matter of divorce and remarriage, but it is an entirely different thing to discuss what will probably take place in the immediate future. Predictions about what will happen in the future are risky, but on the basis of my assessment of the relevant factors the Roman Catholic Church probably will not change its official teaching on divorce in the near future. The number of Catholics who are divorced and remarried, however, will continue to grow. The shortcomings in the tribunal system will become more evident. Pastoral solutions will be utilized almost as an ordinary procedure so that many divorced and remarried Catholics will continue to participate in the sacramental life of the Church. Non-canonical celebrations in conjunction with second marriages will occur more frequently. One can conclude that even now Roman Catholic practice in the United States has turned an important corner—in practice remarriage with full participation in the sacramental life of the Church is now a possibility for many Roman Catholics.

Tensions will grow as the separation between the official teaching and the pastoral practice becomes more pronounced. It is important to realize that theoretical teaching will at times tend to lag behind the actual practice, but the good of the Church demands a congruity between the practical life of the Church and its more theoretical teaching. I hope that, despite my own somewhat pessimistic prognostication, the hierarchical Church will seriously come to grips with this question. In my judgment the best solution would be to assert in both theory and practice that the indissolubility of marriage is a radical demand of Jesus that must beckon all those involved in Christian marriages, but at times people will not be able to live up to the fullness of that ideal and remarriage can be accepted.

Index

Abell, Aaron I., 87, 88n., 89, 145n.
Abortion, 8, 41f., 163f.; abortion laws, Supreme Court, 163, 166; A.L.I. Model Penal Code, 170; cancerous uterus, 174; canon law, 173; compromise, 166; conflict situations, 173-4, 189f., 191; craniotomy, 180; delayed animation, 173, 176f., 185; direct and indirect, 42, 172, 174f., 178, 189f.; ectopic pregnancy, 174; feminine liberation, 131; function of law, 167f.; history of church teaching, 175f.; legal aspects, 163f.; moral aspects, 171f.; new methodology, 183; plurality of opinions, 19, 166, 179f.; pluralistic society, 167, 169f.; principle of double effect, 174, 190; proportionate reason, 174; rape, 186; teaching authority of the church, 172f.; toleration of lesser evil, 165; twinning, 188; types of abortion law, 169f.; when human life begins, theories, 173, 180f.
Absolutes in moral theology, 4, 6, 15-17, 20-21, 27, 36, 41, 78, 82, 238, 244, 272
Agape, 31, 51, 74, 265, 266n.
Alphonsus Liguori, 175, 264
Ambrose, 260
American Society of Christian Ethics, 2
Anthropology, philosophical, *see* Natural law
Antoine, Pierre, 9, 11f., 37n.
Antoninus of Florence, 176
Aquinas, Thomas, 6, 27, 32n., 45f., 79f., 80n.; abortion and delayed animation, 173, 185f.; example for

Aquinas, Thomas (cont'd)
dialogue, 45f.; indissolubility of marriage, 264; natural law, 6f., 27; patron of philosophy and theology, 79f., 80n.; private property and sin, 32f.; Thomistic distinction between *lex naturalis* and *jus naturale,* 6f.; Thomistic ethics, 3; Thomistic renewal, 80
Arella, Gerald J., 218n., 222n., 223n., 233n.
artificial insemination, 20, 41
Athenagoras, 260
Aubert, Jean-Marie, 6n., 7f., 79n., 81n.
Augustin, Pius, 37n.
Augustine, 51, 260
Authoritarianism, 22f.
Averill, Lloyd J., 69n.
Azpilcueta, Martin (Doctor Navarrus), 176

Barth, Karl, 63f., 70
Basic stance for Christian ethics, 12, 47f., 131
Bassett, William W., 21n., 212n., 223, 224n., 227n., 228n., 261, 269n., 270n.
Baum, Gregory, 20n.
Beatitudes, the, 126
Beemer, T., 239
Beirnaert, Louis, 182
Bennett, John C., 50n.
Berrigan, Philip, 100
Besret, Bernard, 76n., 129n.
Bevilacqua, Anthony, 258
Böckle, Franz, 1f., 33, 140, 165n.
Boniface VIII, 142
Bonner, Dismas, 246, 248
Bonsirven, J., 254

marriage (cont'd)
265; sacramentality, 213, 228f., 237f.;
spirituality of, 212; theology of, 212,
234, 266, 268, 274; values of Chris-
tian, 226; *see also* divorce, *ratum
et consummatum*
Marx, Karl, 81
Mass, the, 97, 112f., 114
masturbation, 20, 41
Mater et Magistra, 24, 37
Mathis, Marcian J., 214n.
Maurin, Peter, 90, 110
Maximos IV, Patriarch, 269
medical ethics, 40f.; directives for
Catholic hospitals, 40f., 195; *see
also* abortion, sterilization
Mehl, Roger, 2, 5n., 8, 28, 31, 33, 38
methodology, *see* moral theology,
natural law, pluralism
Metz, Johannes B., 12n., 139n.
Meyer, Nicholas W., 214n.
Michel, Virgil, 112
Milhaven, John Giles, 9f., 13, 15, 18
minority groups, 102f.
Mitchell, Basil, 50
Moltmann, Jurgen, 128, 129n.
Montague, George T., 35n.
Montserrat-Torrents, Jose, 252n.
moral theology, absoluteness of moral
norms, 4, 6, 15-18, 20f., 27, 36, 41,
78, 82, 238, 244; authoritarianism,
5, 22f.; change and development,
44f.; direct and indirect, 18, 41f.,
see abortion, sterilization; distinctively Christian ethics, 139f.; growing divergence of opinion, 19, 20,
21f., 27, 37; *magisterium*, teaching
authority of church, 6, 22f., 102,
137f.; methodologies, 9f., 12f., 18f.,
21f., 28f., 41, 59f., 118, 133, 137f., 149,
151, 155, 183, 213; moral judgments
and decision, 151f., 154, 185; newer
ethical approaches, 9f., 12f., 18, 21f.,
118, 137f.; principle of double effect,
18f., 42, 174, 190, 200; proportionate
reason, 174; stances or starting
points, 47f., 131; tendency to absolutize, 78, 82; tensions, 43f.; theo-

moral theology (cont'd)
logical presuppositions, 5, 56f.; *see
also* complexity, dialogue, natural
law, pluralism, sin, teaching authority of the church
Motu proprio, causas matrimoniales,
217
Murray, John Courtney, 76n., 115,
166n., 167
Murtagh, Cyril, 228n.
Mystical Body, 109, 112, 114
Mystici Corporis, 96, 109

natural law, 3, 5; absolutizing, 78;
a priori elements, 7; Aquinas, 6f.;
civil law, 165f.; creation, 57f.; empirical discovery, 7; eternal, divine
law, 164f.; inadequacies, 7f.; indissolubility of marriage, 220, 264;
methodology, 6, 10, 28f.; moral
manuals, 6, 17; philosophical anthropology, 8f., 11, 29; pluralism,
8; reason, 7; sin, 68f.; sterilization,
196; teaching authority of church,
29, 37, 96, 138; Ulpian, 7
nature, 3, 5, 28f., 32, 60f., 68, 85f.
National Conference of Catholic
Charities, 122f.
Neo-Orthodoxy, Protestant, *see* Orthodoxy
Niebuhr, H. Richard, 14f., 30, 49, 70,
131n.
Niebuhr, Reinhold, 47, 70f.
Nolan, Kieran, 20n.
Nolan, Martin, 205
non-violence, 100
Noonan, John T., 173n., 175n., 178,
180, 219n., 220n., 223f., 234, 258f.,
264, 273
Nygren, Anders, 51, 266n.

O'Boyle, Patrick Cardinal, 112
O'Brien, David J., 89
O'Callaghan, Denis, 197n.
O'Connor, William, 253
O'Donnell, Thomas J., 199n., 208
Orsy, Ladislas, 241f., 245n.
Orthodoxy, Eastern, 269f.

Tettamanzi, Dionigi, 165
Theology of Charity, National Conference of Catholic Charities, 122f., 127, 132f., 135f.
Thielicke, Helmut, 32n., 62f.
Thils, Gustave, 76n.
Thompson, Thomas L., 257
Toner, Jules, 51n.
Torreblanca, Franciscus, 176f.
Tracy, David, 55n.
Tracy, Robert E., 249
transcendental method, 10, 12f.
transcendence, 77
Trembelas, P. N., 271n.
Troeltsch, Ernst, 61n.
Troisfontaines, Roger, 85n., 190n.
Trullenchus, John, 177

Ulpian, 7
Unam Sanctam, 142

values, attitudes and goals, 154; Christian marriage, 226; conflict, 34; hierarchy, 15; human existence, 14; priorities, 153

van der Marck, William, 11
van der Poel, C., 239
vasectomy, *see* sterilization
Vatican II, *Constitution on the Church,* 24; *Declaration on Religious Freedom,* 58, 167; *Decree on Ecumenism,* 269; *Pastoral Constitution on the Church in the Modern World,* 29, 125n., 138
Vawter, Bruce, 254f.
Vermeersch, Arthur, 175n.
Villot, Cardinal, 217, 218n.

Walsh, Mary Elizabeth, 111
Wassmer, Thomas A., 201n., 203f., 204n., 207n.
Wills, Gary, 24n.
World Council of Churches, 59
Wrenn, Lawrence G., 215n., 216n., 217-18, 233-35, 262, 272n.

Zalba, Marcellinus, 191n.
Zambellus, Leo, 176
Zoghby, Archbishop, 269, 270n.